Race and Empire

SEMINAR STUDIES IN HISTORY

Race and Empire

JANE SAMSON

PEARSON
Longman

Harlow, England • London • New York • Boston • San Francisco • Toronto
Sydney • Tokyo • Singapore • Hong Kong • Seoul • Taipei • New Delhi
Cape Town • Madrid • Mexico City • Amsterdam • Munich • Paris • Milan

PEARSON EDUCATION LIMITED

Edinburgh Gate
Harlow CM20 2JE
United Kingdom
Tel: +44 (0)1279 623623
Fax: +44 (0)1279 431059
Website: www.pearsoned.co.uk

First edition published in Great Britain in 2005

ISBN-10: 0-582-41837-2
ISBN-13: 978-0-582-41837-0

British Library Cataloguing in Publication Data
A CIP catalogue record for this book can be obtained from the British Library

Library of Congress Cataloging in Publication Data
Samson, Jane, 1962–
    Race and empire / Jane Samson.—1st ed.
       p. cm. — (Seminar studies in history)
    Includes bibliographical references and index.
    ISBN 0–582–41837–2 (pbk.)
    1. Race relations—History. 2. Imperialism—History. 3. Racism—History. I. Title.
II. Series.

HT1507.S347 2004
305.8′009—dc22
                                                                          2004054492

10 9 8 7 6 5 4 3 2
08 07 06

Set by 35 in 10/12.5pt Sabon
Printed in Malaysia

The Publishers' policy is to use paper manufactured from sustainable forests.

CONTENTS

INTRODUCTION TO THE SERIES

Such is the pace of historical enquiry in the modern world that there is an ever-widening gap between the specialist article or monograph, incorporating the results of current research, and general surveys, which inevitably become out of date. *Seminar Studies in History* is designed to bridge this gap. The series was founded by Patrick Richardson in 1966 and his aim was to cover major themes in British, European and world history. Between 1980 and 1996 Roger Lockyer continued his work, before handing the editorship over to Clive Emsley and Gordon Martel. Clive Emsley is Professor of History at the Open University, while Gordon Martel is Professor of International History at the University of Northern British Columbia, Canada, and Senior Research Fellow at De Montfort University.

All the books are written by experts in their field who are not only familiar with the latest research but have often contributed to it. They are frequently revised, in order to take account of new information and interpretations. They provide a selection of documents to illustrate major themes and provoke discussion, and also a guide to further reading. The aim of *Seminar Studies in History* is to clarify complex issues without over-simplifying them, and to stimulate readers into deepening their knowledge and understanding of major themes and topics.

AUTHOR'S ACKNOWLEDGEMENTS

I am grateful to series editor Gordon Martel for inviting me to write this book, and to Casey Mein, Melanie Carter, and the rest of the editorial team at Pearson for seeing it through the press. Thank you also to the many colleagues and friends who assisted me with research and analysis. Special thanks must go to Rebecca Adell, Paul Hengstler, Nathan Lysons, Katherine Prior and the staff of the University of Alberta Libraries.

PUBLISHER'S ACKNOWLEDGEMENTS

We are grateful to the following for permission to reproduce copyright material:

Map 1 from *The Longman Companion to the Formation of the European Empires, 1488–1920* (Chamberlain, Muriel E.), copyright © 2000 by Pearson Education Limited; maps 2 and 3 from *The Longman Companion to European Decolonisation in the Twentieth Century* (Chamberlain, Muriel E.), copyright © 1998 by Addison Wesley Longman Limited.

We are grateful to all other copyright holders whose material appears in this book. However, in some instances we have been unable to trace the owners of copyright material, and we would appreciate any information that would enable us to do so.

The relationship between racism and imperialism has inspired one of the most prominent debates in scholarship today. The deluge of publications can be difficult to master, even for specialists. Disciplinary rivalries and technical jargons can inhibit comparative study and hinder the ready communication of important insights. This is particularly unfortunate because students at the beginning of the twenty-first century are probably more conscious of racism as an issue than any other generation. Policies of multiculturalism, diversity, and tolerance are welcomed by many, yet they raise important questions about the ongoing process of defining various groups of people as fundament-ally different from others. Such distinctions can also generate inequality, resentment, and violence.

The whole process of distinguishing 'us' from 'them' was enhanced (some would say created) by imperialism, and the legacy of imperial racism remains with us today. Despite talk of a 'postcolonial' world, attitudes, vocabularies, and policies prevail whose roots lie in imperial history. The word 'postcolonial' can too easily suggest a linear timeline which allows us to locate our own era safely after a previous 'colonial period'. This teleology has been enhanced by political rhetoric about 'new world orders' since the Second World War or, more recently, since the collapse of the Soviet Union. When I teach imperial history, I emphasise both the differences and the similarities between different historical periods. Imperialism is a topic that can be approached from many different angles; by concentrating on the topical issue of race, this book has a different focus than some of the popular works currently available on comparative imperial history. David Landes argues in his highly acclaimed *The Wealth and Poverty of Nations: Why Some Are So Rich and Some Are So Poor* that imperialism is the 'expression of a deep human drive' (Landes, 1998: 63). Samuel P. Huntington's *The Clash of Civilizations and the Remaking of World Order* takes a more culturally-centred view, stating that only those from 'Western Christian heritages are making progress toward economic development and democratic politics; the prospects . . . in the Ortho-dox countries are uncertain; the prospects in the Muslim republics are bleak' (Huntington, 1997: 29). In this scheme, Western expansion seems as inevitable as the resentment it provokes. What remains unexamined in these popular texts is the way in which people construct definitions of 'progress' or 'development', and the role that race plays in those definitions. If imperialism is natural and inevitable, can people make choices about the use of power? Do theories of progress and development revolve around racial assumptions? Huntington denies making a race-based argument, yet people with 'Western Christian heritages' are confined by him to western Europe and North America. If religious culture is really the key to progress and development, why are Latin American, Asian, and African Christians excluded from its benefits? At a time when there are more Anglicans in Nigeria than anywhere else, how can the location of 'Western Christian heritage' be confined to Europe and North America? How else, except by presuming a link between race and culture?

The definition of race is a very contentious scientific issue. Vincent Sarich and Frank Miele's book *Race: The Reality of Human Difference* (2004) contends that the human genome contains enough racially-specific features to make race a scientific fact. Others disagree, and only those with advanced training in genetic science can hope to make an informed decision for themselves in this highly technical debate. Links between physical appearance and racial ancestry are also coming under scrutiny. In a recent article in *Nature*, scientists note that although individual genomes can reveal information about physical characteristics, there is a huge degree of variation to the point that 'most genetic diversity occurs within groups' and 'very little is found between them' (Feldman, Lewontin, and King, 2003: 1). People with African ancestry differ more from one another than they do, as a group, from people with Asian background. In short, physical appearance and social identification ('black', 'white', Asian) turns out to be a poor guide to actual racial ancestry. The supposed 'fact' of race is subject to a great deal of subjective interpretation. An understanding of the history of racial science, and its connections with imperial expansion, can provide a very useful examination of those subjectivities and their consequences.

There is insufficient space in this small volume to discuss all aspects of the relationship between race and empire, and the need to concentrate on prevailing ideas can create a sense of inevitability that is quite misleading. It can seem as though various race theories exercised a straightforward influence on imperial policy. For example, the coincidence of evolutionary theory and the 'scramble' for empire can suggest the inevitable rise of scientific racism in the late nineteenth century. Biological race theories and imperial expansion had already been around for centuries, however. Likewise, even at the height of the eugenics movement in the early twentieth century, some voices denounced its allegedly 'scientific' assumptions about race and social health. There was nothing inevitable about people's choice to support eugenics, or the racist assumptions of the European slave trade, or the dispossession of aboriginal populations by European settlers. Historians must always ask hard questions about processes that are presumed to be natural or inevitable. We must ask instead why people prefer particular ways of seeing the world at particular times in history, or what kinds of historical events can prompt different choices. Many politicians today proclaim that individual rights and free trade provide the best operating framework for all of the world's peoples. These things are held to be self-evident: they are 'common sense'. It is important to remember, however, that not very long ago politicians were proclaiming very different things to be 'common sense', such as the need for universal Christianisation, or the need to accept the inevitable extinction of inferior human races. The point is that definitions of 'common sense' are dependent on historical circumstances. Future textbooks will examine today's assumptions with the same critical tools that we use to expose and dissect the presumed certainties of past generations.

Defining the scope of this book was a challenging task. Much as I would have liked to explore all modern imperialisms, this would have been impossible to achieve in such a short text. A focus on the European and American empires was more manageable. My desire to make this book as comparative as possible encouraged me to err on the side of inclusion while noting that some of my choices are controversial. Most studies of modern imperialism focus only on the western European empires. This seemed peculiar, given the contribution of American intellectuals to race theory and the process of American continental expansion, as well as the acquisition of overseas colonies by the United States during the nineteenth and twentieth centuries. I hope that this book will demonstrate the many reasons why historical scholarship demands the inclusion of the United States in a comparative study of imperial race relations.

The decision not to include the Russian empire and the Soviet Union therefore requires explanation. These empires could be called 'Western' after 1700, thanks to the modernisation campaigns of leaders from Peter the Great to Stalin, but the Russians are almost never included in comparative studies of modern imperialism. One reason for this might be the fact that their interest in overseas territory rule was brief. Like China, Russia was primarily a continental power. Another reason for neglect might be the uncertain relationship between race theory and imperial expansion in Russia. At certain points tsarism proved tolerant of racial difference, and Soviet policy would claim (rightly or wrongly) that all groups should share in the socialist revolution. Historians of Russian imperialism are debating all of these issues, but with space at a premium in this particular text, it seemed advisable to leave the Russians out of the analysis. I hope that this will not deter others from taking up this particular challenge.

I should also state that moral comparison has not formed part of my study. Some historians have believed that their nation's policies were uniquely humanitarian, and debates continue about whether or not one empire was 'better' than others in its treatment of indigenous peoples, its labour systems, or its attitude toward miscegenation. It seems to me that imperial beauty contests are not winnable. I would never claim that circumstances in the Belgian Congo were the same as those in Australia, but missionaries could point to improved education and health for Africans on their stations in the Congo, while the fate of Australia's aboriginal people included deliberate murder with poisoned food. To weigh one imperial tragedy against another would be perilous. All that I can say for certain is that the unequal power relations of modern imperialism were related to beliefs about racial inequality, and this relationship produced some of the greatest atrocities in recorded history. The deep entanglement between race and empire was so powerful that its legacy remains even in our own 'postcolonial' times.

LIST OF ABBREVIATIONS

ANC   African National Congress
BSAC   British South Africa Company
EIC   East India Company
HBC   Hudson's Bay Company
HMSO   Her Majesty's Stationery Office (Government Printer)
INC   Indian National Congress
VOC   Dutch East India Company

CHRONOLOGY

711	Berber Muslims from North Africa invade Spain
1492	End of rule by the Moors in Spain
1492	Christopher Columbus lands in the Caribbean
1494	Treaty of Tordesillas divides the known world between Spain and Portugal
1541–2	Jacques Cartier's exploration of the St Lawrence area
1608	Founding of New France (Québec)
1622	'Jamestown Massacre' in Virginia
1757	Victory of EIC over Nawab of Bengal in the Battle of Plassey
1756–63	Seven Years War ('French and Indian War' in North America)
1765	The British obtain the *diwani* (civil government) of Bengal
1767	British explorer Samuel Wallis first encounters Tahiti
1774	British *Québec Act* includes native territorial rights
1776–83	American Revolution and War of Independence
1778	Spain requires parental consent to all marriages involving whites under 25 years old
1785	*Northwest Ordinance* enacted by the American Congress
1787	Founding of Sierra Leone as a home for liberated slaves
1788	Penal colony founded on Australia's eastern coast
1788	Governor-general of Bengal Warren Hastings tried for corruption by the House of Lords
1794	First abolition of slavery in the French empire
1803	The world's first black-ruled republic declared in Haiti
1807	Britain outlaws slave trading
1810	Abortive Mexican Revolution
1819	Stamford Raffles acquires coastal village of Singapore for Britain
1821	Mexican independence
1822	Brazilian independence
1830	French invasion of Algeria begins
1831	US Supreme Court's *Cherokee Nation* decision
1833	Emancipation of slaves in the British empire
1840	Treaty of Waitangi brings New Zealand under British rule
1848	Permanent abolition of slavery in the French empire

1857	The Indian Rebellion ('Indian Mutiny')
1859	Publication of Charles Darwin's *The Origin of Species*
1864	Samuel Crowther becomes first black Anglican bishop
1867	Alaska purchased from Russia by the USA
1873–4	Second Ashanti War
1881	French territory in north Africa extended to include Tunisia
1882	British invasion of Egypt
1884	Berlin Conference
1887	American legislation repeals autonomy of 'Indian territories'
1888	Abolition of slavery in Brazil
1890	Italy founds the colony of Eritrea
1891	Publication of Friedrich Ratzel's *Anthropogeographie*
1891	Founding of the Comité de l'Afrique française
1893	German sovereignty proclaimed in German South-West Africa (now Namibia)
1894	Lombok incident in Bali
1895–6	Third Ashanti War
1896	Battle of Adowa
1897	Benin War
1898	Battle of Omdurman
1898	Hawai'i annexed by the United States
1898	Spanish–American War
1899–1902	South African War ('Boer War')
1901	Australian *Pacific Island Labourers Act*
1904	Herero Massacre
1905	Japan defeats Russia
1910	Creation of self-governing Union of South Africa
1919	Amritsar Massacre in India
1924	Native Labour Commission appointed in Belgian Congo
1926	*White Women's Protection Ordinance* enacted in Papua New Guinea
1931	Statute of Westminster grants full independence only to British Dominions
1936	'Italian East Africa' created from Abyssinia, Eritrea, and Italian Somaliland
1939	Libya proclaimed to be part of Italy
1946	Independence of the Philippines
1947	Creation of independent India and Pakistan
1954–62	Algerian War of Independence
1957	The Gold Coast becomes independent as Ghana
1957	Malayan independence
1959	Alaska and Hawai'i become American states
1960	Canada grants unqualified voting rights to Aboriginal peoples

MAPS

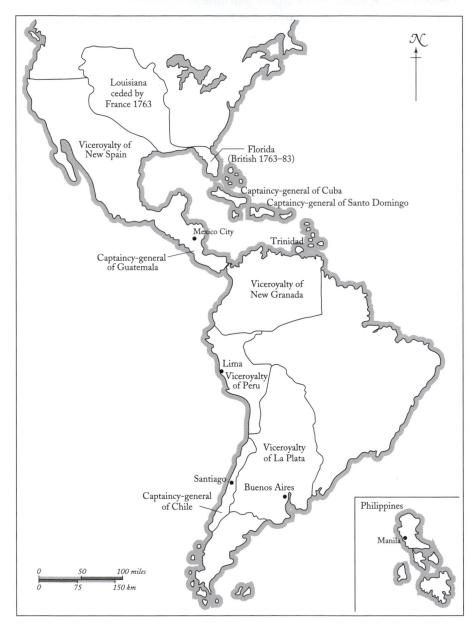

Map 1 The Spanish Empire in the Americas and the Pacific in the late eighteenth century

Source: Chamberlian, Muriel E., *The Longman Companion to the Formation of the European Empires, 1488–1920*, © Pearson Education Limited, 2000

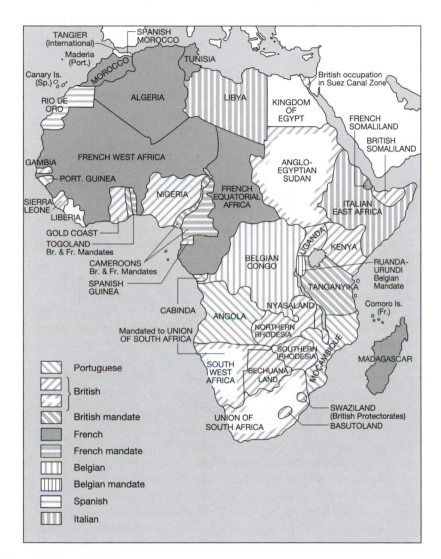

Map 2 Africa in 1939

Source: Chamberlain, Muriel E., *The Longman Companion to European Decolonisation in the Twentieth Century*, © Addison Wesley Longman Limited, 1998

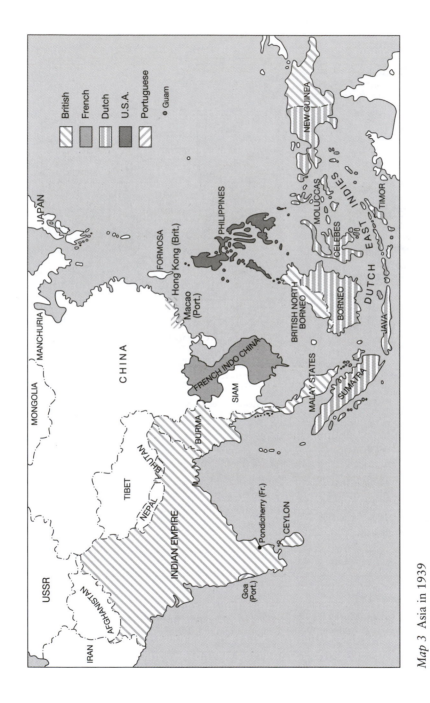

Map 3 Asia in 1939

Source: Chamberlain, Muriel E., *The Longman Companion to European Decolonisation in the Twentieth Century*, © Addison Wesley
Longman Limited, 1998

PART ONE   THE BACKGROUND

CHAPTER ONE

INTRODUCTION

People make race. Differences in skin colour and other physical attributes exist, but on a spectrum rather than in neatly apportioned categories. For centuries, some theorists have noted that it was impossible to determine accurately where one physical type ended and another began. There were too many intermediate colours and forms. Today's genetic science tells us that the situation is even more complicated than this: a person's physical appearance may be no guide at all to ancestry. The 'common sense' belief in the possibility of a consistent, visual identification of race has been constantly questioned. This is why it is so important to emphasise the point that 'race' is a concept created by people rather than nature; it is people who decide how much African ancestry makes a person 'black', or whether 'white' people include Russians, Irish, or Jews. People differ physically from one another in various ways – this is a biological fact – but human beings decide what to make of those differences and how to classify and interpret them.

It is probably helpful to begin with some definitions. Humans seem always to have devised ways of making distinctions between 'Us' and 'Them', but the question is: are such processes inevitably racist, or is modern racism distinctive? Scholars have been examining the difference between ethnicity and race in order to begin to answer this question. The *Oxford English Dictionary* defines an 'ethnic' group as 'having common racial, cultural, religious, or linguistic characteristics' whereas a 'race' is 'a group of persons, animals, or plants, connected by common descent or origin' (*OED Online*). What this tells us is that ethnicity might or might not involve physical characteristics, but race always does. Ethnocentrism is not necessarily based on physically-based discrimination: ethnic groups might identify themselves by language, religion, or other characteristics. Racism, however, is always about physical difference.

The next question to consider is: how and when did physically-based forms of discrimination begin to predominate in European thinking about the world's peoples? There is little agreement among scholars about exactly when racism began, but all would agree that it was evident by 1700. Many would link it to the development of the modern nation-state during the eighteenth century, when political states became increasingly identified with particular 'nations', or peoples. As we shall see, national identities shifted from an emphasis on royal subjecthood or religious affinities to ethnic ties. One aspect of the debate about the origins and nature of racism deserves special mention here. Too often, race is regarded as something possessed only by non-white people. The phrase 'coloured people' is a good example of this: non-whites have colour but, by implication, white people do not. As one scholar puts it: 'as long as white people are not racially seen and named, they/we function as a human norm. Other people are raced, we are just people' (Dyer, 1997: 1). Many scholars today would insist on the inclusion of 'white' as a colour, reminding us that race and racism are not one-way processes. By classifying non-Europeans in various ways, Europeans were classifying themselves as well.

What about the definition of 'imperialism' and 'colonialism'? Imperialism can be defined as 'an imperial system of government . . . esp. when despotic or arbitrary' whereas colonialism is 'an alleged policy of exploitation of backward or weak peoples by a large power' (*OED Online*). 'Colonialism' seems more clearly linked with race, and has acquired a new popularity in recent years as a description of unequal power relations in everything from actual imperial rule to the attitudes that preceded it and lingered after its departure. I prefer 'imperialism' to 'colonialism' because it is broader in historical scope; 'colonialism' usually refers to the modern period. Also, I am uncomfortable with the idea of a timeline which stretches from a pre-colonial period, through colonialism, to today's supposedly post-colonial era. In my opinion, imperialism has been remarkably varied and adaptive throughout human history, reflecting the circumstances of the day without necessarily being tied to territorial rule. Some scholars have even called human beings 'imperial animals' (Tiger and Fox, 1998: *passim*), suggesting that imperialism is both natural and inevitable. The purpose of this book will be to explain and contextualise different theories of race and empire, and the choices people made in order to favour some theories over others. Even if we really are 'imperial animals' (and that is debatable) we are also intelligent, morally conscious beings who can make choices about the way we conceptualise ourselves and others.

What was distinctive about modern imperialism, if anything? One notable characteristic is the widespread alienation of land from the control of indigenous populations. Ancient empires often relied on tribute and military service, favouring the maintenance of indigenous landholding and labour systems in order to maximise revenue. There was migration within and between ancient empires, but not a wholesale dispossession of indigenous populations and their replacement by large numbers of people from distant lands. There is also a question of scope. In ancient times, would-be imperial conquerors already knew the peoples that they hoped to conquer. All of this changed when the Americas and Europe encountered each other. Now, for the first time, vast territories and a wide range of cultures were included in empires that spanned the globe. This produced an increased sense of distance, both geographical and racial, between Europe and its colonies abroad.

Karl Marx was one of the first theorists to notice the relationship between modern capitalism and European imperialism, and his insights remain important whether or not one agrees with his political conclusions. Modern capitalism needs to maintain growth, and after the industrial revolution began in eighteenth-century Britain, the search for resources and markets increased. Overseas operations were financed by metropolitan capital, accelerating modern colonialism's shift away from older notions of imperial tribute-gathering. Modern empires regarded their subjects very differently as a result of this shift. Colonised peoples had once been valuable in their own right, but modern imperial powers sometimes replaced them by others who provided a better return on investment, as in the replacement of indigenous labour by African slaves in the Americas, or the large-scale importation of Asian workers to colonies in Africa or the Pacific. Conditions in the colonies were manipulated where necessary in order to maximise profit. Advocates of this process were quick to point out that it provided increased opportunity for labourers, and that it ensured relatively low prices for consumers at home. Critics maintained that the process relied on racial and geographical inequalities, and on the relative powerlessness of producers and workers outside Europe and North America. Debate about these issues continues, although the word 'imperialism' is usually replaced by 'globalisation' these days, suggesting a new and (possibly) improved state of affairs, and disguising the deep historical background of many of today's most serious problems in international relations.

Questions about the relationship between racism and imperialism are fraught with controversy. Many have believed that both of these things were the inevitable result of natural European superiority, and only fairly recently have these concepts been extensively criticised by people unwilling to take such superiority for granted. My own belief is that chicken-and-egg debates about which came first – racism or imperialism – are ultimately fruitless. Rather than a linear progression from one to the other, it is easier to imagine the two as part of a symbiotic relationship. Each needed the other; each supported the other.

When did racism and imperialism first begin to collude in this way? Some scholars would push racism back into the ancient world; others deny that modern racism has any counterpart. What is clear is that by 1700 the two things were already powerfully related. Unexpected encounters with new peoples in the Americas and the Pacific forced Europeans to create new ways of explaining physical and cultural differences. The rise of print culture, and rising literacy levels in the European world, gave these theories an audience of unprecedented size. For the first time, race relations became the subject of popular interest and, eventually, popular political pressure. There is no doubt that these features of the modern world enhanced the ability of race theory to interact with imperial rule.

There is another dimension to this debate. Is racism really the most important factor in imperialism? Might imperialism exist even if the rulers and the ruled share a common racial origin? English and Scottish colonisation in Ireland was not hindered by the fact that English, Scots, and Irish were all 'white'. Other questions concern the role of class and gender issues. Are there cases in imperial history when race has been less important than social rank or gender? Some recent scholarship has drawn attention to alliances between upper-class gentlemen across the racial divide, as when Indian royal families sent their sons to Oxford and Cambridge, or when British knighthoods and other honours were shared with aristocrats in Africa, Asia, and the Pacific. Other work has pointed out the crucial role of gender, as when cross-racial sexual relations, including marriage, were far more acceptable for white men than for white women. As we will see, white women's reproductive power was usually fiercely protected, suggesting that they were perceived as the guardians of racial purity.

Many historians would say that race relations were always less important to empires than making money. The issue of economics certainly helps to explain the rapid disintegration in the twentieth century of most of the modern territorial empires: they had become increasingly expensive to maintain. New regional trading organisations, and Cold War geopolitics, enabled countries to find materials and markets without the expensive business of imperial rule. Colonial nationalism was difficult and costly to suppress. Open racism was in decline in much of the West after the Second World War, but the reasons for both imperialism and decolonisation cannot be reduced to the single causal factor of racism. Spain's empire in the New World had been accidental at first, created when unexpected continents stood between the Spanish crown and the riches it hoped to exploit in Asia. Racial attitudes certainly helped to facilitate and justify Spanish conquests, but it was the lucrative spice trade, not racism, which had propelled Columbus across the Atlantic. The exploitation of racial 'inferiors' was not necessarily the first priority of imperial powers. David Cannadine has suggested that in many cases there was a 'homogenising convergence' between metropolitan and colonial social structures, at least in the case of the British empire (Cannadine, 2001, 13). This convergence allowed useful connections to be built between men of similar class background and aspirations across the racial divide.

Is expansionism always racist? Critics of globalisation would say yes, pointing to ongoing structural inequalities between white and non-white people around the world. Some ask whether 'decolonisation' has ever really taken place. On the other hand, human rights advocates believe that European and North American influences can be beneficial. What seems clear is that the independence of many former colonies has not removed racism from the world stage, and the words 'colonialism' and 'imperialism' continue to appear on the opinion pages of newspapers and in political debate. Will race and empire always be with us? It might seem so, but my belief is that little is inevitable about human interaction. We make choices about ways of seeing one another, and choices about how to act on those conceptions. Perhaps the only way forward is to recognise the subjectivity of all our world-views, resisting calls to see each other only in one way or another: 'us' or 'them'. To do this responsibly, it is essential to be better informed about the deep history of these ways of seeing one another, and their implications for our shared histories.

PART TWO   ANALYSIS

CHAPTER TWO

THE EARLY MODERN PERIOD

During the fifteenth century, Portuguese explorers sailed along the African coast, establishing trade relations and crossing the Indian Ocean to the markets of south and south-east Asia. Spain, Portugal's great rival, sent its own navigators to Asia by what it believed to be a faster western route, not realising that the American continents stood in the way. These pioneering voyages vastly extended Europe's commercial and political influence, bringing substantial new territories under European rule in the process. The largest of these colonies were in the 'New World' of America, and here the Spanish crown drew on Roman imperial doctrines to create the concept of a global Roman Catholic empire. This concept was reinforced by the Treaty of Tordesillas which divided the known world between Spain and Portugal in 1494. Latecomers to the Americas such as the British and Dutch, who were Protestant, had to find other ideologies for colonial rule. The most prosperous overseas operations, however, were the small trading depots established in Africa and Asia by various European nations. The Portuguese were eventually joined by the French, Dutch, English, and others as European nations scrambled to compete in a new era of globalised trade. In the process, they were forced to find ways of describing and explaining their intensifying encounter with non-Europeans.

RACE IN THE MIDDLE AGES

By the Middle Ages there had already been a shift away from the fairly tolerant polytheisms of the ancient Mediterranean world to the missionary faiths of Christianity and Islam. Distinctions between 'Us' and 'Them' became more explicitly religious: Christians and heathens; Muslims and infidels. Berber Muslims from north Africa invaded Spain in 711, conquering most of it along with parts of south-western France. The 'Moors', as they became known, encouraged the development of a sophisticated culture in the Iberian peninsula. During the eleventh century, Christian leaders from northern Spain began a reconquest, but Moorish power lingered in some coastal areas, including the kingdom of Granada which remained under Muslim rule until 1492 (the same year that Columbus landed in the Caribbean). After the reconquest, royal and aristocratic families became very concerned with *limpieza de sangre* ('purity of blood'), praising whiter complexions as evidence that particular families had not intermarried with Moors or Jews. Family trees were examined closely, and sometimes altered to disguise unacceptable miscegenation. It is difficult to see this process as anything but a physically-based system of discrimination: racism.

In the meantime, a series of Crusades had taken large numbers of European soldiers to the Middle East in an attempt to ensure that Christian holy places stayed under Christian rule. Historians have pointed out the role of European sectarian and political rivalry in the Crusades; Roman Catholic crusaders even sacked the Eastern Orthodox capital of Byzantium at one point. Many other people saw the crusades as an opportunity to expand commercial markets in the eastern Mediterranean. Atrocities were practised by both sides, yet many contemporary accounts by Christians praise the honourable conduct of their Muslim opponents. Nevertheless, the Conquest and Reconquest, along with the Crusades and various forms of commercial and political rivalry in north Africa, produced entrenched hostility between the Christian and Muslim worlds. One pioneering historian of Portuguese imperialism has suggested that centuries of conflict 'kept alive the traditional Portuguese hatred of the Muslim' and 'predisposed them to regard all the followers of the Prophet as mortal enemies, whether they were Moors, Arabs, Swahili, Persians, Indians, or Malays' (Boxer, 1963: 6).

Another group regarded as problematic by Europeans were the Jews. Scattered by the Romans during the first century, Jews had settled in Europe and elsewhere with varying degrees of success. Because Christians were forbidden to lend money for interest, Jews became associated with money lending, becoming a focus for the resentment and anxiety that always surrounds this necessary but unpopular activity. Jewish dietary restrictions inhibited social interaction with Christians, and intermarriage was relatively rare. Sometimes Jewish communities coexisted peacefully with Christians for centuries, only to find that they provided a convenient scapegoat for changing economic or political conditions. The periodic expulsion of Jews from various European cities during the Middle Ages combined with images of them as an alien people, suggesting that they were not truly European. Like the mutual hostility between the Christian and Muslim worlds, tense relationships between Christian and Jewish communities created longstanding patterns of suspicion and hostility that sometimes erupted into violence.

Were the traumas of Muslim rule, the Crusades, and the persecution of Jews the primary reasons for the development of racism in Europe? Current debates focus on the question of whether religion or skin colour was the most important difference between Europeans and others. One point of view insists on 'the problem that dark skin . . . posed for a [Christian] culture that believed that God made man in his own image' (Hall, 1995: 13). If black skin was perceived negatively, how could black people have been created in the image of God? Religious identities must indeed be taken seriously in their ability to challenge racial distinctions. Christianity is not a 'western' faith; Europeans had been converted by darker-skinned missionaries from the eastern Mediterranean and northern Africa. Some scholars contend that Christians conceptualised 'the idea of the Moor and the Jew as infidels, unbelievers whose physical differences are signs (but not causes or effects) of their unbelief' (Appiah, 1995: 278). This interpretation was reflected in medieval medical theories, which suggested that physical appearance could be affected by climate, or by shocks experienced during pregnancy. It also helps to explain Spanish racial fears following the Reconquest. It fails, however, to deal with the question of how non-European Christians should be regarded; a problem which became increasingly acute after Spain's discovery of the Americas. Could Christianised Indians be regarded as equals?

THE SHOCK OF THE NEW WORLD

Christopher Columbus landed in 1492 on what he believed to be a south-east Asian island. After claiming the area for Spain, he remained convinced that he had discovered a western route to the 'Indies' (hence the name 'West Indies' for the Caribbean islands). It quickly became clear, however, that he and his successors had stumbled upon new and unexpected lands. Spain's vast empire in the 'New World' was unprecedented, overturning earlier world-views based on biblical geography, and introducing Europe to a range of new human societies. It was a defining moment in the history of European imperialism, and an enormous challenge to existing views of human difference. There was no existing framework within which to identify new peoples. The Americas were not mentioned in the Bible. Medieval travellers' tales about the Orient, or stories about 'wild men' in the mountains of Europe, had not prepared Europeans for the intellectual challenge of an unexpected New World. Ancient philosophers had speculated about the possible existence of monstrous peoples in other parts of the world; others had insisted that the climatic extremes at the polar and equatorial zones would rule out the development of human life there.

Columbus's first reports told of human beings with few material possessions who were content with nakedness, suggesting the biblical innocence of the Garden of Eden. However, these indigenous societies also featured familiar characteristics such as social rank and warfare. If they were not inhabitants of an unknown Eden, what were they? Some theorists suggested that they were 'pre-Adamites': peoples descended from humans created before Adam and Eve and living in a state of innocence. It is clear that the earliest visitors to the Americas were unsure about how to interpret what they saw and, at first, tended to represent Indians using the standard conventions of European art without emphasising their physical distinctiveness. Idealistic fantasies about the Indians did not survive long in the colonies, not least because of the precipitous decline of Indian populations after European contact. The usefulness of the concept of a 'noble savage' persisted in some strands of European thought, however, and would be revived when Europe encountered another set of unexpected peoples in the south Pacific in the eighteenth century. As with earlier images of primeval innocence, these interpretations were profoundly Eurocentric: critiques of the corruption and decadence of Europe based on little (if any) actual knowledge of indigenous societies.

Spanish and Portuguese colonisation in the Americas featured two goals: economic exploitation and religious conversion. Both of these aims required extensive involvement by the indigenous population, and there was debate about whether or not they possessed rights which Europeans should respect. The outcome of this debate was not inevitable. The ancient Greek philosopher, Aristotle, had identified civility with urban life, claiming that there were natural and obvious differences between 'irrational' and 'rational' men (all women and children being irrational). Aristotle pronounced the Greek city-states to be rational, but all other peoples were irrational 'barbarians'.

The Americas had been unknown to Aristotle and the rest of the ancient Mediterranean world, however. Theorists created additional categories of 'barbarians' in order to cope, using standards of political and social organisation to locate different peoples in a scale of civilisation. The lowest category included peoples 'without king, without compacts, without magistrates or republic, and who changed their dwelling-place, or – if it were fixed – had one that resembled the cave of a wild beast' (Elliott, 1992: 49). Ranking schemes also distinguished between literate, monotheistic peoples such as Christians and Muslims, and the followers of polytheistic faiths such as Hindus. This hierarchical approach to human difference would remain intact into the twentieth century, although explanations of difference would change. For the moment, both cultural and physical distinctions were important, but it is no coincidence that white people were always at the top of the hierarchy. In a substantial departure from Aristotle's work, white skin was becoming identified with civilisation. As Spanish conquests proceeded in central and south America, evidence of human sacrifice joined the list of characteristics that allowed Europeans to regard indigenous Americans as inferior and therefore suitable for exploitation. In some cases they were hunted with dogs, as though they were animals. 'What manner of being are the Christians?' wondered the inhabitants of what is now Nicaragua. 'Christians do not want to work: they are liars, mockers, gamblers, perverts, and blasphemers' (Dickason, 1997: 134).

Not everyone agreed about the inferiority of non-Europeans; in 1537 the Pope declared Indians to be fully human, making them appropriate subjects for conversion. For the Jesuits and other missionaries, it was essential to emphasise human equality before God. It is true that missionary accounts often noted cannibalism or other evidence of 'bestiality', just as the reports of the *conquistadores* had done, but the purpose of this ethnography was to demonstrate that Indians were men and women with the same spiritual needs as any other subjects under Catholic rule. Some individuals went further: the Dominican friar Bartholomé de las Casas became a particularly staunch advocate of indigenous rights. In 1550 he debated with a spokesman for the colonists, Juan Ginés de Sepúlveda, in the presence of Spanish theologians [*Doc. 2*]. Both men drew on an impressive range of ancient and contemporary authorities in order to argue for or against Indian rights, and the outcome of the debate was not immediately clear. All further conquests in the New World were ordered to be suspended while the ideological battle raged. De Sepúlveda followed Aristotle in declaring that some people were naturally slaves, adding that the conquest of Indian kingdoms would facilitate the spread of Roman Catholicism. Las Casas also hoped for the conversion of the Indians, but not their conversion from a state of natural slavery. He believed in the fundamental equality of all human races.

The theological judges of this famous debate were unable to decide on their verdict: a telling moment of hesitation between 'othering' and 'brothering'. What eventually decided the Spanish government was a fear that the colonists of Peru, and perhaps other colonies, would openly rebel against the Spanish crown if it failed to uphold their ability to exploit indigenous labour as they saw fit. Las Casas's universalist approach to indigenous rights gave way to an emphasis on hierarchies of superiority and inferiority.

RACE AND NEW WORLD GOVERNANCE

Continental imperial expansion often involved a combination of settlement and the colonisation of extensive areas of land. In Spain's New World colonies the category *Indio* ('Indian') became an administrative designation indicating someone who lived in an Indian village, was counted on the census as Indian, and paid tribute to the colonial state in the form of labour or goods. Racial categories were created and enforced by the state; they were not merely 'natural' designations. Various words were used to describe mixed-race people in the Spanish colonies, but in many cases general terms such as *casta* (breed) were used for everyone who was not Indian, or a slave (of African ancestry), or Spanish (Wade, 1997: 29). Despite some local differences, there was always a *sociedad de castas* (social organisation of breeds) in which Spaniards or those of Spanish descent were always at the top. The *encomienda* system of the early Spanish empire granted land to successful military leaders along with the right to collect tribute from the Indians and to command their labour. Only after the crown abolished Indian slavery in the 1550s did the Spanish empire turn to African slavery. Indians were still forced to supply labour to the crown, but they were no longer technically slaves, and now ranked higher in the *sociedad de castas* than black people did. The greater recognition of Indian rights came at the price of withholding those rights from African slaves.

There is considerable debate about how racist the Spanish empire intended to be. The frequent use of the phrase *obedezco pero no cumplo* ('I obey but do not execute') in official correspondence reveals the way in which local colonial rulers resisted directives with which they disagreed. The Spanish crown's attempts to regulate and humanise the *encomienda* by abolishing Indian slavery is one example of this process: local governments simply introduced forced labour instead. The relative success of Catholic missionaries in the New World had been one reason for the crown's increasing concern about Indian rights, but missions could be raided for forced labour or land. The horrific impact of European diseases on the New World could be interpreted in various ways, prompting statements of compassion and protection from Spain, and inviting an accelerating seizure of Indian lands in the colonies. For all these reasons, colonial rulers felt justified in using *obedezco pero no cumplo* 'to postpone indefinitely the execution of royal wishes' (Phelan, 1960: 60). As we shall see, other empires featured the same split in opinion between the metropolis and the colonies. Colonists often resented what they saw as the ill-informed idealism of their distant imperial masters, and took action to subvert it.

In Portuguese-ruled Brazil, the early coasting trade had required much more collaboration with the indigenous population; in fact, 90 per cent of Brazil's population lived within one hundred miles of the coast before 1900 (Burns, 1995: 2). Before the eighteenth century the common language of Brazilian commerce was Tupi, a coastal indigenous language. The subsequent influx of African slaves led to the replacement of Tupi by Portuguese because this was the language that blacks were forced to learn. Epidemics of smallpox, and a diminishing economic importance in a slave society, combined to reduce drastically the size and influence of the indigenous population in Brazil. Today, only small groups of Indians are left, mainly in the interior of the Amazon basin, and their livelihood continues to be threatened by deforestation and dislocation.

Other early empires sent more substantial numbers of settlers to their colonies than the Spanish or Portuguese did. England governed the largest overseas settlements, having already experimented with plantation systems in Ireland where English or Scottish Protestant landowners exploited Irish Catholic peasant labour. But the colonisation of Ireland had involved making distinctions among different types of Christian Europeans; the colonisation of North America was a very different prospect. Not only were the English dealing with a non-European indigenous population, but they did so on territory already claimed by Spain. As a Protestant country by the seventeenth century, England discounted the various papal directives giving territory to Spain and Portugal, and the English were not initially dismissive of Indians rights, not least because they wanted to distinguish their empire from that of the Spaniards. Some English settlers struggled to overcome language barriers and other obstacles in order to attempt to comprehend and describe Indian society, but theorists back in Europe were more interested in creating hierarchies in order to legitimise colonial conquest [*Doc. 3*]. The title of one English study clearly reveals its purpose: *The Scale of Creatures*, published in 1676, maintained that 'the Europeans do not only differ... in colour [but also] in natural manners and in the internal qualities of their minds' (Lindqvist, 1996: 100).

Some scholars have argued that it was the English philosopher Thomas Hobbes who did most to overcome the old Aristotelian debates in favour of a new methodology which would enable the development of modern notions of race and racial hierarchy. Hobbes's *The Leviathan* (1651) proposed that humanity was naturally disposed to warfare and conquest. Civil states arose as defence mechanisms, allowing their citizens to escape continual conflict through a shared identity and goals. Peoples whose form of government was unrecognisable to European eyes were therefore fit for conquest, making English colonies 'voyds by warre' whose indigenous inhabitants did not possess rights to the soil (Hannaford, 1995: 193). Hobbes repudiated Aristotle's claims about the fundamental importance of law and governance, claiming instead that men governed through strength of arms. Although he did not use the word 'race' in the modern sense, he did discuss the existence of a 'race' for power which had positive implications for expanding imperial rule. Such thinking was by no means universal in the early English empire. Samuel Purchas's account of early English exploration and colonisation contained the following classic statement of Christian universalism: 'The tawney Morre, black Negro, duskie Libyan, ash-coloured Indian, olive-coloured American should with the whiter European become one sheepe-fold, under one great shepheard' (Hannaford, 1995: 171). Hobbes, however, had described unequal power relations as natural and inevitable, providing a significant alternative to older schemes based on more inclusive political or spiritual imperatives.

The English depended too much on Indians to discount them entirely. They might be deemed 'savages', but their hunting and agriculture saved many an early settlement from starvation, and their military assistance was critical in conflicts with rival imperial forces in North America. The Hudson's Bay Company (HBC), chartered in 1670 to pursue the fur trade in northern North America, relied on indigenous trapping for its profits. It also had few 'settlers' as such, preferring to use the indenture system to bring young men from Britain to work in the trade for a limited period of time. Many of these men married into Indian families. To the south, in the British settlement colonies, treaties were negotiated in order to codify and facilitate relationships between indigenous leaders and the British; a very different situation from that in the Spanish empire. There is a clear difference between Spanish or Portuguese proclamations of prior sovereignty in the New World, and England's more negotiated presence; there is also a difference between the largely self-governing English settlements and the centralised metropolitan control Spain hoped to impose on its empire.

Nevertheless, treaty relationships did not automatically convey racial equality in North America. The 'Jamestown Massacre' of 1622 demonstrates the early date by which some indigenous peoples decided that the newcomers were becoming too numerous and too land-hungry for their liking. As the pace of settlement grew, interracial relationships had grown increasingly strained and in 1622 Indians attacked the settlers, killing 247 men, women, and children. The impact on race relations was immediate. One account denounced 'the bloudy and barbarous hands of that perfidious and inhumane people' who had committed a massacre 'contrary to all lawes of God and men, of Nature and Nations' and had dismembered the corpses 'with base and brutish triumph' (Samson, 2001a: 46). A vicious cycle of retaliation and fresh attacks would mark the frontier of settlement from this point on, enhancing the impression that Indians were fundamentally alien peoples whose savagery demanded conquest and control.

The French also used treaty relationships to facilitate settlement in the St Lawrence valley, in what is now Canada, and to extend fur trading operations to the west and south as far as Louisiana [*Doc. 4*]. Explorer Jacques Cartier's activities in the St Lawrence area in 1541–2 had not boded well: an eyewitness reported that 'When we landed, some of our brainless young bucks cut off arms and legs from several of these poor people, just to see, they said, if their swords cut properly. This was in spite of the fact that these barbarians had received them well, in friendship' (Dickason, 1997: 171). France's claim to rights of discovery and settlement in Canada and elsewhere was based on missionary aspirations; Cartier's expeditions were meant to 'establish the Christian faith in a savage land far from France . . . even though [the King] knew full well no gold or silver mines were to be found there, nor any other gains save the conquest of souls for God' (Dickason, 1997: 172). This strategy was meant to challenge the Pope's division of the world between Spain and Portugal by claiming that French imperialism would also enhance the growth of Roman Catholicism.

France sent Jesuits and other missionaries to their North American territories, where they made slow but steady progress in converting indigenous groups to Christianity. French statesmen were also interested in profit and settlement, however. New France (now Québec) was founded in 1608, and by the end of the seventeenth century its population was about 20,000. New France's Huron allies were particularly crucial to the defence of the colony, especially against the British-allied Iroquois, and the French fur trade was as dependent on Indian trapping as its British counterpart. This was inevitable in colonies dedicated to exploiting indigenous trade networks and settling colonists. As one French statesman put it, the Spanish had 'wished not to cultivate, but to devastate' (Pagden, 1995: 93). Nevertheless, French rule was not free from racial distinctions. Indigenous leaders complained that the French had stopped sending their children to live with them: a system of mutual adoption and education that was a feature of indigenous alliance-making. The French remained keen to obtain Indian children, but as 'hostages . . . for the safety of the French who are among them, and for the strengthening of our commercial relations' (Dickason, 1997: 259). Because New France never became heavily populated, and the pressure on land remained relatively low, the implications of this attitude never became apparent. Those Indians who converted to Christianity became French subjects, holding land from the French crown, but the bulk of the indigenous population remained relatively unaffected by this policy; in 1665 the French king himself ordered New France 'not to usurp the lands on which [Indians] habitually reside on the pretext that they would be improved by the French' (Dickason, 1997: 274). Whether or not native people possessed full sovereignty was never put to the test until much later.

SLAVERY

African slavery began long before Europeans began to explore the African coasts at the end of the fifteenth century, but the European trade would vastly exceed earlier precedents in both scope and brutality. What effect did this have on European concepts of race? There is much debate about which came first: slavery or racism. Did the enslaved condition of Africans create the notion of Africans as inferior, or did a pre-existing racism encourage the enslavement of Africans? Religious and racial identities seem to have varied in relative importance, as in Shakespeare's *Othello* (1622) where a Christian black man is able to become a military and political leader, and marries a white woman, but then degenerates into a wife-killer amid metaphors of bestiality and savagery. Recent scholarship seems to incline toward a 'racism first' explanation which declares that 'The racist beliefs that Iberians and others would later refine to a "science" were firmly entrenched before Christopher Columbus made landfall in the Americas' (Sweet, 1997: 144).

Early modern Europeans consulted Aristotle, who had believed that slavery was natural because some peoples were irrational and others were not. For the civilised to enslave uncivilised 'barbarians' was therefore proper. Aristotle had not been speaking specifically about Africans, however; slavery in the ancient Mediterranean world was widespread, and unrelated to skin colour. The global scale of early modern imperial expansion was unprecedented and the traditional classical authorities were inadequate guides to its novel features. Some historians see Europe's enslavement of Africans as unique, featuring forms of discrimination which were 'noticeably new, whose stark racial character makes the study of the philosophy and practice of enslavement a useful vantage point from which to track the growth of racial identification' (Blackburn, 1997: 66).

A particularly useful scholarly debate concerns the biblical story of the sons of Noah. After the biblical flood, Noah's three sons received different divinely ordained fates. Ham accidentally saw his father's nakedness while Noah was drunk, and his descendants were condemned to serve those of the other two sons, Shem and Japheth. This story was interpreted to refer to the division of the known world between the descendants of these three sons: Europe to Japheth, Asia to Shem (hence the word 'Semitic'), and Africa to Ham. Although this interpretation was ancient, the use to which it could be put in an age of European expansionism was modern. The 'Curse of Ham', one historian argues, was re-examined in a new light following Europe's discovery of new peoples in America and sub-Saharan Africa and 'more attention was given to Genesis 9 [the story of Noah] . . . in the sixteenth and seventeenth centuries than had been the case, arguably, in the entire history of Christian exegesis' (Braude, 1997: 141). As more and more European colonies purchased African slaves from the Portuguese, and began to establish their own slaving operations on the west African coast, the link with apparent biblical endorsement grew stronger. Purchas, the English chronicler of exploration and early colonisation, changed his own interpretation of the Noah story from one emphasising the unity of humankind to one specifically identifying the inferiority of the descendants of Ham. 'These are descended of Chus [Canaan], the Sonne of cursed Cham [Ham]; as are all of that complexion, Not so by reason of their Seed, not heat of the Climate; nor of the Solye . . . but rather from the Curse of Noe [Noah] upon Cham' (Braude, 1997: 137). The interpretation of the curse as slavery was familiar from ancient Christian thought, but in an age of imperial expansion and widespread African slavery, an old story received significantly new emphasis. Other thinkers would elaborate this concept of divinely ordained African inferiority, as when the French philosopher Charles de Montesquieu introduced an aesthetic judgement: ugly, black bodies deserved to be enslaved. 'One could not imagine that God, who is a very wise being, would have placed a soul, especially a good soul, in a body entirely black', he declared (Hannaford, 1995: 197).

Since it was the Portuguese who first established a widespread slave trade for Europe's expanding colonies, we should take a particularly close look at Portuguese attitudes toward race and slavery. The notion that Portugal's empire was uniquely tolerant of racial difference has come under scrutiny in recent years: 'it is an article of faith with many Portuguese that their country has never tolerated a colour-bar in its overseas possessions', but although these beliefs might be sincerely held 'it does not follow that they are always well grounded on historical fact' (Boxer, 1963: 1–2). One advocate of Indian slavery in Brazil attempted to link Indians with the curse of Ham in order to facilitate their enslavement, adding that they were 'not true human beings, but beasts of the forest incapable of understanding the Catholic faith', and that many of them 'killed themselves out of spite like barbarians' to avoid enslavement (Boxer, 1963: 96–7).

Such views were often criticised by the Portuguese government, and by some of the more humanitarian missionaries, but no widespread protest greeted similar beliefs about Africans. Early Portuguese ties with the Christianised king Dom Affonso I of the Congo were quickly succeeded by mutual hostility as Portuguese slaving operations expanded in the area. Far from objecting to this process, missionaries and clerics needed little encouragement to begin 'preaching with the sword and the rod of iron' and even to profit directly from the slave trade (Boxer, 1963: 22). In their coastal enclave of Angola, the Portuguese were shipping out 6,000–7,000 slaves per year by the mid-seventeenth century in order to sustain the development of plantations in Brazil. The Portuguese king's advisers reminded him in 1688 that there was nothing natural about this state of affairs: west Africans 'loathed our rule . . . and only out of fear and respect for our arms did they allow the preaching of the gospel and the admission of our trade' (Boxer, 1963: 37). The royal court made attempts to curb the violence of the slave trade but, as one Portuguese governor of Angola put it, Africans 'fear nothing save only corporal punishment and the whip' (Boxer, 1963: 27). The occasional missionary protested about the essential injustice of widespread slave trading, but most Portuguese humanitarians during this period were concerned about the treatment of slaves, or their access to religious instruction, rather than the institution of slavery itself. As we can see from the earliest account of a shipment of African slaves to Europe [*Doc. 1*], amid conflicting theories about the origin of Africans, their consignment to a 'lower hemisphere' enabled them to be regarded as natural slaves. When combined with the enormous profits to be made in slaving, and the accelerating demand for slaves in the Americas and elsewhere, such explanations were increasingly convenient.

Other European countries entered the slave trade later than Portugal. Dutch settlers arrived in south Africa during the seventeenth century where they enslaved Africans from groups they identified as particularly inferior. Like other trading empires, the Dutch needed indigenous knowledge and trading networks and 'for the Dutch blackness was not a core attribute' as yet (Van Den Boogaart, 1982: 53). They were contemptuous of the 'Hottentots' (Khoi), however, whom the first Dutch commander at the Cape called 'dull, stupid, lazy, and stinking' (Marks, 1981: 16). Nevertheless, miscegenation with Khoi and other Africans near the Cape Colony was extensive enough to generate a debate about intermarriage during the later seventeenth century, and a formal ban on mixed-race marriage by the Dutch East India Company (VOC) in 1685. Racial distance increased at the Cape Colony by the eighteenth century, especially after growing demands for land led to the 'Hottentot Wars'. The near-extermination of many Khoi communities by smallpox in 1713 enhanced the picture of an inferior people giving way before European expansion. As the scale and frequency of warfare increased between the Dutch and various African groups, enslavement helped to guarantee a labour supply for the colony. This, in turn, generated greater superiority and hostility by the Cape Dutch toward Africans in general: a classic example of the interrelationship between expansionism and racism.

English slavery followed a similar pattern with some exceptions. The defeat of Dutch forces during several maritime wars during the seventeenth century brought England into greater international prominence. By the later seventeenth century, English overseas commerce was expanding rapidly and the growing colonies in America and the West Indies were now dependent on African slave labour. Rather than rely on the Portuguese to supply slaves, the English established their own trade and were able to enhance it in the teeth of Spanish opposition thanks to their growing power at sea. By 1700 England would dominate the European slave trade, ousting Portugal from its preferred position as supplier of slaves to the Spanish empire.

One of the best-known explanations of changing English attitudes toward black slavery comes from the work of Winthrop Jordan, who points out that economic demand, coupled with European military power, were crucial to the establishment of slavery. They are not sufficient explanations, however, of why it was Africans who became 'special candidates for degradation' (Jordan, 1974: 50). During the seventeenth century he notes a shift in the terminology by which English colonists referred to themselves: 'From the initially most common term *Christian*, at mid-century there was a marked shift toward the terms *English* and *free*. After about 1680, taking the colonies as a whole, a new term of self-identification appeared – *white*' (Jordan, 1974: 52). The equation of whiteness with freedom, and blackness with slavery, was so well established by the end of the century that a Virginia law code of 1705 decreed 'That all servants imported and brought into this country, by sea or land . . . shall be accounted and be slaves, and as such be here bought and sold notwithstanding a conversion to Christianity afterwards' (Jordan, 1974: 51). It was clear that Christianity was no longer a common bond across racial lines; blackness, not heathendom, was the sign of slavery, and in opposition to blackness a new emphasis on whiteness was arising to symbolise freedom and superiority.

MISCEGENATION

The scale of early modern expansionism provided many opportunities for cross-racial sexual contact, and produced increasingly large mixed-race groups. Sexual relations, whether willing or otherwise, usually took place between

European men and non-European women, although there were exceptions. Recent scholarship has explored the many ways in which 'Colonialism . . . was not only a machine of war and administration, it was also a desiring machine' (Young, 1995: 98). The legal status of cross-racial relationships, or of mixed-race children, provides important insights into imperial power relations. Were marriages common between European men and non-European women, or were sexual relationships usually more informal or coercive? Were mixed-race children recognised by their European fathers, and if so, did they enjoy the same social status as children of entirely European ancestry? Were degrees of racial intermixture recognised by law, or was one non-European ancestor enough to classify a person as 'black', 'Indian', or 'aboriginal'?

Spain had no official objection to miscegenation at first, but its colonial officials often tried to maintain Spanish blood purity in the New World: a good example of 'I obey but do not execute' (Phelan, 1960: 59). These attempts were largely ineffective. By the eighteenth century, specific mixed-race identities arose to reflect the consequences of widespread miscegenation. The question is: were these various groups considered equals? The answer is definitely no. As we have seen, the different *castas* were ranked in a hierarchy with European-born Spaniards at the top and black slaves at the bottom. Although *mestizos* (Spanish-Indians) could sometimes rise to prominence, especially if they were descended from a high-ranking Spanish ancestor, the vast majority of them were poor and forbidden either to hold *encomiendas* or to enter the priesthood. *Mulattos* (Spanish-Africans) and freed slaves were even more marginalised, and the reason is not far to seek. African ancestry was more of a disadvantage than Indian ancestry. Indians enjoyed specific legal rights and protection, especially after Spain abolished their official enslavement, and some very high-ranking Indian nobles had African slaves. For blacks to have owned Indian slaves was impossible.

There were similar trends in Portugal's mixed-race colonial communities. The early Portuguese trading operations in Brazil relied extensively on *cunhadismo*, or 'in-lawism', by which marriages into Indian families gave Portuguese traders a wide range of social and economic connections. The enslavement of Indians, and later Africans, enhanced the position of the *mamelucos* (Portuguese-Indians) who formed the backbone of Brazilian commerce and administration. Nevertheless, it is important to note that the word *mameluco* comes from the east African slave trade where it was used by the Portuguese to describe the African overseers that they used to discipline other Africans. This suggests that the *mamelucos* were useful to the Portuguese, even essential, but not necessarily equal. In Portugal's east African and Indian outposts, European-born Portuguese were always favoured, even in the Church, where decrees had been issued banning racial discrimination. By the eighteenth century even the metropolitan government had become openly discriminatory. A directive of 1715 concerning the south Asian outpost of

Goa warned that Indians 'should on no account be preferred to nor equalled in any way with the Portuguese, because such is convenient for my service, and the authority and prestige of our nation' (Boxer, 1963: 73). Far from being equitable about mixed-race groups, Portuguese policy did not even treat locally-born Portuguese with the same respect granted to those born in Europe. Blood and breeding mattered.

In the French and English fur trading operations in North America, on the other hand, prosperity depended on the Indians who caught most of the furs and provided most of the food. The scale of civilisation might rank Indian societies below those of Europe, but during the killing northern winters these intellectual schemes scarcely mattered. Europeans relied on the indigenous population, marrying Indian women in order to gain access to geographical information and trading networks, and signing treaties with Indian chiefs in order to guarantee their security. The fact that Indians had social practices and political organisations that Europeans could recognise, with leaders who could be negotiated with on behalf of the group, made interaction easier. Mixed-race relationships did not reflect racial equality, however. The famous marriage between John Rolfe and Pocahontas in 1614 is a case in point: their relationship reflected the quest for peaceful coexistence between some settlers and some Indians in colonial Virginia, but it also reflected Rolfe's wish to Christianise Pocahontas and the government's attempt to construct Pocahontas's powerful father as a vassal of the English crown. Rolfe was urged to couch his permission to marry not in terms of two people who wished to share their lives, but 'for the good of the plantation, the honour of our country, for the glory of God, for mine own salvation, and for the converting to the true knowledge of God and Jesus Christ an unbelieving creature' (Canny, 1998: 159). When Pocahontas visited England with her husband she dressed appropriately for a high-ranking woman of the English nobility, yet was disappointed when she failed to be greeted with the cere-mony and tribute she believed to be due to her status. We know the rest of the story: such intermarriages remained extremely rare in the British settlement colonies, and race relations deteriorated rapidly into open warfare on some parts of the settlement frontier. Although the British forged military alliances with Indian groups against their European competitors, especially France, they usually did not welcome Indians into their families as equals.

The key was the presence or absence of substantial settlement. In colonies with relatively few Europeans, there were not enough white women to allow the creation of all-white enclaves. European empires in Asia were character-ised by extensive *métissage* during this early period. A distinctive Eurasian clan system developed in Batavia where extensive intermarriage had been actively assisted by the VOC in Java. Higher-ranking officials could afford to support families, but soldiers and clerks could not, and the VOC encouraged them by providing dowries for Asian brides and even paying for the freedom of enslaved women so that they could marry Dutch husbands. The only caveat was a decree of 1617 banning marriages between Dutch men and non-Christian Asian women. The ultimate goal of this policy was to encourage the Christianisation of Java through the creation of a Europeanised mixed-race community. The outcome was questionable, however, since contemporary observers noted that 'After having been married for years, the [Asian] ladies are often, therefore, as ignorant of the world and of manners as upon their wedding day' (Boxer, 1965: 224). Commercial and political expediency were much more important in the end than the education and Europeanisation of wives. Likewise, Britain's East India Company (EIC) had no objection to intermarriage, especially if it conveyed obvious political or economic benefits. This view would change in the later eighteenth century, as we shall see. In the meantime, differences between the trading empires in Asia, and the expanding British and Dutch settlements in North America and southern Africa, were clear. Where there was widespread settlement involving European families, and an increasing demand for land, racial distance increased.

CHAPTER THREE

THE MODERN EMPIRES, 1700–1820

The vast Spanish and Portuguese empires were under siege by the eighteenth century. Spain remained anxious to retain its hold on the most profitable areas of its empire, namely the central and south American colonies, but rising *crillo* (colonial-born European) nationalism in the late eighteenth century became full-blown independence movements by the early 1800s. Meanwhile, France was reviving its overseas empire while Britain rose to a global industrial and maritime dominance that would not be challenged until the late nineteenth century. The loss of the American colonies after 1776 did little to slow the growth of British imperialism. Explorers, merchants, and missionaries produced a flood of information about non-European peoples, and an increasingly literate public was eager for publications which would explain and interpret the outside world. Some theorists sought universal laws of progress which would explain human development while others emphasised the inborn destiny of particular ethnic groups. These scientific developments reinforced existing tensions between human universalism and human difference; between and 'brothering' and 'othering'. This produced a situation in which 'two pre-Darwinian ethnological hypotheses were formed: "race is nothing" and "race is everything"' (Hannaford, 1995: 236).

ENLIGHTENMENT, RACE, AND EMPIRE

One of the characteristics of the Enlightenment was a growing emphasis on empirical observation and analysis; this process enabled the gradual replacement of theological and metaphysical conceptions by more secular theories of race and culture. Information flowed back to Europe from explorers and colonists, leading to the formation of groups such as the Société des Observateurs de l'Homme in France. Europeans had already created schemes with which to rank the various peoples they had encountered during the process of imperial expansion. They had already speculated about possible relationships between humanity and the animal world, imagining unknown continents populated by monsters. As knowledge of the outside world grew, however, Europeans developed new ways of understanding and justifying the expansion of their empires.

The publication in 1748 of Montesquieu's *Spirit of the Laws* was a landmark. Montesquieu believed that it was necessary to move beyond the old, classical texts to find new ways of understanding the world's peoples. Instead of the political characteristics that Aristotle had emphasised, Montesquieu tried to find natural explanations of human difference. He introduced the word 'races' as a way of describing three stages of human development, from political, to feudal, and finally to the commercial, northern European societies he admired. By linking social development to ethnicity, Montesquieu and others allowed northern ethnic groups (such as French or Germans) to claim superiority over Moors, blacks, Jews, and even the classical civilisations which had formerly been regarded as models [*Doc. 5*]. It was Montesquieu who introduced the word 'savage' as a specific category in a social evolutionary scheme. Previously, almost all Africans, native Americans, and Pacific peoples had been called 'savages' or 'barbarians' in a generalised and not necessarily negative way. Montesquieu used the word 'savage' more precisely to describe the lowest type of barbarian. This usage made the word increasingly pejorative, especially where Africans and other darker-skinned people were concerned. Enlightenment preoccupations with classification and notions of progress produced a range of ranking schemes which placed Europeans at the top of human hierarchies and the darkest-skinned peoples at the bottom.

This might seem to be a clear-cut case of the 'othering' of non-Europeans, but the situation was more complicated than this. The place of intermediate groups between 'white' and 'black' was sometimes difficult to define. From the earliest days of Spanish and Portuguese colonisation, the concept of the *bon sauvage* ('noble savage') appealed to idealists wishing to criticise the decadence and authoritarianism of Europe. The 'noble savage' was revived by a number of French Enlightenment philosophers, including Jean-Jacques Rousseau, who believed that institutions corrupted humanity, and that a natural, even primitive state was preferable. Rousseau's contemporaries were deeply divided about the supposed superiority of the 'noble savage', especially since a longstanding acquaintance with indigenous peoples had challenged its assumptions, but the concept received an unexpected boost when Europe encountered new, exotic peoples in the south Pacific during the later eighteenth century. Racial hierarchies could be used both to glorify and to criticise the civilisations at the top of the scale.

Tension between 'othering' and 'brothering' notions of race was clear in the work of two leading Enlightenment theorists, Georges-Louis Leclerc, comte de Buffon, and Johann Blumenbach. Buffon's *Natural History* (1749–67) emphasised the unity of the human species, pointing to the fertility of mixed-race offspring as evidence of this. He proposed an environmental theory of degeneration to explain differences in human appearance and culture: non-Europeans did not live in the same favourable circumstances that Europeans enjoyed [*Doc. 8*]. Europeans represented the high standard from which others had declined. This theory had enormous appeal because it removed the biblical Middle East from the centre of attention (a problem when Middle Eastern peoples were considered inferior to Europeans) and offered a more modern scheme apparently based on scientific observations. Although clearly Eurocentric, Buffon's scheme held time and distance – not race – responsible for the development of human difference. There was no essential, biological difference between human beings.

Blumenbach, one of the founders of physical anthropology, published *The Natural Variety of Mankind* in 1775 to show how skeletal forms, especially skulls, differed between the races. White-skinned people, whom he named 'Caucasians' in the 1781 edition, were (naturally) considered to have the largest and most attractive skulls. Blumenbach's work derided those who sought links between Africans and apes or other animals. Nevertheless, his pioneering work would allow others to take the implications of physical anthropology much further, to the extent of denying fundamental human unity. One colleague remembered that Blumenbach's study included the skull of a mentally ill man 'which, not without meaning, lay side by side with that of the orang-utan; whilst, at a little distance off, the surpassingly beautiful shape of that of a female [Caucasian] attracted everyone's attention' (Hannaford, 1995: 213).

Scientific attempts to prove a 'link' between apes and humans go back at least to 1700 when William Tyson, an anatomist, became interested in the newly discovered orang-utan of south-east Asia. Comparing orang-utans with the pygmy peoples of southern Africa, Tyson concluded that 'in this chain of creation for an intermediate link between ape and man I would place our pygmy' (Lindqvist, 1996: 100). Enlightenment theorists were mainly concerned with material observations about social organisation and economic activity, however, and many rejected the sort of speculation that Tyson indulged in. The French anatomist Georges Cuvier repeatedly stated that it was impossible to rank animal species: 'The further I have progressed in the study of nature, the more convinced I have become that this is the most untruthful concept ever brought into natural history' (cited Lindqvist, 1996: 99). Nevertheless, Cuvier felt able to rank different types of human beings, saying of Africans that 'The hordes belonging to this variant of human being have always remained in a state of total barbarism' (Lindqvist, 1996: 99).

The point of all this was supposed to be an emphasis on the changeability of different human societies, and some Enlightenment thinkers saw in this a warning against European interference in the wider world. Where scholars once connected Enlightenment science with imperial expansion in a fairly direct way, recent work has begun to question the assumption that Enlightenment and empire went happily hand-in-hand. An important new book on the subject proposes that anti-imperial writings should receive as much attention as others in order to show that the Enlightenment was 'a genuine and contentious struggle among eighteenth-century thinkers about how to conceptualize humanity, cultural difference, and the political relationships among European and non-European peoples' (Muthu, 2003: 264). Peoples could rise or fall in the scale of civilisation over the course of history, as Edward Gibbon's famous *Decline and Fall of the Roman Empire* made clear. The tendency was to emphasise rising rather than falling, however, in a linear process by which peoples would progress from lower to higher stages. This was both an optimistic view of human history, and a discriminatory one. John Millar echoed many Scottish Enlightenment theorists when he wrote that 'There is in human society a natural progress from ignorance to knowledge and from rude to civilised manners, the several stages of which are usually accompanied with peculiar laws and customs' (Bayly, 2003: 34). As information poured into Europe about those 'peculiar laws and customs', such theories seemed to be confirmed. For philosophers sceptical about traditional European political organisation and religion, however, European culture was itself in need of progressive development. Instead of reforming its own archaic monarchies and religious structures, wrote Denis Diderot, Europe had imposed its barbarities on the outside world: 'ruins have been heaped on ruins; countries that were well peopled have become deserted . . . It seems as if from one region to another prosperity has been pursued by an evil genius that speaks our [European] several languages, and which diffuses the same disasters in all parts' (Muthu, 2003: 87).

Such sceptical secular voices were drowned out in Britain by the evangelical revival which began in the early eighteenth century and reached its height during the early nineteenth century. It provided a powerful new motive for emphasising humanity's shared origins and destiny, and it raised pressing questions about the justice of slavery, but it also generated new strategies of overseas expansion. As Protestants, British evangelicals paid particular attention to the Bible, noting the New Testament verse which said, in the translation they would have used, that God 'hath made of one blood all nations of men for to dwell on all the face of the earth' (Acts 17: 25–6). The powerful image of 'one blood' spoke of a profound physical unity that made skin colour a superficial distraction. It gave new life to universalist ethnologies such as that of the anatomist James Cowles Prichard. Philology, the historical study of language, was particularly important in this endeavour. British Protestant missionary societies proliferated during the late eighteenth and early nineteenth centuries, making it easier than ever to obtain detailed linguistic and cultural information about non-European peoples. The missionaries themselves were motivated to find evidence of biblical accuracy, and produced word lists that suggested relationships between, say, Tahitian and Hebrew, to demonstrate that the world's people all shared an origin in the biblical Middle East.

None of this means that ethnologists like Prichard did not discriminate between different peoples, however. An emphasis on essential unity did not rule out notions of advancement or backwardness, and there had always been biblical authority for such views, as we have already seen in the interpretation of the story of Noah and his three sons. Some societies had stayed in closer touch with their Middle Eastern (i.e. Judaeo-Christian) roots, and were therefore more civilised. Others had degraded and were now barbarous or savage. It is particularly important to notice the significance of such thinking for the development of a 'civilising mission' in imperial rhetoric. When horrified missionaries reported cultural practices such as widow suicide or cannibalism, their observations served a double purpose. They emphasised non-European 'otherness' and inferiority, and they also implied the existence of universal moral rules and the possibility of social change under European guidance.

Europe's response to information about non-European societies also helped to encourage notions of national character or 'genius' that were emerging from the Romantic movement of the later eighteenth century. Different groups of Europeans began to regard themselves as unique, and therefore entitled to an independent political destiny. One of the earliest theorists of Romantic nationalism was Immanuel Kant, whose 1775 study *On the Different Races of Men* issued a clear challenge to the universalists. Kant emphasised links between temperament and inheritance, concluding that human races possessed different fundamental characters. Generalisations could by now be made about the biological nature of national character, sharpening fears about the dangers of miscegenation. 'This much we can judge with probability,' wrote Kant, 'that a mixture of races (by extensive conquest) which gradually extinguishes their characters, is not beneficial to the human race' (Hannaford, 1995: 222). Kant believed in the power of human reason, and in the ability of education to create better citizens, but his work also suggested that character lay more in the blood than in the brain. Johann Gottfried von Herder introduced a new concept – *kultur* ('culture') – in his multi-volume *Outlines of a Philosophy of the History of Man* (1784–91). For Herder, history was about the formation of particular national cultures around language, religion, ritual, education, and other social phenomena. Cultures could be strong and youthful, or weak and degenerate, depending on their place in history. Human beings might be a single biological species, but culture divided them; no state, no civic identity could ever transcend the culture that was bred in the bone through inheritance.

This Romantic tradition of racial character emphasised fundamental differences between peoples. Nevertheless, it would be misleading to describe Romantic nationalism as conservative in today's political terms. During the eighteenth century, nationalism developed to counter the absolutist rule of traditional monarchies. Folk nationalism had profoundly democratic implications, and this is why nationalism and liberalism often went hand-in-hand during this period. Hindsight tells us that the new emphasis on folk culture would fuel racism and imperial expansion in Europe and overseas, but nationalism also prompted democratic political reform in Europe along with liberalising unification movements in Italy and Germany. As we shall see in later chapters, European imperial powers would eventually reap what they had sown when their non-European subjects began to make nationalist claims of their own.

ANTISLAVERY AND AFRICANS

Enlightenment philosophy often featured ideals of equality and liberty, and when these were combined with the British evangelical revival, a substantial antislavery movement emerged by the later eighteenth century under the Latin slogan *Ab une sanguine* ('of one blood'). Some Europeans had always spoken out against slavery, but their minority view was never able to make a wider impact. Now new ideas were in the air, many of them emphasising human universality, and it was easier than ever to share those ideas: literacy was increasing in Europe, and the publishing industry was growing. Some historians have drawn attention to the declining economic value of slaves in order to argue that slavery was abolished because it was no longer profitable. Most scholars, however, would agree that changing views of race and Christian duty also contributed significantly to widespread abolition in the late eighteenth and early nineteenth centuries. 'Slave-ownership, for example, conflicted with the obligations of charity and evangelization; slave status removed the liberty for moral choice and ethical behaviour. For British evangelicals especially, slavery and sin were regarded as synonymous, equally individual and national evils to be rooted out' (Porter, 1999: 202). Since the overseas empires had been built largely by slave labour, this was a remarkable development. It is important to note, however, that the abolition of slavery did not necessarily bring about equality for blacks under European rule, nor did it rule out theories of human development which emphasised European superiority.

By 1810 almost one million blacks lived in British territories (another 1.4 million lived in the USA). Life under slavery was extremely varied, including conscript soldiering, domestic service, agricultural labour (especially in the sugar fields), and a range of trades. Slaves sometimes escaped, forming communities such as the Maroons of Jamaica, or sometimes they earned enough through trade or clerical service to buy their freedom, especially if their fathers had been Europeans. Such experiences were not the norm, however. The killing demands of sugar production in the West Indies, along with the frequent segregation of the sexes in slave barracks, ensured that the black population could not replace itself naturally and had to be constantly supplemented by new slaves from Africa. Caribbean planters were therefore unlikely to regard Africans as potential equals. Edward Long's *The History of Jamaica* (1774) [*Doc. 7*] proclaimed that 'they can scarcely differ from the wild beast of the wood in the ferocity of their manners' and revived speculations about links between Africans and apes (Samson, 2001a: 128). The religious practices of slaves were of particular interest, and could be used to support both sides of the argument. Slaves came from a variety of places in Africa, while others had been born in the Americas, but they created a hybrid culture which reflected many traditions. The development of *voudoun* ('voodoo') from west African beliefs is one example. It is no surprise to find that, amid the vastly unequal power relations of slavery, the means of working harm to enemies was of particular interest to slaves. Beliefs called 'witchcraft' or 'sorcery' could easily be used as evidence of African savagery, however, and they could also act as a powerful call to the emerging evangelical missionary societies.

Britain abolished the slave trade in 1807 and all slaves in the British empire were emancipated in 1833. Financial compensation was paid, not only to the Caribbean planters, but to west African chiefs whose local economies had been dependent on slavery for generations. Emancipated blacks expected access to land, education, and political power, but were frequently disappointed, and protests such as the Morant Bay rebellion in Jamaica encouraged the identification of blackness with antisocial violence. Meanwhile, abolition also had important implications for imperial expansion in Africa itself. As one antislavery campaigner put it: 'it is the duty of the people of this empire to take up the cause upon Christian grounds, as a measure of atonement for the injuries we have done' (Samson, 2001a: 127). Economic alternatives had to be found for slavery: 'legitimate commerce' in the form of palm oil, cocoa, and other tropical products, as well as older trade goods such as ivory and gold. Missionaries were sent, hoping for the rapid Europeanisation and 'improvement' of Africans, and their initial successes were symbolised by the consecration of a former slave, Samuel Crowther, as the first black Anglican bishop in 1864.

It is important to realise that, laudable as the antislavery movement's aims were, they were not free from assumptions about European superiority. A leading abolitionist denounced the racist basis of African slavery, insisting that 'Had nature intended negroes for slavery, she would have endowed them with many qualities which they now want' such as being 'born without any sentiment for liberty' and 'incapable of resentment or opposition; that high treason against the divine right of European dominion' (Craton *et al.*, 1976: 244). Nevertheless, abolitionists took a paternalistic view of Africans, defining them as abused children in need of Christianisation and Europeanisation in order to take their rightful place in international affairs. Even black aboli-tionists took this view, emphasising the greater commercial rewards to be reaped in African markets which consisted of free and productive citizens. One of the most famous of them, the former slave Olaudah Equiano, wrote in 1789 to the British queen, pleading for unjust enslavement to cease, but adding that a trade in British manufactures in west Africa would be successful 'as the native inhabitants will insensibly adopt the British fashions, manners, customs &c. In proportion to the civilization, so will be the consumption of British manufactures' (Craton *et al.*, 1976: 259). Equiano, who married a white Englishwoman, was convinced that English commerce and culture would be the salvation of Africa if slavery was abolished; he did not suggest that African culture itself was worth saving.

Cultural interaction was more complicated than these idealists realised, however. Britain's west African colony of Sierra Leone, founded in 1787 as a home for liberated slaves, became mired in civil conflict between the coastal Christian communities and the increasingly resentful indigenous population of the interior. British missionaries enjoyed considerable success among non-Muslim Africans, but made little headway in Islamic areas. Similar disap-pointments greeted the establishment of Liberia by American abolitionists in 1815. Founded by an African-American entrepreneur, Liberia was intended to be a base for Europeanised blacks who could raise their fellow Africans in the scale of civilisation. As in Sierra Leone, conflict grew between these newcomers and the existing population and migration was never as substan-tial as planners had hoped. Most free blacks wished to stay in the Americas, where most of them had been born, and to fight for abolition in the southern United States, where slavery lingered until after the American Civil War. It had become clear that there was no quick, straightforward method for undoing the racist structures enhanced and entrenched by slavery, or for 'improving' Africa through European trade and acculturation. As we shall see, many began to think of Africans less as brethren 'of one blood' and more as inferiors in need of Western tutelage.

Antislavery in France was likelier to emphasise political rights: after the French Revolution, how could the new republic possibly endorse slavery? The new national motto, after all, was *liberté, egalité, fraternité* ('liberty, equality, brotherhood'). Nevertheless, things were not as simple as that. Women dis-covered that brotherhood was gender-specific; slaves and their advocates found that race was still a barrier to equality. Uprisings by blacks, especially in French colonies in the Caribbean where slaves were numerous, led to racial conflict. Only in 1794 was slavery abolished in the French empire, and more out of practical necessity than anything else: the Revolution had prompted Britain and its allies to declare war on France. The French government hoped that grateful blacks would end their rebellions and choose instead to enlist for military service against the British. This strategy was only partly successful. In

Saint-Domingue, the leader of a slave rebellion, Toussaint L'Ouverture, helped France to repel a British invasion. He wanted much more than the abolition of slavery, however, and began leading his people in a fight for political independence. In 1803 the world's first black republic proudly changed its name to Haiti. This was fortunate for Haitian blacks because Napoleon re-established slavery in some of the other French plantation colonies. Not until 1848 would slavery be abolished for good in the French empire.

EXPLORING THE PACIFIC

Although Spanish galleons had been plying the Pacific for centuries, current technology did not permit accurate mapping and the galleons simply followed a selected line of latitude straight across the ocean. As a result, the continent of Australia and most of the island groups of the Pacific, including New Zealand, remained uncharted until the 'Second Age of Discovery' in the eighteenth century and the pioneering voyages of the British explorer James Cook. These voyages would also bring new indigenous peoples to Europe's attention, challenging or confirming various theories of race and inviting imperial expansion in the Pacific.

The British explorer Samuel Wallis first encountered Tahiti in 1767, and a host of other European explorers followed. Some of them tried to understand Tahiti and the other Polynesian islands in terms of the classical education that they had all received. Was the beautiful island of Tahiti the classical paradise, Arcadia? Pacific islanders became a popular example of the 'noble savage' whose virtues could be used to highlight the decadence and failings of European civilisation. One French explorer saw only 'hospitality, ease, innocent joy, and every appearance of happiness' in the south Pacific (Marshall and Williams, 1982: 267). Such accounts were eagerly consumed by philosophers in Europe, especially those influenced by the idealised primitivism used by Jean-Jacques Rousseau and other political theorists. Rousseau's work had drawn on accounts from North America and elsewhere, extolling 'natural man' and his egalitarian, communal societies. Some writers were prepared to push this to its logical conclusion: the eventual displacement of Europe at the summit of civilisation when 'New Zealand may produce her Lockes, her Newtons, and her Montesquieus; and when great nations in the immense region of New Holland, may send their navigators, philosophers, and antiquaries, to contemplate the ruins of *ancient* London and Paris', wrote one of them (Howe, 1993: 249).

Captain James Cook and his successors wondered how the Pacific had been populated, and how the different peoples related to each other. It was a French theorist who divided Pacific islanders into three groupings: Polynesian ('many islands'), Micronesian ('small islands'), and Melanesian ('black islands'). Only the latter were identified by skin colour rather than geography: a revealing example of how much the lighter-skinned Polynesians had become the base-line against which the colour of other islanders would be measured. Similar attitudes were shared by the (mainly Protestant) missionaries who began arriving in increasing numbers at the end of the eighteenth century. They were drawn there by Cook's accounts of human sacrifice, cannibalism, and other 'heathen' practices: information skirted by the primitivists in their more ideal-ised accounts of islanders. They were also drawn by Christian universalism: in order to preach the gospel they had to believe that the islanders were fully human, and equal before God. Nevertheless, they also followed the ethnolo-gical traditions that related all of the world's peoples to biblical history. Many missionary ethnographers called Polynesians and Micronesians 'Semitic', relating them to Noah's son Shem and to the peoples of the Middle East. The darker islanders in the western Pacific were often labelled 'Hamitic', associating them with the cursed descendants of Ham. Melanesian spirituality was 'sorcery' or 'witchcraft': the same terms used to describe indigenous African practices.

The link between ethnology and empire was clearer in some cases than in others. The Pacific islands were of the least immediate interest: they contained no precious metals, no coal deposits, and were too small to support large-scale plantations. France annexed Tahiti and neighbouring islands in the mid-nineteenth century, along with the south-western island of New Caledonia, but more to protect its Catholic missionaries from British Protestant harass-ment than anything else. Britain showed no inclination to annex islands until the later part of the century when an alleged of slave trade in islanders seemed to require its intervention.

The newly-discovered continent of Australia, and the fertile islands of New Zealand, were another story. In New Zealand, Captain Cook had observed that the numerous and warlike Maori lived in settlements and cul-tivated the soil. The Maori converted rapidly to Christianity once British missionaries reached them in the early nineteenth century, and the British recognised the Maori as a sovereign people, signing with them the Treaty of Waitangi which placed New Zealand under British rule in 1840. The situation in Australia could not have been more different. Blacker in colour than the Polynesian Maori, speaking a plethora of ancient languages, sparse in num-bers, and touching the land lightly with their efficient modes of subsistence, the aborigines seemed backward and primitive. Unattractive to European eyes, they were also resistant to Christianisation; something that was often used as evidence of their savagery. When Britain decided to found a penal colony on Australia's eastern coast in 1788, it needed land, and by unspoken agreement it was decided that the existing inhabitants were too primitive to be entitled to treaty negotiations.

This decision seems peculiar since Cook was given specific instructions to claim land only with the consent of the inhabitants. Nevertheless, eighteenth-century philosophy had been linking land with agriculture in ways which allowed non-agricultural peoples to be constructed as 'wandering' over the land, rather than possessing title to it. The English political philosopher John Locke had talked about the 'mingling of labour' with the soil as a means of defining land title, and lawyers claimed that lands could be considered *res nullius* ('empty things') if no such agricultural labour was evident (Pagden, 1995: 78). This legal fiction enabled British colonists to circumvent the usual need to establish possession either by conquest or by treaty. In the words of Colonial Office legal advisers in 1819, Australia was possessed by Britain 'as desert and uninhabited, and subsequently colonized from this country' (Reynolds, 1989: 67). The absurdity of this went largely unquestioned, except by minority humanitarian voices, until the later twentieth century. Pacific exploration had increased Europe's knowledge of a range of new peoples, and ethnographic observations flowed in which seemed to confirm the assumption that Australia's aboriginal people did not work the land in a recognisable way. At the same time, Britain was in desperate need of a new penal colony for the transportation of convicts. As ever, the development of racial hierarchies was influencing, and being influenced by, the needs of an expanding empire.

NORTH AMERICA

By the eighteenth century, almost all of the indigenous Caribbean islanders were gone: killed by disease, economic dislocation, and persecution. The islands were now inhabited by large numbers of African slaves and a smaller number of European planters and traders. British and French West Indian possessions included some islands seized from Spain, such as Jamaica, but also a range of never-inhabited islands without an aboriginal population to comment on or dispossess. North America was a different story. British settlement continued to expand on the eastern seaboard, generating confrontations with the indigenous population that frequently became violent. The British also warred with European rivals such as the Dutch, Spanish, and French. New Amsterdam became New York, and by 1763 and the end of the Seven Years War, New France (Québec) was under British control. Captain Cook charted most of the west coast of what is now British Columbia in Canada, and the rapid influx of British traders precipitated the 1789 Nootka Crisis with Spain. Spain's concession of British trading rights on the west coast was the beginning of a steady erosion of Spanish claims to predominance in the Pacific region. Russian activities also benefited from Spain's withdrawal, but were much more limited in scope than British commerce. In most cases, indigenous military and economic support was critical to European success.

Much would change by the end of the eighteenth century. 'The Original great tye between the Indians and Europeans was Mutual conveniency', wrote a colonial official in 1761, but as increasing numbers of settlers sought increasing amounts of land, the balance of power tilted further in favour of the colonisers (Richter, 1998: 348). As in Latin America, settlers and their descendants often had harsher views of native people than did their home governments in Europe. For a brief time after the victory of 1763 the British government seemed willing to impose British rule, law, and Protestantism on all of its new territory, including that inhabited by French Catholics. Nevertheless, special provision was made for Indians, who were promised that British settlement would not proceed beyond a certain point. When the borders of this Indian territory were vastly enlarged by the Québec Act of 1774, and Catholicism and French civil law were permitted to remain in force in Québec, British settlers were outraged. Their accusations of favouritism obscured the fact that Indians living within colonial borders were already increasingly dispossessed and marginalised figures, and that this – not the unenforceable Québec Act – was the true sign of things to come.

The decisiveness of the British victory in 1763 removed the opportunity for Indians to play Britain and France against each other, and matters became worse after the thirteen American colonies declared their independence in 1776. The resulting war featured Indian allies on both sides, but this time Indians were the losers no matter which side they had been on. The Peace of Paris of 1783 drew a border between British North America and the United States without native involvement, leaving Indian allies of the British abandoned to their fate in the territory of their enemies. Many migrated north, to find what land they could on the territory of others, and in competition with the Loyalists of European descent for whom the best agricultural land was reserved. There were also the Métis to consider. In New France they had been *capitaines des sauvages* ('native leaders'), acting as translators and facilitators for French traders and administrators, speaking French and adopting the Roman Catholic faith. The French explorer Samuel de Champlain had once said, 'Our young men will marry your daughters and we shall be one people' (Brown, 1988: 1344). The British fur trade, still under Hudson's Bay Company control, also featured a large number of mixed-race traders and administrators. By the early nineteenth century, however, mixed-race groups tended to form self-contained communities and were increasingly under siege by European immigration and changing economic patterns. Prairie Métis were still crucial to the fur trade, and could still conduct their own buffalo hunt, but the founding of the Assiniboia colony in 1811 signified the beginning of a shift in British commercial activity from fur trading to settled agriculture on the prairies. It also invited comparison between Protestant settler-farmers and the Catholic, 'wandering' Métis whose mixed blood was increasingly regarded as evidence of degeneracy. The proud and innovative *capitaines des sauvages* had become 'half breeds', struggling to maintain both identity and livelihood in colonies no longer dependent on their support.

It is also important to note the divergence in attitudes toward Africans between the British settler colonies in North America and the British and French colonies in the West Indies. The Caribbean islands had always featured free people of African ancestry, whether runaway slaves like the Maroons of Jamaica, or mixed-race children who had been freed by their European fathers. Because of the climate, the islands had tended to attract single European men rather than families. By the time the British empire emancipated all slaves in 1833, free blacks – usually known as 'coloureds' to distinguish them from enslaved 'blacks' – would outnumber Europeans in some cases. Colonial administrations dealt with this situation by focusing on gradations of colour to the point of absurdity, as in the French colony of Saint-Domingue (now Haiti) where there were nine legal categories of person depending on the exact combination of African and European ancestry. Terms such as 'quadroon' and 'octoroon' reflected this process of classification. The existence of a range of racial categories did not mean the absence of discrimination, however. A French commentator in the Antilles believed that 'the souls of the free colored are elevated in proportion as their skin color lightens' (Lowenthal, 1973: 338) and European men controlled the process by which their mixed-race children could become free coloureds rather than enslaved blacks. They also controlled the system of patronage which determined their education and employment. Coloureds had to struggle for full political rights, and often remained virtually segregated in particular jobs and residential areas.

In the American colonies, where white immigration had been so much more substantial, cross-racial sex resulted in few legally recognised children. The masters of slaves were usually married to European women who lived with them in the colonies. Such men usually consigned their mixed-race children to slavery along with their African or part-African mothers. In the West Indies, a free 'coloured' person might actually have darker skin than an enslaved 'black' one; the labels referred as much to social status as to physiology. In America, on the other hand, 'one drop' of African blood rendered a person 'black'. Many of the founders of the American constitution were opposed to slavery; others were ambivalent. All were agreed that the American Revolution should create a new and better system of social and political relations. Nevertheless, the sudden, seismic shift in identity from colony to independent republic was profoundly challenging. One historian suggests that this 'wonderful and terrifying prospect of social fluidity' meant that race continued to be a central identity issue; Americans had 'little else to cling to' after discarding so much of what had defined them in earlier generations (Malcomson, 2000: 290). It was certainly clear that blackness, regardless of slave status, was inferior to whiteness. 'One drop' of black blood was enough. Someone of very light skin might try to 'pass' for white, but in doing so they confirmed the fact that no other categories were available besides 'black'. Whiteness was about absences: 'The sum of what you were not – Indian, black, slave – made you what you were, in that you were white' (Malcomson, 2000: 291). We will see later on that this precariousness made it difficult for anthropologists and eugenicists to define the true essence of whiteness in terms of ethnicity or physical type.

RACE RELATIONS IN ASIA

Only in the eighteenth century can we begin to speak of a 'British India', and scholars continue to debate the reasons why the East India Company turned from commerce to conquest. Its trade had usually been prosperous, though limited by Indian power and by the rival operations of other Europeans such as the Portuguese, French, and Dutch. India's peoples had not been of much interest to European scholars; as one historian notes, '"Asia" for most seventeenth-century Englishmen had probably been synonymous with the Asia of the Bible and of the ancient world, that is with the Near East; by the end of the eighteenth century it had become almost a synonym for India' (Marshall and Williams, 1982: 67). Reasons for these shifts in attitude toward India include the creation of an East India Company army, with mainly Indian soldiers, which began operating alongside Indian allies against their enemies. In other words, the company entered Indian politics, taking advantage of victory to secure trading concessions from the Indian leaders it had supported. Enlightenment interest in the history and development of humanity was also an important factor. The study of Asian languages and literature, known as 'orientalism', was no longer limited to the study of biblical peoples. European scholars learned Sanskrit in order to study ancient Hindu scriptures, philologists pondered the relationships between Indian and European languages, and East India Company officials used the administrative language of the Muslim Mughal empire – Persian – to govern their growing Indian territories.

By the middle of the eighteenth century, the EIC began to adopt a more aggressive expansionism in India. In 1744, the powerful Nawab of Bengal refused an ultimatum on trading rights from the EIC and in 1756 captured Calcutta, imprisoning some British officials and traders in a tiny room. By morning, many were dead. As one survivor recalled, the group struggled to be able to sit down and tried to do so in shifts to create sufficient room, but many 'could not immediately recover their legs, as others did when the word was given to rise, [and they] fell to rise no more. For they were instantly trod to death or suffocated' (Judd, 1972: 36). Later media reports in Britain about the 'Black Hole of Calcutta' fed on generalised images about alleged Asian cruelty and barbarism inherited from earlier centuries. They also seemed to endorse Robert Clive's victory over the Nawab at the Battle of Plassey in 1757. After further conflict, the British obtained the *diwani* or civil government of Bengal from the Mughal Emperor himself in 1765.

Twenty million Indians were now under direct British rule for the first time, and the British inherited all of the traditional tax-gathering rights and other powers formerly enjoyed by the Mughals. Nevertheless, there was nothing inevitable about British rule throughout all India. On the contrary, the *diwani* came from the Emperor, affirming his ultimate authority and requiring an annual tribute by the British of 2.6 million rupees. Bengal was governed largely by Indian institutions using existing administrative systems. Islamic titles given to Clive and others reinforces the point that the British were operating more as Indian rulers than British ones. Controversy raged about how this huge, new imperial responsibility should be met. The EIC became so wealthy that its operations were of national interest: it loaned money to the British government and its policies came under increasing parliamentary scrutiny.

A turning point came in 1788 when Warren Hastings, governor-general of Bengal, was recalled and tried for corruption by the House of Lords. An orientalist, Hastings respected India's cultures and helped to support Hindu and Muslim scholarship and worship [*Doc. 6*]. He once wrote that 'It would be a grievance to deprive the people of the protection of their own laws' (Samson, 2001a: 96), but this view was at odds with the growing opinion in Britain that European law and culture – especially Christianity – were naturally superior and should be exported to India. Critics accused Hastings of failing to inculcate 'the good of the people as much as possible in the spirit of the Laws of this Country, which intend in all respects their conservation, their happiness, and their prosperity' (Samson, 2001a: 97).

Although Hastings was acquitted after a lengthy trial, one of his successors, Lord Cornwallis, created a new, improved administration from 1786 by increasing salaries in order to decrease corruption. The result was a higher yield in tax revenue, producing an annual drain of wealth from India to Britain of around 1,500,000 pounds sterling every year from 1783 to 1793 – an enormous sum of money. The new emphasis on cultural supervision and improvement was reflected by a new codification of landholding practices: interference of a sort that the old EIC had avoided. British rule was now about British values; not Indian ones. A relatively fluid situation which had traditionally permitted some upward mobility to wealthier farmers, or acknowledged the common use of waste lands or forests outside villages, was now severely restricted. The British wanted an established rural elite and clearly demarcated (and taxable) parcels of private land. Later they began banning traditional cultural practices such as *sati* (widow suicide), and British missionaries were allowed into India for the first time. Intermarriage between British men and Indian women was now discouraged, and mixed-race Eurasians were no longer promoted to high rank in the EIC. Indians themselves could still enter the EIC administration, but tended now to become clerks rather than managers. An Indian petition to the British parliament made matters plain:

The better classes of the natives of India are placed under the sway of the Honourable East India Company, in a state of political degradation which is absolutely without a parallel in their former history. For even under the Mahomedan conquerors, such of your petitioners as are Hindoos, were not only capable of filling but actually did fill numerous employments of trust, dignity and emolument, from which under the existing system of the Honourable Company's government, they are absolutely shut out. (Marshall, 1998: 524–5)

By 1800 Governor-General Richard Wellesley (brother of the Duke of Wellington) generalised about 'Asiatic treachery and falsehood'; for him the rule of law could only be effectively established in India through autocratic rule by himself and his hand-picked council, with the inevitable consequence 'that we excluded our native subjects from all participation in the legislative authority' (Marshall, 1998: 525). Although there was no large influx of white settlers, as in Australia or Canada, the British reorganisation of India was profoundly disruptive. Although welcomed by some, especially the landowning elites, the pace of change brought only war, famine, and growing resentment to many others.

Imperial governance in the Dutch East Indies was noticeably different at this time. By the eighteenth century, the Dutch had largely driven the Portuguese out of south-east Asia. At first the VOC operated only small coastal trading posts, as the Portuguese had done; a large European presence was not required in order to exploit the well-established spice trade of the archipelago. But Dutch trade became Dutch rule; especially in Java, where a steady flow of tribute known as the 'culture system' (as in 'cultivation') ensured enormous profits. The system encouraged cash crops which were then handed over as tribute to the Dutch, making it increasingly difficult for the area's growing population to feed itself. As one historian has observed, 'Free from all romantic illusion, this oldest of bourgeois countries reckoned silk-worms, pepper-plants, peasants, all as items in a balance-sheet' (Kiernan, 1969: 88). There was an attempt in the 1830s to restrict cash crops to less than 20 per cent of village land, and to return surplus revenue to the villagers, but things soon went back to normal.

By the early nineteenth century, income from Java comprised almost 20 per cent of total Netherlands revenue. The capital, Batavia, reflected the degree to which this wealth depended on interracial networks. Mixed-race Eurasians were the backbone of the VOC administration, although this was not necessarily approved of by visiting Europeans. One traveller was repelled by 'the extreme splendor and hauteur which the women in Batavia – Dutch, Mistiza and Half-Caste too – display, especially upon going to and from church . . . even the most inferior has her slave follow behind to carry a parasol or sunshade above her' (Taylor, 1983: 41). Most incoming Dutch quickly adopted local practices, however, and wound up marrying Asian or Eurasian women. By the later nineteenth century, improvements in transportation and communications meant that senior officials were usually transients with no need to marry into the local society, and mixed-race marriages became increasingly associated with lower-ranking Europeans. Hardening racial classification and prejudice were taking their toll on older, more pragmatic commercial accommodations. Like the Métis of British North America, Eurasians found themselves increasingly marginalised during the nineteenth century.

CHAPTER FOUR

SETTLEMENT AND CONSOLIDATION, 1820–1880

This period featured the most extensive European diaspora in history. European immigrants poured into the British colonies of settlement and the United States while French *colons* ('settlers') crossed the Mediterranean to Algeria. Such extensive settlement required the investment provided by the accelerating development of industrial and finance capitalism in Europe and the United States. It also required land – land already populated by indigenous peoples – and a reliable labour supply. The official abolition of slavery by most empires in the nineteenth century prompted the creation of alternative labour systems, many of which were coercive. Conflicts erupted over land, labour, and the rapid pace of social and economic change under imperial rule. Cross-racial gender relations revealed an increasing sense of racial distance between superior Europeans and inferior others, reflecting the proliferation of theories explaining the role of race in human development. Not all theories featured biological determinism, but Christian universalism and Enlightenment ethnology were on the wane during this period in favour of newer fields such as physical and social anthropology. These developments gave an increasingly scientific gloss to the apparent inevitability and desirability of European expansion.

THE RISE OF ANTHROPOLOGY

The developing social sciences continued to provide scientific endorsement for the idea of race by investigating language, folklore, religion, and kinship structures. So close became the link between race and culture in this period that a range of European sub-categories were created such as 'Anglo-Saxon' (English) and 'Gallic' (French). These groups were compared and contrasted, and their origins re-examined. Instead of the classical world of Greece and Rome, a more fundamental and biological origin was identified in the ancient 'Aryan' race which had supposedly produced the Indo-European language family. Non-European cultures like India's were linked with the past, providing evidence of cultural practices long discarded by the more advanced Europeans. Before the full impact of Darwin's evolutionary theory was felt in the social sciences, European progress was still constructed mainly in historical and developmental terms. By implication, any culture could rise or fall in the scale of civilisation. Long before Darwin, however, Romantic nationalism began to locate cultural essence in the blood, rather than in the political or economic institutions of a people. Darwin's theories would strengthen existing notions of biological, ethnic identities and rivalries.

The study of philology was well established by the nineteenth century, identifying various cultures in relationship to one another using language. The German linguist Friedrich Max Müller identified Aryan and Dravidian 'races' in the ancient Sanskrit scriptures of India. Debate continues about whether Müller and others mistranslated certain words. Of particular relevance here, however, is Müller's conclusion that the Aryans dominated the Dravidians to create the Indo-European language family. The Aryans must therefore have been a superior race, an idea that would be taken to its most hideous extreme in the ideologies of Nazi Germany. In the meantime, interest in 'Aryans' created an intriguingly complex interest in Indian history and culture. On one hand, Europeans could congratulate themselves on reaching the pinnacle of modern development as the descendants of the supposedly superior Aryans. On the other hand, the birthplace of this superior culture lay in India, not in Europe. Müller knew that his theories challenged traditional views 'and upset all their stratified notions, like a sudden earthquake' because it 'changed millions of so-called barbarians into our own kith and kin' (Müller, 1899: 27). Cultural advantage enhanced by the passage of time, rather than racial superiority, explained the development of European civilisation.

British India was a popular laboratory for theories of human development. Henry Maine used an appointment to the Indian legislative council to pursue his interests in social history, later becoming a professor of jurisprudence. Like many others, he believed that India contained vestiges of a more primitive stage of human development. His pioneering work, *Ancient Law: Its Connection with the Early History of Society and its Relation to Modern Ideas* (1861), proposed a theory about the progress of political and legal organisation from early, village-based stages to modern, industrialised nation-states. Maine put his academic work into practice in the form of India's first comprehensive law code: a natural outcome of his belief in ideas of social progress and improvement. As C.A. Bayly explains, 'The official mind consequently became conservative. A rush of legislation and administrative initiatives . . . represented attempts to shore up what were taken to be traditional Indian institutions' (Bayly, 1991: 391).

The role of German theorists was crucial to growing identification of culture with race. By the time Germany became a unified nation in 1871 there was already an established anthropological elite at several German universities, and a large group of explorers, botanists, and anthropology students who gathered information for analysis. German humanism had been extremely powerful in the early nineteenth century, giving rise to the liberal nationalism that (among other things) had enabled German unification. This humanism was most often expressed through literature, history-writing, and a study of the classics: the traditional humanities. At the same time, the experience of empire, both within Europe and without, was challenging universal humanist beliefs. Considered liberals at home, many early German anthropologists – like others throughout Europe and the United States – saw nationalism as biological and imperial expansion as natural. European cultures were studied through the established disciplines of the humanities, but non-Europeans were studied by anthropologists. In other words, Europe had civilisation (history and the arts) while 'they' had culture (kinship structures and primitive religions). The Royal Museum of Ethnography opened in Berlin in 1886, featuring massive collections of non-European artefacts, and the Berlin Anthropological Society was founded. An observer explained that social science had been impossible 'until modern voyages of discovery had brought the necessary comparative materials from the newly opened regions of the world' (Zimmerman, 2001: 6). This process generated distinctions between *Naturvölker* ('natural peoples'), non-Europeans, and European *Kulturvölker* ('cultured/civilised peoples'). Adolf Bastian, professor of anthropology at the University of Berlin from the 1860s, explained that anthropology used 'the lowest organisms of human society' – colonised non-Europeans – to discover the universal laws which had brought Europeans to the pinnacle of human development (Zimmerman, 2001: 47).

The philology professor Friedrich Wilhelm Nietzsche believed that the blood-and-soil nationalism of the Romantic movement had not gone far enough. Nietzsche worried that modern Germany might lose touch with its roots in *Volk* genius; constitution-making seemed a cold business when compared with the passionate folk nationalism of Nietzsche's friend Richard Wagner. Nietzsche and his followers wanted to reinvigorate German genius by creating a new nobility of *Übermenschen* ('supermen') whose will to rule should transcend all barriers including those of race. Contrary to popular belief, Nietzsche was not anti-Semitic. He believed that Jewish survival was a testament to the strength and determination of the Jewish people. Germans, on the other hand, had become mediocrities under the influence of democracy and capitalism, and he was disgusted by the way that some of them blamed Jews for German social problems, concluding that 'it might be useful and fair to expel the anti-Semitic screamers from the country' (Hannaford, 1995: 314). Nevertheless, anti-Semitism, like Wagner's operas, became much more popular than Nietzsche's disturbing, demanding texts.

British anthropology was less institutionalised than its German equivalent, though it too relied on the activities of missionaries, explorers, and colonial officials for its raw data. *Notes and Queries on Anthropology, for the*

Use of Travellers and Residents in Uncivilized Lands and the *Admiralty Manual of Scientific Enquiry* were reprinted frequently in order to keep informants focused on information that would be useful to theorists. Of interest is the fact that the frequently reprinted *Admiralty Manual* featured a chaper on ethnograpy written by James Prichard, the iconic figure of British evangelical ethnology. In this way, older universalist approaches to the study of humanity (however Eurocentric) had an extended shelf-life in British anthropology. This, as usual, did not mean that theorists could not find ways to justify imperial rule and exploitation. H.T. Buckle's *History of Civilization in England* (1857–61), reprinted well into the twentieth century, declared that environmental determinism was the leading factor in human development, concluding that people from tropical areas were, if not natural slaves, at least natural low-wage workers incapable of higher achievements. Sir Charles Wentworth Dilke travelled North America and Australia before producing *Greater Britain* in 1868 [*Doc. 10*]. For him, economic and political success was due to the special leadership qualities of Anglo-Saxons: a reflection of Romantic preoccupations with the unique 'genius' of various cultures and peoples.

Theories about comparative religion, marital institutions, and kinship systems proliferated, but all of them placed Europeans at the top of a developmental scheme [*Doc. 11*]. Profound inequality between white and non-white people was therefore both natural and inevitable. A classic example of such reasoning was visible in Australian ethnography. No treaty was ever signed with Australia's aboriginal peoples, as we know. Even after more information was obtained about aboriginal cultures, the outcome remained the same: dispossession. Missionaries reported a strong resistance to Christianisation and a tendency to 'wander' rather to form settled communities. Explorers used the geographical and survival knowledge of aboriginal guides while at the same time condemning the backwardness of aboriginal societies. A particularly revealing issue concerned aboriginal beliefs about the conception of children. A number of ethnographers recorded legends and explanations about women conceiving children through dreams, or by bathing in certain streams or pools. This suggested that aborigines did not understand the role of sexual intercourse in conception and, as the pioneering psychologist Sigmund Freud put it, 'People who had not yet discovered that conception is the result of sexual intercourse might surely be regarded as the most backward and primitive of living men' (Wolfe, 1999: 197).

Many anthropologists in Europe and the United States began to regard Australia as a laboratory in which to observe the lowest state of savagery: a state which Europeans had long outgrown, but which lingered, frozen in time, in the Australian outback. In the meanwhile, settlement continued to expand, sparking humanitarian protest in Britain and, to a much lesser extent, in the Australian colonies. A special parliamentary committee on aboriginal relations was convened in 1836 and its report denounced the dispossession of indigenous peoples throughout the British empire, lamenting their depopulation through disease and dislocation. Already most full-blood Aboriginals in Van Diemen's Land (now Tasmania in Australia) had been killed or removed, and the committee noted the comments of one governor who said that the complete disappearance of the aboriginal population was being eagerly anticipated by settlers. Nevertheless, he warned, 'it is impossible not to contemplate such a result of our occupation of the island as one very difficult to be reconciled with feelings of humanity, or even with principles of justice and sound policy', adding that 'the adoption of any line of conduct, having for its avowed or secret object the extinction of the native race, could not fail to leave an indelible stain upon the British Government' (Great Britain, 1837: 14). Some scholars today give that 'indelible stain' a more specific name: genocide.

One more theme needs to be mentioned in this section: the gendered concepts of 'manly' and 'effeminate' races. This was a more popular pastime than some of the anthropological theorising we have been considering, demonstrating that people did not have to be scholars to find ways of identifying and comparing different groups of people. For example, British observers often considered people from the north-west of India superior to other Asians. The decadent Chinese empire had given Chinese 'little opportunity for exerting manly talents in their lives' (Marshall and Williams, 1982: 144). In contrast, north-west India was associated with the Mughal empire which had ruled over much of India for centuries before the British came. It took the British a long time to subdue what became known as 'the North-West Frontier', and they learned by hard experience to respect the troops they encountered (many of whom had resisted Mughal rule as well). Bengalis, on the other hand, were considered effeminate even though many of them were also Muslim. An educated Bengali middle class had developed to pose an uncomfortable problem. British-educated Bengalis, wearing European clothing but remaining Muslim or Hindu, and speaking accented English, seemed more comical than admirable. Their hybrid behaviours were interpreted as unnatural, and were associated with feminine qualities such as vanity and flirtation. As one official put it: 'as the Bengalis are disqualified for political enfranchisement by the possession of essentially feminine characteristics, they must expect to be held in such contempt by stronger and braver races' (Sinha, 1995: 35).

The Bengal Army, the largest part of the EIC forces, was not actually manned by Bengalis but by Hindustanis and others from the northern provinces around Delhi. The highest backhanded compliment that the British empire could bestow was to conquer a resilient people and put its warriors to work in special regiments in the imperial forces. Thus Highland Scottish, Sikh, and Gurkha regiments remain among the most prominent and highly-decorated units of the British army. Nevertheless, an underlying tone of anxiety can be detected beneath gendered constructions of the world's people: 'India and China had become effete societies, inert victims for invaders. Britain should take note' (Marshall and Williams, 1982: 151). British imperial manliness required constant reinforcement lest the British empire meet the same fate as that of Rome, China, and the Mughals.

RACE AND LAND

When colonial governments needed ever-larger amounts of land for settlement or commerce, they often obtained the land by treaty from its indigenous inhabitants. Sometimes treaties were signed after European military conquest; sometimes they were concluded more amicably. Later on, the terms of treaties were frequently ignored when the colonising power began seizing land in retaliation for rebellion, or by declaring it to be uncultivated and therefore 'waste'. In Australia, as we know, there were no treaties at all. What links these very different approaches together is the assumption in every case that the incoming Europeans were entitled to be there. Thanks to social evolutionary theory, the progress and improvement of humanity was believed to depend on the spread of Europeanisation [*Doc. 12*]. Rising population growth in much of Europe combined with problems generated by urbanisation and poverty to generate interest in the export of surplus populations overseas. The accelerating pace of industrialisation demanded new sources of raw materials and new markets, and although this process did not necessarily require overseas settlement, it always invited the exploitation of overseas territory. All of these things combined to produce an insatiable hunger for land and resources.

Britain was one of the first imperial powers to attempt to regulate the acquisition and disposal of colonial lands in the nineteenth century. The Cape Colony, taken from the Dutch during the Napoleonic Wars, was one early experiment. The Cape already featured a relatively small number of settlers, mainly of Dutch descent, who already thought of themselves as a distinct people: Afrikaners or 'Boers'. They had been farming and grazing in the area since the seventeenth century, and by the time the British took over, Afrikaners were colliding regularly with the Xhosa on the colony's eastern borders and the Zulu to the north. For a variety of reasons, including humanitarian pressure and a concern with profitability, the new British administration sought to regulate landholding in colony. The Afrikaners resented this interference with a flexible traditional system which had allowed them to acquire new land where they pleased, and to pass it on to their children as they saw fit. British meddling with land and slaveholding were two of the primary motives for the Great Trek of Afrikaners out of British territory in the 1830s and into Xhosa- and Zulu-ruled land to the northward.

The British now found that they could not separate humanitarian concern from territorial expansion, nor could they control the behaviour of their settlers in southern Africa. Securing colonial borders often meant conflicts of their own with Africans which were followed by land seizures and a further extension of borders. The new colony of Natal was created in 1843 partly to block Afrikaner access to the coastal port of Durban, but also to protect British settlers and missionaries in the area. By the end of the century the Afrikaners and the British would find themselves in open conflict during the South African (Boer) War of 1899–1902. In the meantime, British entrepreneurs sought more territory to the north of the Cape Colony where British regulations did not apply. In the 1880s, in what is now Zimbabwe, the British South Africa Company (BSAC) fought with the Ndebele people to obtain land subsequently parcelled out to white immigrants. During a Ndebele uprising in 1896 the BSAC went bankrupt and was forced to negotiate. The chief of the Ndebele recalled sitting for hours with his retinue, waiting for the British magistrate to agree to see him. He chided the magistrate for his lack of good manners and hospitality, telling him, 'I did not wish to hurry him in any unmannerly way; I would wait his pleasure; but my people were hungry . . . The answer that came from the Chief Magistrate . . . was that the town was full of stray dogs; dog to dog; we might kill those and eat if we could catch them' (Lindqvist, 1996: 62). Later, the chief said to Cecil Rhodes, head of the BSAC, 'You came, you conquered. The strongest takes the land. We accepted your rule. We lived under you. But not as dogs! If we are to be dogs it is better to be dead' (Lindqvist, 1996: 62). Military defeat was a familiar concept to the Ndebele; racism was not.

In Canada and New Zealand, much of today's land title litigation concerns the erosion (rather than the absence or illegitimacy) of treaty rights during the nineteenth and early twentieth centuries. In the province of Alberta there has been recent litigation about Treaty 8, signed in 1899 between the British and various indigenous groups, which covers an area of about 840,000 square kilometres (more than three times the size of Britain). The litigation did not concern the treaty itself, but rather with its attempted violation by governments, as in a proposed withdrawal of tax exemptions in perpetuity as granted by the treaty. An unprecedented memorandum of understanding signed in 2001 between the government of Alberta and Treaty 8 First Nations states that future agreements must 'not abolish or diminish the Aboriginal or treaty rights' of Alberta's native people (Alberta, 2001: 1), following a Supreme Court decision which declared that the honour of the Crown was at stake in upholding the original intentions of the treaty.

This example, like the recollections of the chief of the Ndebele, shows that the business of treaties has to be treated with caution with regard to racism. A treaty that represents a partnership between sovereign nations need not have racist implications. Failing to honour the terms of a treaty, however, may well involve assumptions about a hierarchy of rights and priorities based on race. Amid the westward continental expansion of the United States,

President Thomas Jefferson once argued that 'all the lands within the limits which any particular society has circumscribed around itself are assumed by that society and subject to their allotment only' (Williams, 1990: 271). After the American Revolution, some writers had argued that the British Crown's jurisdiction over western lands had automatically devolved to the new American government, while others declared that Indian rights were based on natural law and could not be overturned. A crucial moment came in 1785 when the *Northwest Ordinance* announced that Congress would use newly-acquired frontier lands to repay the war debt 'with utmost faith . . . observed toward the Indians' (Williams, 1990: 306). What did 'utmost faith' mean in practice? The United States government turned to paternalism to define its relationship with indigenous populations. The US Supreme Court's *Cherokee Nation* decision of 1831 was a crucial turning point in the definition of this relation-ship and, to some extent, it continues to set the terms of debate about Indian rights and governance. The Cherokee had argued that treaties endorsed their status as a sovereign state and the Supreme Court agreed, adding that any sale of Indian lands could take place only with Indian consent. In deference to the perceived superiority of American sovereignty, however, Chief Justice John Marshall created the concept of 'domestic-dependent nations'. A relationship of 'pupilage' should exist between Indian groups and the more civilised Amer-ican. Marshall added that the need for their consent in land sales might prove to be temporary if Indian populations continued to decline. The importance of seeing these developments in a global context is clear when we realise that the Marshall judgment was cited by Australian and New Zealand colonial courts in cases seeking to limit indigenous land title.

By the later nineteenth century, even 'pupilage' was too much for some American settlers, who resented the recognition of any sort of indigenous territory. Residential schools for children, often run by churches, were one form of forced assimilation. In other cases, reservations were encouraged to develop a system of private ownership whereby land could eventually be sold to non-Indians. In the meantime, the concept of 'Indian territory' was eroding; federal legislation in 1887 repealed the independent status of these territories, replacing them with systems of private land ownership. Treaties continued to be signed, but were sometimes marked by confusion, and even deception. Such documents often greeted the relevant Indian chief as 'friend and brother', but their contents were not always translated accurately into the indigenous language. 'Friend and Brother!' one chief observed bitterly, 'You may judge how our chiefs felt when they returned home and found that the Governor . . . got them to sign a Deed for their lands without their knowledge' (Khodarkovsky, 2002: 69).

The US-Mexican Wars of the 1840s and 1880s also involved racial issues in an expansionist context. Blacks and Indians were already conceptualised as inferiors, but the status of Hispanics (many of them of mixed race) was less clear. Should the desire for Mexican land involve colonial rule, or should it prompt the incorporation of the land's inhabitants with full American rights? Both options were extensively discussed with regard to the threats they posed to democratic values on the one hand and racial purity on the other. In the end, the USA shrank from extending its borders into the more heavily populated areas of Mexico; as one senator pointed out, 'Ours, sir, is the Government of a white race . . . we have never dreamt of incorporating into our Union any but the Caucasian race' (Horsman, 1981: 241). Not all Americans agreed with the emphasis on Caucasian identity and destiny, and some politicians were concerned about the rising tide of racism in American politics. One remarked that 'If anything was wanting to prove that this age is an age of imbecility and false philosophy, it is furnished in this drivel about races' (Horsman, 1981: 249).

The examples of Alaska and Hawai'i show how powerful racial issues remained throughout the nineteenth century in American expansionism. The Americans purchased Alaska from the ailing Russian empire in 1867 when its population was still mainly indigenous. A white minority arrived during the gold rush of 1897–8, and Alaska's first legislature was dominated by immigrant whites who were the only ones able to meet the strict requirements for American citizenship. Hawai'i, whose indigenous monarchy had become increasingly indebted to American traders, and whose population was in steep decline, featured desirable land for plantations. A reciprocity treaty with the United States in 1875 helped to ease the economic predicament of the Hawai'ian government, and American investors began importing Chinese labour in order to develop plantations. Indigenous Hawai'ians had constituted 82 per cent of the population in 1878, but only 25 per cent by 1900. Their increasingly powerless monarchy conceded defeat, permitting the country to be annexed by the United States in 1898. As we will see, racial concerns delayed full statehood until 1959.

The French empire had lost interest in colonies of settlement for some time before circumstances prompted King Charles X to consider their merits again. Charles's reign was wracked by political and economic protest, and he decided to distract his people's attention by means of an imperial venture in north Africa. France had been trading with Algiers and other ports for centuries, but had become increasingly dismissive of Algerian rights during the early nineteenth century. The Algiers traders had destroyed French trading outposts in their city in retaliation for large unpaid debts and other grievances. Algiers was under French blockade in the late 1820s, yet French moderates recommended an armistice to avoid open war. Unfortunately, when the Algerians saw French naval vessels arriving in 1829 they fired on them, believing them to be a French invasion force. This gave King Charles the excuse he had been looking for to replace moderates with conservatives in his government, and to launch an assault against Algiers in 1830 to restore

French pride. He committed over 30,000 soldiers, and in ten days Algiers surrendered amid scenes of carnage: 'French soldiers, despite official policy to the contrary, pillaged Algiers, committed violence on men and women, desecrated mosques and cemeteries, and confiscated land and houses' (Aldrich, 1996: 26). When Charles X was deposed by Louis-Philippe, Algiers still remained in French hands. Slowly but steadily the French conquered other coastal and inland towns during the 1840s, burning villages and crops and destroying herds of livestock as they went. Because these were military operations, the lands acquired were regarded as French by right of conquest and were given to French settlers. The French politician Alexis de Tocqueville called on his countrymen to imitate the expanding American continental empire, and in only 30 years between 1841 and 1872 the European population of Algeria rose from 37,000 to 279,700. Later in the century France annexed Tunisia and Morocco. The resulting conflict and land seizure was constructed as the natural outcome of civilised progress; as one newspaper proclaimed: 'for a city of barbarians, to be burned by France is to begin to be enlightened' (Cohen, 1980: 274).

John Weaver observes in his comparative study of 'The Great Land Rush' that 'modern states augmented their culture of legality' by these means, using the Lockean concept of material improvement 'at the risk of harming those people who resist professionalized functional processes or who are denigrated as unimproving' (Weaver, 2003: 351). We know that some humanitarian voices were raised in protest about the consequences of this process. One observer of early nineteenth-century Australia wondered, 'what will future generations think of our Christianity . . . when they find recorded that our proprietorship to the soil has been purchased at such a Costly Sacrifice of human happiness and life' (Reynolds, 2001: 141). Unfortunately for indigenous peoples, even humanitarians rarely questioned the benefits of European expansion in the larger sense of 'civilisation', and therefore had little sense of how expansion and acculturation might proceed without the negative impact they deplored.

LABOUR SYSTEMS

After slavery was abolished in most of the European empires in the early nineteenth century, an immediate need arose for replacement labour; especially in the plantation colonies. The problem was particularly acute for the British: some imperial powers, such as Portugal, had negotiated an exemption from the abolition of slavery, and although no new slaves were brought to the southern United States, the institution of slavery continued there as well. The British attempted to persuade freed slaves in the West Indies to become apprentices on the plantations, but this was a disastrous failure. Newly-freed slaves wanted land of their own, to work for themselves; not to remain on the same plantations they had worked as slaves. Desperate for alternatives, the British used the newly-conquered island of Mauritius, a former French colony, as the site of an experiment in indentured labour. Indentures were nothing new: white labourers in the Hudson's Bay Company and in the early American and West Indian colonies had gone out under contracts which guaranteed them transportation, pay, clothing, and other benefits for a specific contract period. African slavery had eclipsed the indenture system, which at any rate was never particularly popular among Europeans. Now, in the wake of abolition, new labour diasporas from south and east Asia would change the face of empire in many tropical colonies.

In the British case, the immediate need was to supply labour to replace African slaves on plantations. Workers from British India signed indentures to work for a fixed period of time in exchange for wages, transportation, housing, and other basic benefits. The system worked so well in Mauritius that it was quickly exported to the West Indies and, eventually, throughout the empire. Why did the British choose south Asians for such work? The idea of indentured African labour never gained much ground, in part because the antislavery movement had made the whole question too sensitive. Other empires would come to different conclusions about African labour, as we will see. In the meantime, theories about climate and race continued, as ever, to suggest that people from tropical parts of the world were naturally suited to heavy plantation labour, and since much of south Asia was now under British control, its population seemed a natural choice. The so-called 'hill coolies' from the mountains of Ceylon were particularly favoured, but large numbers of workers came from the Indian mainland too. Wherever they went, indentured labourers faced a range of working conditions, some of them brutal. The British government attempted to regulate the recruitment, transportation, and rights of these workers, but there were always abuses that escaped the regulations. There was also an attitude of paternalism that underlined even the most benign employment: 'There is an Indian term, Mai-Bap, "Mother-Father", which the planter liked to be accorded' (Tinker, 1977: 24).

Not every British colony used indentured labour: different approaches were determined by the size of the indigenous population, whether or not indigenous people were willing to undertake agricultural labour, and the relative importance of European settlement to economic exploitation. In Malaya, for example, British settlement was not extensive and the indigenous Malays were reluctant to leave their own lands for wage labour on plantations or in mining. But Stamford Raffles's acquisition of the small coastal village of Singapore in 1819 was meant to become the heart of a new, British commercial network in south-east Asia. Tin and other minerals were already mined in the region, and British botanists discovered that rubber trees transplanted from South America would grow well in Malaya. As the demand for both rubber and tin grew during the nineteenth century, thanks to industrialisation, the British encouraged a large-scale immigration from south Asia, and later from China, to fill colonial labour requirements. The chartered Company of North Borneo had a private army whose soldiers displayed the severed heads of rebels on the tennis lawn of Government House, and whose plantations featured 'coolie' workers who died in their hundreds of fever and neglect. 'Dividends of one hundred per cent appeared in a new and horrid light' wrote one disgusted visitor (Kiernan, 1969: 87). The West's greed for rubber and tin, for which North Borneo was a major source, would continue to grow amid the Second Industrial Revolution and the massive rearmament which helped to produce the First World War. Investors held their noses, and took the dividends.

Although most indigenous Malays remained on the land, and thus were not equated with 'coolie' labour, this situation did not necessarily gain them the respect of their new rulers. British missionaries and other reformers often wrote about the alleged vices of the Malay 'race': sexual promiscuity (harems and polygamy), drug-taking, indolence, piracy, and a host of other supposedly inborn characteristics. Some Malay rulers still welcomed British involvement as a way of securing their own thrones, or of obtaining British help against their enemies, and cared little at first about the increasing use of indentured (rather than Malay) labour. The predicament of Malay peasants was of little interest to them, but the peasants themselves grew increasingly resentful about the influx of immigrant workers. Hostility toward the descendants of Indian and Chinese labourers would hamper Malayan decolonisation in the 1950s, and would do little to resolve ethnic tensions.

France had abolished slavery once and for all in 1848, and resolved the resulting labour problems in a variety of ways. In the same year, inhabitants of its older colonies, Martinique, Guadeloupe, Guyane and Réunion, the Society Islands (including Tahiti), and the four oldest parts of Senegal, became French citizens. In all other cases, citizenship could be obtained only by marriage, by the legal recognition of parentage by a French father, or by naturalisation; the latter was extremely rare because requirements included renouncing customary law (Islamic law, or traditional customary law in the Pacific islands, for example). This meant that most French colonial populations were subject to a special *code de l'indigénat*, even in Algeria where the colony had been proclaimed to be part of metropolitan France in 1848. The *code* gave colonial officials and police forces direct powers of arrest, imprisonment, and punishment as they saw fit. In theory the codes of the various colonies were not arbitrary; they were regularly published and outlined the local offences they covered, as in French Indo-China (now Vietnam, Laos, and Cambodia), where the inhabitants were forbidden to buy umbrellas in order to enforce a racial divide in clothing standards. Even more attractive was the regular supply of *engagés forcés* (forced labour) guaranteed by the *code*. Offences were frequently punished by sentences of forced labour. While not technically slavery, the system of *engagés forcés* was coercive and racially selective: the *code* applied only to indigenous non-Europeans, and remained in place in Algeria until 1928, and until 1946 elsewhere in the French empire.

Indigenous groups sometimes responded violently to the imposition of forced labour. In the Algerian interior, where the influence of Sufi Muslim leaders was strong, uprisings directly challenged French power. By the later nineteenth century, *colon* farms averaged 124 hectares while indigenous farms averaged 12: too small to provide family subsistence. This was very convenient for the *colons*, who could offer wage labour to people who had formerly worked for themselves. Where wage labour was insufficient to meet demand, successfully suppressed uprisings guaranteed a steady stream of prisoners whose labour could be forced.

In modern Angola the situation was somewhat different; slavery was not abolished in Portugal's African colonies until 1910. Europe's first slave-trading empire was also its last. The trade had declined rapidly during the nineteenth century, although demand continued to come from Brazil until 1888. The Portuguese increasingly turned to the exploitation of Angola's natural resources, and began to consolidate their hold on the interior in a series of military campaigns in the nineteenth century. The new resource extraction economy required labour resources to be retained in Angola; not shipped overseas for plantation work in Brazil. This labour was ensured through a system of compulsory state employment. The Portuguese assumed that conquered peoples had an obligation to work for their new masters, and created the terms *libertos* (liberated slaves) and *serviçaes* (employees of the state) to distinguish former slaves from current government employees. The Department of Native Affairs in Angola divided the black population into *assimilado* ('civilised' or assimilated) and *não-assimilado* ('uncivilised' or unassimilated) in order to facilitate labour recruiting. *Não-assimilado* were supposed to earn 'civilised' status by working for the state or for a European settler. The pay was so poor, however, that families could only pay their taxes by selling their family's food, the seeds for next year's crop, and even their children.

A fundamental contradiction emerges from this comparative study of colonial labour practices. Whether or not slavery was involved, European attitudes about indigenous labour were simultaneously pragmatic and disdainful. Systems of indentured labour were justified on the grounds that Asians or Africans were rational people capable of choosing labour contracts to better themselves and their families. On the other hand, many colonies featured extremely coercive labour practices accompanied by rhetoric about African or Asian laziness. Only the discipline of work for European-run governments, or European farms and businesses, could 'cure' non-Europeans of their congenital indolence. Into this contradictory picture came the indigenous leaders who might, or might not, wish to help colonial officials to allocate land and labour. An elderly African recalled the situation in colonial Uganda under British rule: 'When the government arrived, they made Abak an important man. People were ordered to work in his fields. In the old days, people only went into other men's fields when beer was going to be made. But after the government had arrived, people were forced to work' (Isaacman and Roberts, 1995: 27). Ordinary people could not necessarily rely on their own leaders to protect them from exploitative colonial labour practices.

COLONIAL WARFARE

The word 'consolidation' in this chapter's title can be very misleading, suggesting an orderly process based on coherent policy. European power was decisively challenged many times during the nineteenth century. European military technology eventually prevailed, but only after serious losses and protracted battles in some cases. Imperial policy had to be rethought afterwards, with significant implications for race relations.

As we know, there had been conflict between Europeans and indigenous groups in North America almost from first contact. A whole series of wars characterised the 'opening' of the western frontier following American independence; perhaps the most famous example is the defeat of General Custer's cavalry forces by the Lakota people under the leadership of Sitting Bull in 1876. Sitting Bull denied the US federal government's right to define 'Indian territory', and crossed the border into Canada to evade capture by the US authorities. In the end, like so many others, he wound up living on an American reservation where indigenous government was supposed to prevail. If reservation land proved too valuable, however, settlers would be brought in and the indigenous population forcibly relocated elsewhere, as the Dakota discovered. Treaties were no barrier to greed either. The British often boasted of the relatively peaceful nature of westward settlement in their Canadian colonies, and it is true that there were far fewer armed conflicts north of the border. The needs of the fur trade, which depended so heavily on indigenous goodwill, delayed substantial settlement in the Canadian west before the late nineteenth century. There was no room here for the American general's view that 'The only good Indian is a dead Indian' (Miller, 2000: 210). During the later nineteenth century, as western settlement expanded, the Canadian treaty commissioners declared that their treaty system was 'the cheapest' means to facilitate settlement, and 'a humane, just and Christian policy' (Miller, 2000: 210). Nevertheless, the outcome was the same on both sides of the border: dispossession, depopulation, and – until fairly recently – despair. Good intentions were no remedy for disease and loss of livelihood.

In Asia, the first substantial challenge to imperial rule came in 1857 with the Indian Rebellion. The conflict began with mutiny in parts of the Indian Army. Despite the critical importance of the army for British rule, respect, let alone equality, for Indian officers was extremely rare (in those days few people respected the common soldiers of any race). Indian officers tended to be of high caste and often from proud military families, but they might be led by English cadets such as 'Subaltern', the author of a published journal about the conquest of the Punjab, who 'felt shocked at scenes of carnage, quickly consoled at the prospect of medals – played cricket and the flute, scribbled verses, did his duty, and was not overly interested in Indians, who were *niggers*, or Sikhs, who were *rebels*' (Kiernan, 1969: 43). At the beginning of the nineteenth century one colonial official had remarked that Indians 'are excluded from all posts of great respectability or emolument, and are treated in society with mortifying hauteur and reserve . . . What must the sensations of this people [be] at our thus starving them in their native land?' (Dalrymple, 1998: 273). Grievances about increased discrimination joined rumours that the British were introducing new rifle cartridges whose papers were greased with forbidden beef and pig fat. Army mutinies rapidly spread to civilian groups, especially in the north of India, demonstrating that the rebellion's motives were much more complicated than the story of the rifle cartridges suggests.

EIC officials of the older type lamented the administrative and cultural meddling which they believed had provoked Indians to rebellion. Missionaries, on the other hand, claimed that the rebellion demonstrated the need for even more intensive Christianisation and Europeanisation. This intellectual debate was sidelined by stories of the atrocities committed by rebel troops in the north where British women and children had been sexually assaulted, killed, and dismembered. These incidents were used as evidence of the treacherous, sexually threatening nature of Indians as a group. Although the British government realised that too much punitive action would be counterproductive, and adopted a conciliatory policy toward all but the actual organisers of the rebellion, atrocities had to be avenged if British prestige was to be upheld. Punishments for captured rebel troops included being tied alive to the mouths of cannon in order to be blown apart and therefore denied the possibility of a proper Hindu or Muslim funerary rites.

The rebellion was finally brought under control in 1858, and the government of India was placed directly under British parliamentary authority. The pace of Europeanisation increased, and although talk of 'improvement' continued, the day was now considered very far off when Indians would be able to rise in the scale of civilisation sufficiently for independence. Even if many district officers and other colonial officials were honestly devoted to their welfare, Indians were still very clearly regarded as inferior. 'India was never forgiven for what it did in 1857, still less perhaps for what it exasperated the English into doing, or allowing to be done . . . The bitterness that India had always felt was now felt on both sides, and the gulf had become impassable' (Kiernan, 1969: 47).

In New Zealand, this type of gulf produced a protracted civil war. At first glance, the imperial Europeanisation project seemed to have succeeded rather well: most Maori had been Christian for at least one generation, and many attended mission schools. Ironically, this identity could work against British interests. Maori grievances about treaty violations, and concern about the large numbers of *pakeha* (previously translated at first use) arriving in their country, combined with images and stories from the Old Testament to produce prophetic movements aimed at shaking off British oppression. In a pointed reversal of the usual biblical ethnology, Maori prophets sometimes saw their people as Semitic and therefore superior to the incoming settlers who had a different racial ancestry. Maori tradition had always emphasised the importance of genealogy, and this identification of their people with the divine destiny and persecution of Jews would continue into the twentieth century.

A 'king movement' arose to provide a centralised response to British rule, and although not all Maori supported the movement, it became an important rallying point for the more disaffected tribes. As with land disputes in other colonies, the Maori quarrel was not with the British people as such, or even with the British government, but with the way that their rights were not being respected as the Treaty of Waitangi had guaranteed. The first Maori king was crowned with these words: 'Potatau, this day I create you King of the Maori People. You and Queen Victoria shall be bound together to be one. The religion of Christ shall be the mantle of your protection; the law shall be the *whariki* mat for your feet, for ever and ever onward (Ballantyne, 2002: 162). Similar identities also motivated some Maori groups to remain loyal to the colonial government; the battles that dominated the 1840s and 1860s were not only race wars, but civil wars as well.

At first, the British found it hard to believe that their regiments could be defeated by 'savages'. Rather than give Maori fortifications and bravery too much credit, reports emphasised surprise ambushes, or the presence of unexpectedly large numbers of Maori and therefore overwhelming odds in their favour. In the end, as so often, Britain's ability to send reinforcements from Australia and elsewhere, and the role of artillery and gunboats, eventually ensured victory. By the late 1860s British officials were able to stand down many of the military reinforcements, and to begin a process of consolidation involving, among other things, the confiscation of millions of acres of land belonging to the defeated tribes. Nevertheless, as the governor observed, 'after all the expenditure of blood and treasure which has taken place in this country, the Queen's writ can hardly be said to run in the purely Maori districts' (Samson, 2001a: 133). The guaranteed Maori seats in the New Zealand parliament were preserved, putting New Zealand's indigenous people in a very different position from those of Australia or Canada who would not even be able to vote until the 1960s.

By the later nineteenth century, the imperial powers had significant new technologies with which to extend their influence. In earlier centuries, Europeans had not enjoyed much (or any) advantage over non-Europeans in military combat. Muskets were widely traded, ensuring that Europeans often faced troops armed to some extent with European weaponry, and besides, muskets were difficult to load quickly, had a limited range, and were notoriously unreliable in damp weather. By the end of the nineteenth century, however, industrialisation had produced military technologies of vastly greater destructive scope. Breech-loading rifles and machine guns joined the imperial arsenal along with even more sinister developments such as dum-dum bullets (named for the Indian village where they were invented). Banned for use against Europeans because of their horrendous effects, dum-dum bullets exploded on impact, creating fearful internal wounds. Imperial soldiers and adventurers considered them ideal for elephants, tigers, and savages. Death was virtually guaranteed even after a relatively inaccurate shot, making big-game hunting and colonial warfare safer than ever (for Europeans). Gone was the massive loss of European life through disease in the 'white man's grave' of western Africa, or in colonial garrisons from the Caribbean to India. Along with improvements in inoculation and preventative medicine, European weapons technology made empire-building seem more like an adventure than a life-threatening risk. A few examples from Africa will illustrate processes that were at work around the globe.

Britain's empire had already been expanding before the 'scramble' began, but the pressure of international rivalry increased the pace of territorial expansion. In west Africa, for example, relatively small coastal colonies were rapidly extended inland thanks to improvements in transportation technology, medical treatments for tropical fevers, and military firepower. There was also a powerful tradition of imperial adventure and masculinity to consider. Warfare against 'savages' was often described in terms of a thrilling sport. Lord Garnet Wolsey, commanding officer of British forces during the Second Ashanti War of 1873–4 in the Gold Coast colony, described his experiences in frankly sexual terms: 'It is only through experience of the sensation that we learn how intense, even in anticipation, is the rapture-giving delight which the attack upon an enemy affords . . . All other sensations are but as the tinkling of a doorbell in comparison with the throbbing of Big Ben' (Lindqvist, 1996: 54). Men had thrilled to the experience of battle long before this, of course, but now they had uniquely powerful weapons. The regimented warfare of Europe could still involve hand-to-hand combat with bayonets, but in the colonies the opposition was usually so poorly armed that big guns were often all it took. The Ashanti learned their lesson, and in 1896, as British troops under Robert Baden-Powell marched toward their capital city in the Third Ashanti War, they chose simply to surrender. Although this produced gratifying images of Ashanti chiefs crawling at the feet of the British leaders,

Baden-Powell, founder of the Boy Scouts, missed the glory of combat and told his mother: 'I thoroughly enjoyed the outing, except for the want of a fight, which I fear will preclude our getting any medals or decoration' (Lindqvist, 1996: 57).

The conquest and pillage of Benin offered plenty of thrills, however. Part of what is now Nigeria, the inland kingdom of Benin had imposed trade restrictions on the British. Earlier in the century, the British government had refused requests from traders and consuls for an attack on the Benin interior, so in 1897 consul Lt. James Phillips decided to take matters into his own hands. On the principle that it is easier to ask forgiveness than to seek permission, he sent the usual request for intervention to the Foreign Office and, without waiting for a response, set out with 200 attendants on an unannounced visit to the king at Benin City. The king asked them to postpone the visit because an important religious festival was about to start; in reply, as a deliberate insult, Phillips gave the messengers his walking stick and resumed his journey to Benin. When Phillips and seven other white men were killed in an ambush the next day, the British public demanded revenge; the Foreign Office's reply to Phillips's request for military intervention – negative, as usual – was now overtaken by events. In a savage punitive expedition driven by public opinion, the British defeated Benin's forces and sacked Benin City before burning it. In the process, British troops observed 'Altars covered with streams of dried blood' and a sacrificial tree near the royal compound where 'there were two crucified bodies, [and] at the foot of the tree seventeen newly decapitated bodies and forty-three more in various stages of decomposition' (Pietz, 1999: 54). Only a minority worried about whether the situation at the royal compound was representative of all of west Africa, or pondered the viciousness of the British attack which had led to the king's desperate sacrifices. What mattered most was that the horror of 'fetishism' had been proven for all to see, inviting a more forceful military presence and an even greater sense of European superiority and imperial responsibility in Africa.

Similar dynamics surrounded British wars in the Sudan. Led by a Muslim nationalist, Mohammed Ahmed Ibn-el-Sayed (known to the British as the 'Mad Mullah'), many Sudanese reacted sharply to rising European influence in Egypt. The Suez Canal had opened in 1869 and, to protect their investment, British and French advisers dominated the Egyptian government and their soldiers garrisoned the Canal Zone. Having only recently shrugged off Ottoman domination, the Egyptian government was unable to Europeanise at a pace that would satisfy its new imperial masters and, bankrupt, was forced to sell its shares in the Canal to the British. Under such conditions, the purified Islamic state envisioned by Ibn-el-Sayed – revered as the Mahdi, or 'expected one' – attracted a great deal of support. The tottering Egyptian regime and its ill-trained army sustained a number of defeats at the hands of the Mahdi and his 'dervishes': intensely loyal troops prepared to embrace martyrdom. Britain invaded Egypt in 1882, but its forces were also defeated, and General Charles Gordon died besieged at Khartoum in 1885. Cultural memories of Islamic invasion in Europe and the battles of the Crusades gained new currency in the modern context of anti-European Islamicist movements like this one. Gordon became a heroic martyr of empire whose bravery was overcome only by the fanaticism of the Muslim hordes.

A relief expedition reached Khartoum too late to save Gordon, and the British forces withdrew; a tide of racial humiliation swept Britain and helped to drive the governing Liberals from power during the subsequent election. Gordon, the empire, and white pride had been betrayed at Khartoum. The Mahdi died of fever shortly afterward, throwing the Sudanese nationalist movement into turmoil, and providing an opportunity for the British to return in the 1890s to defeat its weakened forces. Memories of Gordon's martyrdom and of the decapitation of his corpse by the Mahdi's forces were still fresh. In 1898 General Horatio Kitchener defeated a large 'dervish' army at Omdurman, opened the Mahdi's tomb, and removed the skull before throwing the rest of the corpse into the river. He planned to turn the skull into an inkwell, but some of his officers pointed out that this might undermine British claims to moral superiority over Islamic fanaticism. Kitchener reluctantly agreed to bury the skull at a site still revered today by Sudanese nationalists.

Watching with boyish enthusiasm was the young Winston Churchill, then a newspaper reporter, who recalled that 'To the great mass of those who took part in the little wars of Britain in those vanished light-hearted days, this was only a sporting element in a splendid game' (Lindqvist, 1996: 54). Even Churchill confessed that he pitied the thousands of Muslims who rushed at the British machine guns while armed only with spears. No Sudanese got within 500 yards of the British position, and within a few hours nine thousand of them were dead. The subsequent killing of thousands of the Sudanese wounded was based on the fear that their fanaticism would make them strike the British from behind while being taken prisoner. Images of Muslim treachery were reinforced in British minds by the Sudanese campaigns, enhancing the idea of people who would be 'improvable' if removed from the sinister influence of their mullahs. Meanwhile, the only real cost to the British was a diplomatic crisis with France, who wanted a share of the spoils based on their own presence at Fashoda in the southern Sudan. France conceded, Kitchener and his officers got their medals, and the British public praised the restoration of imperial pride.

Germany's *Schutzgebietsgesetz* ('colonial law') declared that non-Europeans were subjects of empire rather than citizens; no African in the colonies ever became a German citizen, and few people of mixed race could meet the stringent requirements for German naturalisation. Africans were forbidden to leave their home colony, ostensibly to guarantee labour supplies, but also to control African emigration to Germany. Whipping, outlawed in

Germany since the 1870s, was commonly used in the colonies. A district commissioner from Cameroon dismissed the promises about indigenous rights made in the original 1884 treaty with the Duala people, explaining that his strict regime was 'justified because of the importance of the white race and its antagonism towards the black' (Stoecker, 1987: 126).

The proclamation of German sovereignty in 1893 in German South-West Africa (now Namibia) did not necessarily ensure a role for African leaders that was acceptable to them. Treaties were not always signed properly, or at all. The nomadic Nama people refused to negotiate because their traditional lifestyle would be eliminated; the more settled, cattle-raising Herero regarded the Germans with greater favour at first, but grew increasingly hostile as the influx of Europeans increased. Some settlers enjoyed the visits and gifts of their African landowners when a child was born or baptised. Others objected to being reminded that they were intruders. One settler woman wrote down the song that a Herero nursemaid sang to her baby son: 'You are lonely because your home is a foreign country. Your family is far away and your grandparents long to see you again' (Bley, 1996: 91).

The colonial government was taking the best land for colonisation and forcing the Herero onto reserves; when they refused to go, General Adrian Dietrich Lothar von Trotha ordered their extermination. Rather than waste too much valuable ammunition, the German forces drove the Herero and their allies into the desert where they died of thirst. The official history of this 'war' describes how 'The death rattles of the dying and their insane screams of fury . . . resounded in the sublime silence of infinity. The Hereros had ceased to be an independent people' (Lindqvist, 1996: 149). Tens of thousands of skeletons were found around holes scrabbled in the sand, many of them the remains of children. There was outrage in some political quarters in Germany, but an immigration agent for the colony was clear about the advantages of the massacre: 'No false philanthropy or racial theory can convince sensible people that the preservation of a tribe of South African kaffirs . . . is more important to the future of mankind than the spread of the great European nations and the white race in general,' he wrote. 'Not until the native learns to produce anything of value in the service of the higher race . . . does he gain any moral right to exist' (Linqvist, 1996: 150–1). Dissent, voiced in Germany and elsewhere, could be identified by the 'sensible' majority as naïve 'false philanthropy'.

In one notable case, European force failed to overcome indigenous resistance. Italy wanted to achieve Great Power status, and created the colony of Eritrea in eastern Africa in 1890, followed by the establishment of a protectorate over the coast south of British Somaliland in east Africa and settlements in Libya. Meanwhile, an attempted invasion of Abyssinia was repelled in 1896 at the Battle of Adowa, and Italy was forced to recognise Abyssinian independence. This was the only example of a conclusive defeat for European forces in Africa, but Italy's marginal position among the Powers prevented this from creating larger shock waves. For one thing, the prevalence of Christianity in Abyssinia provided a comforting rationalisation of the kingdom's unique ability to repel imperial invaders. Still, one young politician, who would become minister of colonies under Benito Mussolini's fascist government, remembered defining his political career as 'the reaction to Adowa, the revenge for Adowa' (Segrè, 1974: 18). Under Mussolini, Abyssinia would be conquered and Italy's African empire expanded. The Italian example shows how much imperial expansion could be driven by domestic concerns, such as military prestige. Such motives were perpetually at odds with European claims about assimilation and civilisation. Perhaps this is what one British observer meant when he said, 'We demoralize and we extirpate, but we never really civilize' (Kiernan, 1969: 88).

MISCEGENATION AS CONTAMINATION

European men had been finding non-European women sexually attractive for centuries and, as we have seen, early empires often featured significant intermarriage as well as less formal forms of sexual interaction. By the nineteenth century, however, attitudes were changing. During and after the Mexican wars with the United States, some Americans fantasised about the way in which they would be welcomed as liberators by Hispanic beauties frustrated by the effeminacy of their own men: 'The Spanish maid, with eye of fire, / At balmy evening turns her lyre / And, looking to the Eastern sky, / Awaits our Yankee chivalry / Whose purer blood and valiant arms, / Are fit to clasp her budding charms' (Horsman, 1981: 233). Defeating the enemy and stealing his women was a time-honoured approach to warfare, but marriage for higher-ranking American men meant 'suitable' marriage, and Hispanic women were rarely found suitable. Enjoying their 'budding charms', and regarding them as social equals, were therefore two very different things.

In Spanish America itself, miscegenation had been widespread in the Spanish and Portuguese colonies of the New World, especially between individuals of European and Indian ancestry. As one official put it, '[Indian] origin is not vile like that of the other *castas*', in other words, like those with African blood (Wade, 1997: 30). In all of the Latin American colonies, however, the highest rank in society consisted of the European-born, followed by the locally-born *crillos* (or *mazombos* in Brazilian Portuguese), the *mestizos* (Indian-European), Indians, and blacks. *Mestizo* children were often raised with the status and privileges of whites, depending on whether or not their European fathers officially recognised them. Other mixed-race children were usually raised by their mothers, and were therefore barred from advanced education and employment. By the nineteenth century, the status of *Indios* was itself in decline; after the expulsion of the Jesuits in the eighteenth century, mission stations became plantations and their Indian inhabitants found themselves rented out as labourers. The Indian population went into precipitous decline through economic dislocation and disease, falling from about 5 million at first contact to about 1 million by the end of the nineteenth century. The Spanish government, usually more lenient in its attitude than its more race-conscious colonial governors, began to discourage mixed-race unions. From 1778 parental consent was required to all marriages involving whites under 25 years old, in an attempt to deter 'unsuitable' matches. Nevertheless, *métissage* continued, continually undermining attempts to construct the colonies as transplanted Spanish communities.

In a few areas, such as Argentina, extensive immigration from Europe during the nineteenth century put additional downward pressure on the status of the *mestizos*. Not so in Brazil, declared a Brazilian statesman, where 'they went on to make up the very core of the nation' (Ribeiro, 2000: 71). Miscegenation continued when Brazil expanded into the South American interior, leading one observer to declare that the various ancestor-races were hardly distinguishable. 'We are destined to national unity', he said, and in these racially mixed Brazilians he saw 'the hardy nucleus of our future, the bedrock of our race' (Burns, 1995, 3). Nevertheless, most of the vast Brazilian plantations and ranches remained in the hands of families with substantial European ancestry.

In northern North America, French and British men had married into indigenous families in order to ensure success in the fur trade during previous centuries. The resulting mixed-race children were integrated into British colonial life by the HBC, but by the mid-nineteenth century even this pragmatic trading company was changing its approach to miscegenation. The case of Amelia, Lady Douglas, is instructive. She was the wife of Vancouver Island's second governor, Sir James Douglas, and she was part Cree. Douglas, also of mixed race, had married a woman whose indigenous connections would help to advance his career. Nevertheless, a settlement colony like Vancouver Island (founded in 1849) was very different from the traditional fur trade communities. There were many more Europeans around, including European women and children. Settler communities did not require indigenous trapping or survival skills; they wanted indigenous land. Lady Douglas, who had expected to make good marriages for her daughters, encountered ridicule instead. Incoming settlers, even those from working-class backgrounds, resented the fact that 'half-breeds' occupied a higher place in the colonial hierarchy than they did. After a Government House ball in 1861 one young Royal Navy officer sneered: 'Most of the young ladies are half breeds & have quite as many of the propensities of the savage as of the civilized being' (Van Kirk, 1999: 229).

Colonial society in India made a similarly dramatic transition. The eighteenth century had featured a considerable number of mixed-race families in

India, notably marriages between high-ranking EIC officials and Indian women. By the early nineteenth century, the number of mixed-race marriages in India had become insignificant. More white women were going out to India with their husbands or fathers, and there were other considerations as well: 'young Indian men were often handsome, in a raffish Italian style; they were believed by prudish Victorians to be inordinately, unnaturally lascivious' (Kiernan, 1969: 57–8). Such images fed anxiety about white female purity. The practices of the old EIC had built some limited bridges across the cultural divide; but now, with only rare exceptions, Indians and British inhabited increasingly separate worlds. High-ranking gentlemen of both groups might socialise at Oxford or Cambridge, study for their bar exams at London's Inns of Court together, play cricket or hunt tigers. Nevertheless, it is significant that they did not usually marry one another's daughters, and when they did meet, it was usually on British terms. British power expanded throughout the Indian subcontinent through a series of wars of conquest, and although many Indian princely families retained some political power, the British term for their territories was 'client states'.

In the Dutch East Indies, mixed-race marriages were made on increasingly Dutch terms. After 1848, Dutch law applied to both partners in the marriage; before then, Asian women had been able to retain indigenous legal status for themselves and their children with the intention, for example, of maintaining traditional inheritance rights. By the later nineteenth century, it was assumed that such women would wish to pass Dutch rights and identity along to their children: a clear departure from earlier attitudes, and a reinforcement of both patriarchal and European power in the Dutch East Indies. The colonial administration in Java debated whether or not to ban marriages between Dutch women and Asian or Eurasian men; the racial 'loss' of white female reproductive capacity was of concern in all modern empires. The government decided simply to maintain their position that women should acquire the identity and legal rights of their spouses, regardless of racial difference. This might sound tolerant, but the lawyers who promoted this decision did so because 'The European woman who wants to enter into such a marriage has already sunk so deep socially and morally that it does not result in ruin' (Stoler, 1992: 542). Where a thriving Eurasian community had once controlled the colonial capital of Batavia, Dutch administrators now tended to arrive already married to Dutch women. Like so many other mixed-race groups, the Eurasians discovered that they were no longer considered necessary to the smooth and profitable extension of empire, and found themselves in an increasingly marginal place between 'authentic' native communities and the Dutch administration.

Changing French attitudes toward *métissage* in Indo-China are equally revealing. Like the Dutch East Indies, French Indo-China featured a substantial mixed-race population. Relatively few French people settled permanently in Indo-China – only a few hundred by 1900 – with predictable results in terms of mixed-race unions and their offspring. In later nineteenth-century France, however, immigration from north Africa, a declining birth-rate, and defensiveness in the wake of the loss of Alsace-Lorraine to the Germans in 1870, contributed to an increase in racism. Frenchness was seen as something transmitted through culture, especially through language, but it was also seen as an inherited birthright. The trial of a Eurasian boy for assault against a German citizen in Indo-China is instructive. The trial, which took place in 1898, resulted in a harsh six-month sentence of imprisonment, and led to an appeal by the boy's father, who resented the treatment of his son as a 'vulgaire annamite' (a common Annamite or Vietnamese; Stoler, 1992: 522). Publicly acknowledged by his French father, the boy was legally entitled to the rights of a Frenchman. The appeal was denied, however, because the boy spoke little French, was illiterate, and his father (a sailor) was away much of the time. Non-French ancestry could contaminate a person, especially if he or she was insufficiently acculturated and had therefore failed to overcome the inherited disadvantages of mixed race.

Some historians have suggested that the arrival of white women turned tolerance into racism in the colonies. 'It's a well-known saying that the women lost us the Empire. It's true', wrote one commentator in 1985. The historian Margaret Strobel has called this 'the myth of the destructive female' (Strobel, 1991: 1). Men who might once have taken indigenous wives or mistresses were increasingly likely to bring families with them from the mother country as the nineteenth century progressed. The emigration of single, 'marriageable' women (i.e. women of childbearing age) was encouraged by imperial govern-ments in order to redress the imbalance between the sexes and to enable more all-European families to grow. It was considered indelicate to refer to such matters directly; one advertisement for women to go to Australia emphasised 'that desirable [jobs], with good wages, are easily obtained' but only 'Unmarried Women or Widows . . . between the ages of 18 and 30' need apply (Samson, 2001a: 146). The shift toward populating colonies with Europeans certainly did not rule out sexual relationships with indigenous women, but it relegated them to more clandestine ones, reducing indigenous women's power further.

White women's sexual chastity was always a major concern in the col-onies, and was protected by increasingly harsh legislation. In Australian-governed Papua New Guinea, the *White Women's Protection Ordinance* of 1926 imposed the death penalty for any indigenous man convicted of the rape or attempted rape of a white woman. White rapists of indigenous women, on the other hand, were rarely brought to trial and certainly never faced the death penalty. The governor explained that 'ordinary native women' were unconcerned about sexual integrity whereas 'a respectable white woman' would be traumatised by rape (Bulbeck, 1992: 192). Women were encouraged to treat their male servants as subhuman rather than risk the danger of sexual attraction. The blatant racism of this situation is clear; what is less clear, however, is whether white women themselves were responsible for it. Were white women more racist than their menfolk because they feared rape, or had their menfolk become more racist through fear that their women might desire non-white men? As research in women's history expands, women's own voices are being disinterred from what was once a debate dominated by men. Women held a range of views about racial issues, including ones which were critical of racism. Writing from the American south in 1835, one woman worried about the effect on her small daughter of growing up attended by black slaves: 'Think of learning to rule despotically your fellow creatures before the first lesson of self-government has been well spelled over. It makes me tremble; but I shall find a remedy, or remove myself and the child from this misery and ruin' (Robinson, 1999: 135). Debate continues about whether white women themselves were responsible for the 'ruin'.

CHAPTER FIVE

THE AGE OF 'SCIENTIFIC RACISM', 1880–1950

The later nineteenth century produced a proliferation of new imperial powers in conjunction with an increasingly biological emphasis in racism. Germany, the United States, Belgium, and Italy increased their international status through the acquisition of overseas colonies. The older empires of Britain, France, Portugal, and the Netherlands continued to expand, and imperial Japan sought admission to the charmed circle of 'civilised Powers'. The Berlin Conference of 1884 allocated enormous new territories to various imperial Powers, yet invited no indigenous representatives. The Powers claimed to be acting in the interest of 'uncivilised' peoples, but rarely allowed those peoples to speak for themselves.

By the end of the First World War in 1918 this 'scramble' for empire had seen most of the world's land surface claimed by one Power or another. The British and French empires grew even larger through the addition of several League of Nations mandates in the Middle East, the Pacific, and Africa. The United States granted independence to the Philippines, but retained many of its other colonies and added others during the Second World War. We know with hindsight that colonial nationalism was growing during this period, but that was not always clear to contemporaries. Too often the twentieth century is seen as inevitably leading to the end of empire, when in fact it featured renewed imperial expansion of various sorts until after 1945. Only then did postwar economic crises, Cold War geopolitics, and changing attitudes force the old imperial powers into decolonisation, willingly or otherwise.

'SCIENTIFIC RACISM'

By the time Charles Darwin published *The Origin of Species* in 1859, intellectuals were already blending culture, biology, and territory together to produce the heady brew of Romantic nationalism. What made the later nineteenth- and early twentieth-century theories different was the belief, in some quarters, that human beings should deliberately manipulate reproduction in order to hasten evolution. The shift began with a noticeable hardening of racial attitudes and prejudices in the later nineteenth century. The pioneer philologist Max Müller warned that specialists like himself 'who know how thin the ice really is . . . tremble whenever they see their own fragile arguments handled so daringly by their muscular colleagues the palaeontologists and cranioscopists' (Hannaford, 1995: 305). Despite these warnings, the popularity of skull-measuring and other techniques of physical anthropology increased. In Britain, a direct confrontation took place between the older, universalist theories of British ethnologists, and the new 'scientific' racial essentialism. James Hunt resigned from the Ethnological Society to form the new Anthropological Society of London in 1862, placing its new headquarters down the street from the Christian Union with a 'savage skeleton' in the front window, and calling meetings of the so-called 'Cannibal Club' to order with a gavel carved in the shape of an African head (Stocking, 1987: 252). The distance between 'brothering' and 'othering' was visibly growing.

The dissemination of Darwin's theory of natural selection, especially after the publication of *The Descent of Man* in 1871, gave race-based theories of human development an apparently scientific sanction. Older theories had emphasised social evolution, but the newer ones stressed the operation of inexorable biological laws in the struggle for survival. By 1889 one French writer could describe Africans as 'thousands of gorillas swarming and vegetating on land which is nevertheless rich in resources' (Aldrich, 1996: 203), relegating Africans to subhuman status and inviting Africa's colonisation by a superior race. Darwin himself had noted the collisions between Europeans and the indigenous population on his travels to Australia, declaring that 'At some future period not very distant as measured in centuries, the civilised races of man will almost certainly exterminate and replace throughout the world the savage races' (Lindqvist, 1996: 107).

Nevertheless, Darwin would not necessarily have endorsed all aspects of the 'Social Darwinism' which followed him. Evolutionary theory dealt with very long time spans, and with the emergence or extinction of entire species. It enabled the development of modern psychological theories which presuppose a basic psychic unity among human beings. Social Darwinists, however, used it to interpret the course of recent human history and social policy. Francis Galton, Darwin's cousin and a pioneering eugenicist, published *Hereditary Genius* in 1869 to promote selective human breeding with an eye to accelerating racial improvement. The British sociologist Herbert Spencer developed a notion of 'survival of the fittest' which was different from Darwin's emphasis on long-term processes of random mutation and natural selection. Spencer and his followers concentrated on finding ways for the 'fittest' human beings to improve their reproductive success. In order to do this, they broke down existing racial groups into ever smaller categories to permit a more precise assessment of the 'fitness' of different ethnic groups and social classes. Spencer's message for the 'unfit' was brutally uncompromising: 'The forces which are working out the great scheme of perfect happiness, taking no account of incidental suffering, exterminate such sections of mankind as stand in their way' (Lindqvist, 1996: 416).

Meanwhile, the modern social sciences were beginning to find a recognised place in academic life, especially on the European continent and in North America, and by the early twentieth century we can speak of anthropology and sociology as professions. Gone were the days of the gentlemen amateurs, although many social scientists continued to rely on others for their field data before the mid-twentieth century. The French sociologist Émile Durkheim often used information from the European empires, especially British India, to illuminate general laws of social development, interpreting elements of Indian culture as survivals from earlier stages of human organisation. Indian customs were artefacts from a shared primitive past that Europe had left behind. The Hindu concept of caste was an important focus of attention, inviting Durkheim to develop theories about religion as the basic building-block of social identity and communication.

Both French and Asian intellectuals contributed to the popularity of Durkheim's approach. For one thing, it emphasised a shared history in which social evolution was accelerated or retarded by various means such as political revolution. For this reason, Durkheimian sociology was often left-wing politically. However, the description of some Asian societies as backward or 'arrested' in terms of development had imperial implications as well. For Karl Marx, India's backwardness had facilitated British conquest; India's village communities were relics of the past, and would need to be swept away in order for India to progress through the stages leading to socialist revolution. For all their opposition to imperialism, Marx and other political radicals were not necessarily free from notions of European superiority. The British radical Edmond Morel, who agitated against the atrocities of the rubber trade in the Congo, was horrified by the use of French colonial troops to garrison parts of Germany after the end of the First World War. He denounced the deployment of soldiers from 'the most sexually developed' of the races, who were bound to assault women sexually because of their uncontrolled passions and who, for 'well-known physiological reasons' (i.e. the allegedly larger penises of black men), would inflict serious injury and even death on their white female victims (Barkan, 1992: 24). This was the same type of anxiety that we have observed in the severity of Papua New Guinea's rape laws, and which had existed for centuries in white attitudes toward black sexuality. It also reflected the notion that non-European troops should not be used in European theatres of conflict; Britain, for example, used relatively few Indian troops on the Western Front (though considerable numbers of Asians and Africans were used as support personnel).

In Britain, by the turn of the century, anthropologists favoured functionalist theories which, at first glance, were considerably more equitable than earlier developmental theories of social evolution. First developed by Bronislaw Malinowski, functionalism emphasised the internal rationality of cultures: one of Malinowski's students described it as an explanation of 'the usefulness of the apparently senseless antics' of 'savages' (Stocking, 1995: 294). Anthropological fieldworkers trained by Malinowski and others were important to colonial rulers for just this reason. If the 'senseless antics' of native people could be analysed in terms of function, colonial governments would be able to identify undesirable elements (such as headhunting) and replace them by other activities (such as organised sport) which would serve the same function. Whether or not this actually worked in practice was less important than the way in which it enabled colonial administrations to rationalise the Europeanisation of subject peoples, giving a scientific gloss to older rhetoric about civilisation and improvement.

In 1866 George Campbell, the British governor of Bengal, declared in the *Proceedings of the Asiatic Society of Bengal* that India 'offers an unlimited field for ethnological observation and enquiry, and presents an infinity of varieties of almost every one of the great divisions of the human race' (Brown, 2003: 204). Indian governors were already appointing superintendents of ethnography to research the 'tribes and castes' of India in order to put colonial administration on an allegedly scientific basis, and to identify potentially troublesome groups. Perhaps the most notorious example of this process was the identification and prosecution of 'thuggee' by Captain W.H. Sleeman with the encouragement of the governor-general of India. Sleeman's department, established in 1830, used doubtful means to collect its information about gangs of 'thugs' who ritually murdered travellers. Informants often confessed under threats of incarceration or hanging. Debate continues about whether 'thuggee' was really an ancient form of ritual worship, or whether it was a later development related to the disruptions of colonialism. Nevertheless, the title of Sleeman's book on 'thuggee' reveals the intimate connection between ethnography and colonial administration during this period: *Ramaseeana, or a Vocabulary of the Peculiar Language used by the Thugs, with an introduction and Appendix, Descriptive of the System Pursued by that Fraternity and of the Measures which have been Adopted by the Supreme Government of India for its Suppression* (1836). Later on, legislation such as the *Criminal Tribes Act* of 1911 would classify particular ethnic groups as possessing inherently criminal cultures, authorising the jailing of individuals simply for belonging to one or other of the so-called 'criminal castes'. This type of interpretation was similar to that involving 'martial races'. Both were part of a process in which Europeans assumed the right to define various groups, to codify them using names of their own choosing, creating hierarchies in which some groups were favoured over others. Anthropological speculation could both explain and justify imperial expansion and control.

As one historian has noted recently, theories based on 'Caucasian' or 'Aryan' superiority remained popular because (ironically) they were non-scientific. Instead, they were 'part of an imaginative geography rather than informed by solid factual knowledge, and hence open to all sorts of association of ideas' (Augstein, 1990: 59). Once those ideas changed, the 'scientific' basis for racism was undermined. In the meantime, however, race theory was as much about politics as science. The liberal German anthropologist Friedrich Ratzel's 1891 publication *Anthropogeographie* specifically refuted ideas about the inevitable extinction of lower races, contending that it had been European military power, not racial superiority, that had led to the decline of indigenous populations in the Americas and elsewhere. After Ratzel joined the nationalist Pan-German league, however, he began to wonder whether other factors provided a better explanation of European power. His *Politische Geographie* (1897) linked the fate of non-Europeans with that of Jews because, despite their prominent contribution to German society, Jews were a scattered people without lands of their own. Territorial expansion at the expense of 'landless' inferiors was therefore both natural and inevitable. It was Ratzel who helped to popularise the word *Lebensraum* ('living space') as a rationale for empire.

Similar views had been promoted by Joseph-Arthur, comte de Gobineau, the French bureaucrat and critic of the French Revolution [*Doc. 9*] and by the Englishman Houston Stewart Chamberlain, whose 1899 book *The Foundations of the Nineteenth Century* stated that races who failed to establish modern nation-states were doomed: 'Wherever, as in India, nations are not formed, the stock of strength that has been gathered by race decays' (Tinker, 1977: 5). Instead of historical explanations of European dominance, these theorists preferred essentialised arguments about the energy or lassitude of different races. Much of this stemmed from eighteenth-century definitions of property rights in terms of 'working' the soil: a French legal text from 1910 declared that 'We cannot recognise the indigenes' right to be the sole possessors of the riches of the soil and to deprive the rest of humanity of them through their ignorance, laziness or incapacity' (Aldrich, 1996: 216–17). Seen from this perspective, the global diffusion of European power and culture was not only natural, but also desirable.

WHITE SUPREMACY?

It was not only 'Europeans' or 'whites' who had triumphed through conquest and imperial rule, but particular kinds of Europeans such as the 'Anglo-Saxons' (English). These sub-racial categories were in use in Romantic theories about national 'genius', but now they were becoming more biological than cultural. William Z. Ripley's *Races of Europe*, published in 1899, used skull measurements and other apparently scientific techniques to identify Teutons, Celts, Anglo-Saxons, and others. Some of these terms are still in use today.

A particularly vigorous school of thought in Britain and the United States regarded 'Anglo-Saxons' as the highest stage of human development. Many went even further, breaking the Anglo-Saxon group down into class divisions, or medical categories, in order to show that some members of the race were 'unfit' and were therefore holding back 'the survival of the fittest'.

By the early twentieth century, therefore, notions of racial superiority rested on two conflicting foundations: confidence and insecurity. In Britain and the United States, proclamations of Anglo-Saxon superiority reached fever pitch, and helped to drown out the rising volume of colonial nationalism. One British statesman declared 'that Irishmen were as unfit for self-government' as the black 'Hottentots' of southern Africa (Kiernan, 1969: 28). Nevertheless, a sense of threat underscored these increasingly shrill claims to superiority. If it was dependent on the distinctiveness of a particular European group, such as the Anglo-Saxons, how would *métissage* affect it? Gustave LeBon's *Les Lois psychologiques de l'evolution des peuples* (1894) warned against the 'decadence' of mixed-race relationships. 'It followed logically', he claimed, 'that all countries with a large number of métis and Jews were for that reason alone condemned to perpetual anarchy' (Hannaford, 1995: 339). It was in this aggressively defensive atmosphere that the eugenics movement thrived. Its founders, Darwin's cousin Francis Galton and the American Charles Davenport, believed that science had demonstrated the natural superiority of white people in general, and of prosperous and educated white people in particular. In our horrified reaction to Nazi Germany's 'Final Solution' to the perceived 'Jewish problem', we must not forget that eugenics programmes also targeted the poor, the mentally or physically disabled, and anyone else defined as 'unfit' to reproduce. Eugenics enjoyed popular support in Britain, Scandinavia, Canada, and the United States, operating in combination with immigration restrictions to preserve the alleged Anglo-Saxon or Nordic purity of the mainstream population. These developments were criticised in some quarters, but it would take the Holocaust to turn public opinion against such measures and, even so, compulsory sterilisation legislation remained on the books in some countries until after the 1950s.

Nervous white supremacists worried most about the demographic, economic, and military threat of Asia. The West had long been constructing the Chinese empire as corrupt and effete, concluding that increasing European domination in China was natural. Various western European countries and the United States had taken advantage of the two 'Opium Wars' to create treaty ports in which their own laws prevailed. The Boxer Rebellion of 1900 reminded the imperial powers that their hold on China was precarious. By the early twentieth century, Asian populations were growing much faster than European ones. From a Social Darwinist perspective, the inevitable flooding of the world's population by Asians would threaten white supremacy. Japan's role in the perceived 'yellow peril' was particularly sinister: its successful modernisation, and its defeat of Russian forces in 1905, forced Europeans to admit that their power could be successfully challenged by non-Europeans. The American socialist Jack London often included 'yellow peril' discourse in his popular novels.

The British Dominions took the same approach to the problem as the United States did. Australia and New Zealand, because of their geographical location, felt themselves to be in the vanguard of white guardianship. One Australian politician worried that it was a question 'whether the White or Yellow race shall gain final supremacy' and that 'Christian civilisation cannot afford the loss of this continent. For Australia is the precious front buckle in the white girdle of power and progress encircling the globe' (Huttenback, 1976: 119). Anti-immigration legislation was carefully crafted to exclude the hardworking Asians who undercut white Australian wages, and one of the new, unified Australia's first pieces of legislation in 1901 was the *Pacific Island Labourers Act* to deport Pacific island workers. The so-called 'White Australia' policy would linger into the 1970s. Even New Zealand, with its relatively liberal treatment of the indigenous Maori, also took a hostile view of Asians.

White people were 22 per cent of the world's population in 1800 and 35 per cent by 1930 (Kiernan, 1969: 27). This would never be the case again, however. Falling white birthrates were already of growing concern. Fears about declining physical fitness among whites also came to the fore, as when the Boy Scout movement arose in response to the poor health of urban soldiers recruited for the South African War. Although white peoples' share of the world's wealth continued to escalate, their demographic position was weakening. Worried governments experimented with eugenics, immigration restrictions, and other measures in order to improve the race. The horrors of the First World War did much to illustrate the futility of all of this: for all their vaunted superiority, Europeans precipitated a conflict of unprecedented brutality and destructiveness. For many intellectuals, the war forever disproved the idea of a racial hierarchy in which white people were different from, and superior to, people described as barbarians or savages. There was little evidence of a superior civilisation on the Western Front.

There had always been scepticism about claims to white supremacy, and doubts about the 'scientific' data used to support them. For many Christian missionaries in the field, for example, Darwin's emphasis on humanity as a single species was a welcome scientific alternative to the skull-measurers and 'missing link' theorists of the day. Links between Darwinian evolutionary theory and Christian missionary activity might seem counterintuitive, but recent research reveals that missionaries were more active scientists than previously thought. At the heart of their researches still lay the 'of one blood' emphasis on the unity of the human family, an idea borne out by the scientific classification of humanity as a single species: *Homo sapiens*. This emphasis led missionaries to anticipate 'what anthropologists would later call the "psychic unity" of humanity: today's "human nature"' (Samson, 2001b: 119). They also sometimes used Darwinian arguments to promote the welfare of groups that they were particularly interested in, as when a Methodist publication declared in 1914 that 'The Maories share with the Hawaians [*sic*] the honour of being at the head of the Polynesian nations. It is not difficult to account for this on the ground of natural selection and the survival of the fittest' (Slade, 1914: 122). Such arguments were easier to sustain in New Zealand, where the indigenous population was growing, than in Hawai'i, where it was in decline. Activists at home also criticised the growing relationship between imperial rule and racial superiority. A Scottish doctor, Theophilus Scholes, published *The British Empire and Alliances or Britain's Duty to her Colonies and Subject Races* in 1899, contending that racism was growing particularly virulent in Anglo-Saxons and, if unchecked, would bring about the downfall of the British empire. These voices were in the minority, however. Much more popular was the notion that 'survival of the fittest' should be used to enhance the fortunes of the white race.

Some signs of change had a more visible impact on European culture. After the First World War, *négritude* ('celebrating blackness') became an aspect of French imperial ideology. After all, the cornerstone of French imperial policy was supposed to be the integration (not the extermination) of blacks and Asians in French culture. Educated blacks in the Caribbean and Africa were contributing to literature in French, and their growing sense of nationalism found support among some French intellectuals and students. In the cafés, amid the heady atmosphere of jazz, a hybrid blending of white and black human creativity seemed possible. But how much of this was genuine equality, and how much simply a consumer-oriented marketing of exoticism? In the United States and Britain, too, there were black jazz bands and movies featuring exotic colonial settings and attractive, dark-skinned women. Children played with Sambo dolls and read about the adventures of Babar the French African elephant. Calls for this cultural engagement to be accompanied by increased legal and political rights still fell on largely deaf ears.

Nevertheless, doubts continued to grow about the concept of 'scientific racism'. The skull-measurers found themselves increasingly ostracised from mainstream academic life. A particularly powerful critique of racism gained ground in the shape of 'cultural relativism' as pioneered by Franz Boas. Boas had trained as an ethnographer in Germany, but left for the United States in 1887, and there has been much speculation about whether his Jewish ancestry, and rising anti-Semitism in Europe, influenced his decision to emigrate. Once in North America, his fieldwork among the Indians of the north-west coast led him to question his training in social evolutionary theory. He began to insist that a search for general laws of human development must always be set into context. Marriage practices in different parts of the world, for example, arose in completely different sets of circumstances. There might be no valid point of comparison between them; each should be studied in its own right. Like many others, Boas repudiated the skull measurements and other features of 'scientific' racism, arguing instead that physiology, language, and material culture were not necessarily related to each other [*Doc. 13*].

Race did not determine culture for Boas, but his was a minority view at the time. Much more popular among white people was the 'common sense' view that race was fundamental to human identity. The imperial Powers were eager to construct themselves as the bearers of the highest levels of civilisation; cultural relativism struck at the notions of superiority which lay at the heart of this view. For the first time, academic opinion was tending in an unwelcome direction: European and American politicians, voters, and consumers continued to prefer racial essentialism. It would take the postwar shock of the Holocaust, and the unpopularity of expensive imperial responsibilities, to disrupt this preference to any substantial degree, and many would argue that essentialised racial stereotyping remains popular (though usually muted) even today.

EARLY DECOLONISATIONS

No more revealing comparison exists than that between the early success of European and *mestizo* elites in achieving self-government or independence, and the prolonged struggle of non-European nationalists. Too often, decolonisation is discussed only in its post-1945 context, preventing the scrutiny of earlier decolonisations and their relationship to racial issues. Only by viewing this issue comparatively, across time and space, do the racial factors come clearly to the fore.

The declaration of independence in 1776 by thirteen of Britain's North American colonies, and the successful war of independence that followed, inspired colonial elites throughout Latin America. *Crillos* resented the policies that denied them their own legislatures, becoming increasingly defiant of centralised imperial regulation. By the early nineteenth century, after a period of extensive warfare which forced Spain to concede, there were several independent republics in Latin America. After *crillos*, the most prominent groups in the newly independent societies were the *mestizos*, and this picture would not change much in subsequent times. This is not to say that Indians and blacks had no role to play in independence movements, but the picture is not a straightforward one of non-white nationalists versus white rulers. In Latin America the racial picture was always more complicated than this, and upwardly mobile *mestizos* were likelier to identify with the *crillos* than with either the black or Indian parts of the population. This has led one historian of Mexico to say that 'It is virtually impossible to say that the movement for independence had a "successful" outcome as a social movement' except in very limited ways (Van Young, 2001: 2).

Almost all of the Latin American colonies had special government departments for Indian affairs, meaning that the position of Indians in colonial identity was complicated. For example, *crillos* in Mexico sponsored research into the Aztec past in order to establish a long, glorious heritage for the colony, but at the same time they denied Indians full equality in their society. Although the standard of living had improved for Indians thanks to Mexico's prosperity in the eighteenth century, they still paid tribute, were forbidden to wear European clothing, and were required to live in designated villages. Much of their land had fallen into the hands of *crillos* by a variety of means, not all of them legal, and their confinement to designated *Indio* villages underscored their separation from other groups in colonial society. Blacks, even free blacks, led even more marginalised lives.

Taking advantage of Napoleon's invasion of Spain in 1810, a Mexican priest named Miguel Hidalgo y Costilla proclaimed a revolution on 16 September. This rebellion had significant support from some *crillos*, but it also involved Indians and *mestizos* who hoped that an independent government would take steps to improve their economic and social condition. Hidalgo's rebel armies enjoyed some early victories, but soon began to resemble an uncontrolled mob. Looting, and the killing of European-born Spaniards, prompted a counter-revolution led by an alliance of Spaniards and *crillos*. Hidalgo was captured and executed in 1811. The successful revolution, when it came in 1821, was firmly under the control of the *crillo* elite. The question must therefore be asked: who was decolonised in 1821? The entire population, or only certain sectors of it?

The same question preoccupies historians of Britain's colonies of settlement. Before the American Revolution, the grievances of American colonists included the injustices of imperial taxation and trade policies; many of them sought a fairer imperial relationship rather than an independent state. British intransigence prompted an increased focus on independence, despite the pleas of some British observers who sympathised with the Americans and believed them to be fighting for basic English liberties: 'This fierce spirit of Liberty is stronger in the English Colonies probably than in any other people of the earth', declared a British statesman (Samson, 2001a: 71). This view emphasised the shared privileges and destiny of Englishmen at home and abroad. It did not extend this concept of shared rights to everyone, however; unlike its French counterpart, the American Revolution did not overthrow the institution of slavery throughout the new United States and, as we have seen, the position of indigenous peoples grew increasingly precarious in the nineteenth century through warfare, the erosion of treaty-making rights, and the creation of reserves. There was no sudden departure from British and other European theories of race. Recent scholarship has been exploring the many and ironic British characteristics of the American Revolution, including the American colonists' aspiration to retain the European cultural identities that 'both established their superiority over and sharply distinguished them from the seemingly rude and uncivilized peoples they were seeking to dispossess' (Greene, 1998: 222). One fundamental aspect of this retained identity concerned arguments about the inborn rights of Anglo-Saxon men: rights based on inheritance which could be constructed as exclusive where women, blacks, or indigenous peoples were concerned.

Although the loss of the American colonies did nothing to diminish transatlantic trade, Britain was not willing to repeat the experience in its other colonies of settlement. Canadian colonists began to achieve responsible government in the late eighteenth century. During the early and mid-nineteenth century there was widespread emigration to new colonies in Australia, New Zealand, and southern Africa. In all cases, British administrators encouraged responsible government and eventual self-government, boasting by the late nineteenth century that Britain was unique among the imperial Powers in its willingness to devolve political responsibility to such an extent.

Britain's generosity was not as conspicuous from the point of view of non-Europeans, however. Only those willing to assimilate themselves to mainstream culture were able to vote, and the widespread creation of reserves in Canada and Australia meant that most aboriginal peoples remained apart and politically voiceless into the 1960s. Worse, they were subjected to various forms of social engineering. Residential schools separated children from their families, and in some cases mixed-race children were forcibly removed from parents in order to encourage their assimilation (as in French west Africa's 'orphanages'). One Australian official declared the purpose of this to be 'to breed out the colour by elevating female half-castes to white standard with a view to their absorption by mating into the white population' (Reynolds, 2001: 151). In South Africa, even 'absorption' was rejected in favour of segregation. In the wake of the South African War, Britain negotiated with Afrikaner leaders to create the self-governing Union of South Africa in 1910. It was clear to the British that black, Asian, and mixed-race rights would face ongoing erosion under white minority rule in South Africa, yet self-government was still granted [*Doc. 18*]. When the new Union began passing a range of racist statutes, *The Times* remarked that non-white peoples must face the fact that 'inequality is inevitable ... not due to inferior status but to facts of race' (Huttenback, 1976: 118).

New Zealand was different: self-government included guaranteed seats for Maori members of parliament, and the Treaty of Waitangi continued to be interpreted as evidence of racial partnership. The high degree of intermarriage between Maori and *pakeha* bore this out but, on the other hand, the dispossession of land in the wake of the Maori Wars, and the disparity in wealth between the two races, suggested ongoing structural inequalities. Substantial acculturation can be seen as a sign of racial equality, but it can also be regarded as an erosion of distinctiveness. During the Maori Wars of the mid-nineteenth century, one Maori chief had warned another that the colonial government was granting full legal recognition to mixed-race marriages and their offspring, 'the result of which will be the destruction of our position and appearance as the Maori people', and that schools were being built 'so that we may be taught the European language; this will also tend to our subversion as a race as at present constituted (our likeness will be destroyed)' (Samson, 2001a: 175). This passionate advocacy of racial and cultural difference reproached the assimilating effect of liberal British policies.

In 1907 the Canadian prime minister suggested the title 'Dominion' as a way of distinguishing Britain's self-governing, white colonies from the rest. South Africa, with its black majority population but white minority government, was included; India – to the dismay of its Europeanised elites – was not. The histories of Dominion decolonisation in the nineteenth and twentieth centuries beg many questions about the extent and inclusiveness of self-government and independence within their borders. The Canadian political scientist Alan Cairns has remarked recently that 'the majority society did not in the past and does not now see itself as an empire ruling over subject peoples' and 'This discrepancy in perception complicates our analysis of where we have come from, where we are, and how we might move forward' (Cairns, 2001: 19). The self-governing Dominions were not necessarily supporters of decolonisation in colonies whose populations were dominated by non-Europeans. Greater freedoms for white people did not mean greater freedoms for all.

IMPERIAL INTEGRATION

During the first half of the twentieth century, empires clung to their overseas territories, using a variety of strategies to justify their ongoing domination of non-European populations. There were important changes to the way in which the West's 'civilising mission' was articulated as the twentieth century progressed. The declining importance of Christianity in public life, especially in Europe, prompted the fashioning of more secular conceptions of human rights and economic development [*Doc. 24*]. Imperial powers spoke less of Christianisation and more of 'civilisation', implying that the achievement of certain secular political and economic goals could win any nation the right to join the exclusive circle of imperial Powers. Nevertheless, new structures of international relations, such as the League of Nations, featured the familiar group of white-governed Powers to the exclusion of almost all others. Talk of economic development, shorn of the traditional link with Christianisation, sounded modern and enlightened, but was it really any different? Generations of left-wing scholarship, beginning with the British political economist J.A. Hobson's *Imperialism: A Study* (1902), linked imperialism with the needs of capitalism. According to this theory, capitalism's need for ever-expanding consumer markets and raw materials was the driving force behind expanding European global influence. For Hobson and his readers (who included the young V.I. Lenin), the changing terminology of 'development' did nothing to disguise the underlying continuity: 'The claim that an imperial State forcibly subjugating other peoples and their lands does so for the purpose of rendering services to the conquered . . . is notoriously false: she neither intends equivalent services nor is capable of rendering them' (Hobson, 1988: 368). Sometimes this claim involved direct territorial rule; sometimes it did not. By the early twentieth century considerable economic and political influence was being wielded by the United States in Latin America, or by Britain in Siam (now Thailand). Hobson's concern was that globalising capitalism would always construct 'development' in its own image and according to its own needs, and that this process would inevitably favour Europeans at the expense of the rest.

Most popular and political opinion in the early twentieth century would have strongly disagreed. Development rhetoric justified imperial power, but it also promised change for the better: tutelage was required so that non-European peoples would be able to participate effectively in a rapidly modernising world [*Doc. 14*]. For several empires, the best way to accomplish this goal was by integrating overseas territory as closely as possible with the metropolitan homeland. Italy between the two world wars is a good example of the vigour of imperial expansionism in the early twentieth century. Dictator Benito Mussolini was fond of comparisons between his regime and the ancient Roman empire, yet he was keenly aware of Italy's humiliating defeat at the hands of Abyssinian forces in 1896. In 1919 he wrote that 'Imperialism is the eternal and immutable rule of life' (Segrè, 1974: 58), adapting the German notion of *Lebensraum* to argue that the eastern Mediterranean was Italy's natural territory. Italy had already increased its influence in parts of eastern Africa, and in 1935 Mussolini salved Italian military pride by annexing Abyssinia itself. The following year Italy combined its eastern colonies to create 'Italian East Africa', and its territory in Libya expanded. Mussolini's plans included a pan-Islamic movement which would rally Muslims in the eastern Mediterranean to Italy's cause; the relative absence of conflict between Italians and Muslims would, he hoped, encourage them to overthrow their British or French rulers in favour of Italians. On the brink of war in 1939 he proclaimed Libya to be part of Italy itself: its 'Fourth Shore'. Italy's defeat by the Allies interrupted Mussolini's plans to forcibly relocate the nomadic desert peoples of Libya to reserves in order to encourage fixed settlement and agricultural development. How this would have affected Muslim support for the Italian empire was never put to the test. What is clear, however, is that 'development' in this context was for the benefit of Italians.

The intensification of imperial control demanded greater knowledge of colonised peoples and their societies, and therefore a greater role for anthropology. In the French empire, links between social science and colonial rule were clear: 'Once assembled in the French mind as a world apart [the colonies] were easily converted from particular places with variegated populations into abstractions: objects of intellectual inquiry, literary fabrication, historical model-building' (Betts, 1982: 66). They were also considered to be part of France itself, although, as we have already seen, integration did not necessarily mean equal access to French legal and political rights. After France expanded its territory in north Africa to include Tunisia in 1881, a college was established at Tunis to provide modern training in languages and social science in order to create an educated elite fit for colonial service. The sociological theories of Durkheim and others were prominent there, and at the new École Française de l'Extreme Orient (1898) and at the Institut Indochinois de l'Étude de l'Homme (1938) when they were founded at Hanoi in France's expanding colony of Indo-China. One of the most popular fields of study was the Cham society of southern Vietnam: people once ruled by a Hindu kingdom from India before the fifteenth century, but now Muslim and marginalised by the Vietnamese. The monumental architecture of ancient Cham suggested a sophisticated culture which had successfully integrated indigenous and Hindu elements just as France itself had originated from a combination of native Celtic and incoming Roman influences. It seemed natural, therefore, that the French should be ruling over the Cham, permitting them once again to flourish as part of a larger empire (Bayly, 2000: 590).

The modern French empire was conceptualised as an integrated unit within which people of various races would be acculturated through French language and culture. Such assimilation would, in theory, lead to equality: colonial populations were to become overseas Frenchmen. This policy built upon earlier aspects of trading communities; 'lingua franca' (literally 'Frankish tongue') is used widely to describe the use of any common language, especially in places where many other languages are present. In Indo-China, the French created a written form of the Vietnamese language, *Quoc-ngu*, using the Roman alphabet, but this was the only example of a French attempt to work with an indigenous language, and the intention was to use *Quoc-ngu* to enable teaching in French (Betts, 1982: 72).

As we know, notions of equality through global Frenchness did not rule out (and even demanded) the belief that other cultures and peoples were fundamentally inferior. The French expression for imperial trusteeship, the *mission civilisatrice* ('civilising mission'), was an implicit denigration of other cultures. 'No nation made universality of attitude and principle a more significant element of its secular ideology than did the French' (Betts, 1982: 65); however, a French visitor to Indo-China in 1886 remarked: 'The common man . . . is quite simply hideous. The bestial face of such a man is always immobile, inert and seems petrified in idiocy' (Aldrich, 1996: 203). Here the supposedly 'expressionless' Asian face of European stereotyping stands between the real Frenchman and his supposed overseas kin. However sincerely France believed in the superiority of its culture, and in the possibility of exporting Frenchness through education, it is clear that racial differences were perceived as obstacles to assimilation. There was a vast gulf between the status of *citoyen* ('citizen') and *sujet* ('subject') under French rule; for the most part, citizens were Europeans and subjects were not.

In some cases, earlier assimilation policies were reversed. Some areas of Senegal were declared 'protectorates', taking them out of the 1848 provisions conferring French citizenship. The new protectorates were also exempt from French antislavery law, allowing forced labour to be practised. In place of the existing Francophone school for the sons of chiefs, known only partly in jest as the 'School of Hostages', the government created the École des Fils de Chefs et Interprètes to train future clerks and administrators for the colony (Robinson, 2000: 69). This school, and the more advanced Franco-Arabic school in Tunis, were of particular significance for French intentions in Islamic Africa. One Senegalese governor hoped that students at the Tunis school would see 'that there is no incompatibility between their beliefs and European science, and that they can become precious auxiliaries of . . . a Muslim civilization which expresses itself in French' (Robinson, 2000: 69). The issue of France as a self-identified Muslim power – a *puissance musulmane* – might seem odd, but is important when we consider how many Muslims were ruled by France by the end of the nineteenth century in west and north Africa, prompting the governor-general of Algeria to write to Mecca to obtain *fatwa* (decrees) stating that submission to French rule was compatible with Islam. As one historian has pointed out, France's African empire involved various 'paths of accommodation' by which the French and their Muslim subjects sought to deal with one another. Between 1880 and 1920 in French West Africa, 'Muslim Sufi orders, a venerable North and West African institution, became pillars of the colonial economy' by concentrating on their local and regional authority while tolerating French rule over the wider political sphere (Robinson, 2000: 1). It is important not to allow the French ethnography of Islamic 'fanaticism' to overwhelm the much more common phenomenon of mutual accommodation during the colonial period.

French policy toward mixed-race groups was also fraught with contradiction. On one hand, it was assumed that white superiority guaranteed mixed-race children greater intellectual and moral advantages. In French colonies in western Africa, special orphanages were established to educate these children, using fictional 'orphan' status in most cases. It was assumed that African mothers and their families were incapable of providing a proper, civilised upbringing; children of mixed blood, therefore, should be removed from this contaminating background and be brought up to see themselves differently in racial and cultural terms. 'It is by creating mulatto races that we most easily Gallicize West Africa', wrote a travel guide in 1902, revealing an acceptance of *métissage* and an opportunistic attitude toward exploiting it (White, 1999:

51). Here was the other half of the contradiction: *métissage* was presumed to produce a new race ideally suited to the civilisation of Africa. This progressivist view was perpetually at odds with the essentialising racism that regarded African mothers as inferior. A French eugenicist would write in 1942 that 'Instability, the dominant characteristic of métis . . . is contagious, it stands in opposition to the spirit of order and method' (Stoler, 1992: 549). Children were taken to 'orphanages' with or without their African family's consent. French officials clearly believed that they were undertaking a civilising mission, but their obsession with children of part European ancestry (as opposed to all children) reveals a belief that blood was more important than education. Colonial officials created administrative registration schemes aimed at documenting the background, births, marriages, and deaths of colonised populations in a process which Gary Wilder has described as 'a scientific-administrative complex that included scholars, teachers and administrators . . . through which practical science and scientific administration constituted one another' (Wilder, 2003: 241). The anxieties about racial mixing evident in this surveillance reveal tensions in both metropolitan and colonial attitudes. In France, fears were growing about racial degeneration and the indigestible 'otherness' of groups like Jews. In the colonies, however, administrators were trying to find ways of working with the local population, and chose to concentrate on the potential 'improving' qualities of racial mixing. Another way of putting it would be to say that at home many French people feared a darkening of their race; overseas, they hoped for the whitening of Africans and Asians.

Racism is at the heart of both attitudes, however. Despite the rhetoric about trusteeship, French colonial administrations remained reluctant to grant citizenship to non-whites. A colonial decree of 1912 restricted citizenship to Africans who 'approach us in education, adopt our civilization and our customs, or distinguish themselves by their service' (White, 1999: 127). Between 1914 and 1922 only 94 west Africans were granted citizenship. A French law of 1910 permitted mothers to demand a declaration of extra-marital paternity, but although the law was ratified in Indo-China and the French south Pacific colonies, its use was restricted to French or other European citizens in Africa. It is clear that black Africans were regarded as particularly alien and undesirable where citizenship was concerned; that said, the expense involved in French litigation made it nearly impossible for non-Europeans to obtain declarations of paternity in any part of the empire. Generations of French colonial subjects heard about trusteeship, civilisation, and improvement, but saw few signs of its supposed rewards. Critics at home regarded this as nothing less than a betrayal of French principles [*Doc. 20*].

In the Dutch East Indies, *métissage* had produced a Eurasian colonial elite essential to the government of the colony, especially in Java. By the end of the nineteenth century, however, colonial officials were more likely to be sent directly from the Netherlands, and to return at the end of their tour of duty.

They were more likely to bring Dutch wives with them than to marry Asian women. The later nineteenth century had also ushered in a new 'ethical policy' which abolished the system of tribute. 'Concentrate on keeping and further developing the East Indies', colonial officials were told (Heywood, 2000: 254). By this time, Dutch rule had expanded far beyond Java to include a range of other islands in what is now Indonesia.

At the heart of the 'ethical policy' lay the belief that a more liberal style of colonial rule would be both beneficial and acceptable to the colonised. However, outside Java, the Dutch were likelier to turn matters over to private companies, or to undertake punitive expeditions to areas that proved reluctant to accept increasing Dutch intervention. A classic example of this was the Lombok incident in 1894 when the Balinese ambushed Dutch officials while they were attempting to negotiate Lombok's entry into the Dutch East Indies. The Dutch retaliated at the cost of over 2,000 Balinese lives, women and children included, when the extended Balinese royal household decided that mass suicide was better than Dutch rule. What was left of the Balinese aristocracy was placed under direct Dutch rule, and back in the Netherlands, political reaction was almost unanimously in favour of this decisive defeat of Asiatic backwardness. In 1922 Dutch legislation declared the Dutch East Indies to be an integral part of the Netherlands itself.

The intensification of imperial control was intimately linked with anthropology. The Netherlands Anthropological Association was founded in 1898, relatively late in comparison with other countries, but Dutch anthropology on Bali and elsewhere was particularly vigorous. Especially important was the search for 'authentic' indigenous spiritualities, such as Buddhism, which could be contrasted with the growing 'alien' intrusion of Islam. The Dutch management of Balinese villages could therefore be constructed as protective and benign. The establishment of an Adat [Indigenous] Law School at the University of Leiden in the early twentieth century reinforced the desire of Dutch authorities to be seen to be governing the East Indies in the inhabitants' best interest. Christianity was as feared as Islam in this context, revealing the ease with which Dutch colonialism could construct itself as modern, scientific, secular, and therefore somehow morally neutral. Like other empires, its use of 'indirect rule' policies in Bali and elsewhere reflected the relationship between anthropology and imperial control. As one Dutch official observed, 'An intellectually well-developed official is useful for administrative purposes', but just as important in ruling local communities were the indigenous leaders who might be 'less talented persons' but 'are natives and possess prestige' (Nordholt, 1999: 257). The question, of course, was whether this combination of scientific surveillance and local political authority would be enough to quench broader processes such as religious change (especially the spread of Islam) or the development of nationalism as an alternative to Dutch integration and development.

'INFANT NATIONS'

European and American anthropology documented and catalogued human differences, allowing the inferior position of colonised peoples to be rationalised as the natural consequence of inferior culture. Colonised peoples were impoverished and vulnerable because their cultures were less civilised; civilised Powers, therefore, had a moral obligation to supervise their development until they were deemed capable of joining the international family of nations. As biological racism increased, Social Darwinist views consigned whole racial groups to the status of children in need of adult supervision. The objective of independence and international partnership appeared increasingly distant, and imperial Powers settled down to what they believed would be a lengthy (perhaps permanent) duty of trusteeship.

Nevertheless, there was an important difference between the position of non-Europeans in an integrated empire, where independent political nationhood was unthinkable, and that of colonised peoples in the British or American empires whose eventual self-rule was at least described as a possibility. The hopes of colonial nationalists were continually dashed, however, by the verdict that they were not yet ready for independence: an elusive readiness which was always defined by the imperial Power. Arguments in favour of delaying decolonisation in these cases therefore focused on the economic, political, or cultural backwardness which justified ongoing colonial rule. The issue of race was intimately connected with this view. As we know, white colonial subjects in the Dominions were quickly found 'ready' for self-government, even in South Africa where they formed only a minority of the population. Non-white populations, on the other hand, faced a lengthy and frustrating process during which they were lectured about development while, at the same time, their European-educated elites were offered little in the way of real political power. Many understandably wondered who exactly was benefiting from the 'development' on offer.

This paradox was perhaps most clearly revealed in British India. By the First World War, a European-educated Indian elite was demanding greater self-government for their country through the Indian National Congress and other organisations. Only a small number of Indians met the stringent voting qualifications and the number of elected political positions was limited. 'We shall not subvert the British Empire by allowing the Bengali Baboo to discuss his own schools and drains', one British official declared (Copland, 2001: 26). Although some British politicians and philosophers had been advocating decolonisation since the eighteenth century, even Karl Marx had believed that British rule would benefit India by forcing it into the modern age. Despite talk of giving India the best of British leadership and culture, Britain continued to exploit India as a market for its own manufactures while making it pay for its own defence. India provided 1.5 million troops and support personnel for the

First World War at enormous social cost, but when the INC demanded that this contribution be rewarded with greater self-government, progress was slow. Nationalist protest expanded, especially under the influence of Mohandas Gandhi and the rising Muslim League. An Englishman living in India in the 1920s said of his countrymen that 'Some people are frightened, others seem really to have undergone a change of heart. But it's too late' (Kiernan 1969: 70).

It was becoming too late to avoid the partition of India along religious lines. The Muslim modernist Sir Saiyyid Ahmad Khan once observed that he couldn't see what was 'national' about the INC: 'Is it supposed to be that the different castes and creeds living in India belong to one nation, or can become a nation . . . ? I think it is quite impossible . . .' (Copland, 2001: 54). Muslim participation in the INC, never large to begin with, declined during the early twentieth century as Hindus such as Gandhi rose to prominence in its leadership. Britain's longstanding fascination with ancient 'Aryans' and the Hindu scriptures, and its relative marginalisation of Muslims after the Indian Rebellion, had intensified sectarian divisions in India. Independence, when it came in 1947 and 1948 to India, Pakistan, Sri Lanka, and Burma, was born in a tragic mixture of triumph and bloodshed.

How did racial issues influence the decision to grant Indian independence? As we have already seen, Europeanised Indian elites found, to their frustration, that they were not usually welcomed as equals by the British. It is true that there were instances of class- and gender-based solidarity, as when England's national team in that most English of sports – cricket – was captained in 1896 by the Indian prince Kumar Shri Ranjitsinhji Vibhaji. 'Ranji' had demonstrated his outstanding talent while a student at Cambridge.

Such high-profile exceptions prove the rule, however, and this was driven home for Indians during and after the infamous Amritsar Massacre of 1919. Frustrated by the distance between India's enormous contribution to the imperial war effort and British reluctance to grant India more extensive self-government, unarmed nationalists gathered in protest in the town of Amritsar and a white, female doctor was attacked during the resulting chaos. The local British army commander overreacted, firing on the unarmed crowd and killing about 400 people. To punish the town for its attack on a white women, a 'Crawling Order' required Indians to crawl on all fours if they wished to pass through the street where she had been attacked. Although this order was deplored by higher-ranking officials, and subsequently rescinded, it was a clear reminder of the racism which underscored Britain's reluctance to grant India independence. Indian nationalists, British left-wing critics, and disdainful Americans protested in vain. Winston Churchill, future Conservative prime minister of Britain, declared in 1931 that 'The faithful discharge of our duty in India is not only a cause, but a symbol . . . What we require to do now is to stand erect and look the world in the face, and do our duty without fear or favour' (Samson, 2001a: 247).

Similar calls to 'stay the course' regardless of the cost have resounded frequently in imperial history. More important in the long run for Indian nationalists, however, was the humiliating defeat of British forces at Singapore in 1942: Europeans defeated by Asians. The imperial retreat from Singapore was exploited by the Japanese, who launched a propaganda campaign encouraging Indians to overthrow their white rulers and join their fellow Asians in Japan's Co-Prosperity Sphere. It is significant that they did not: Indians might wish independence from Britain, but most of them did not wish to join Britain's Asian enemies in order to accomplish their goal. Nevertheless, white prestige had received a substantial blow.

What Churchill and many others failed to realise was the extent to which British popular opinion would shift during the Second World War; a shift which swept him from power in favour of a new Labour government promising change. Left-wing politicans had long been calling for an end to British rule in India [*Doc. 19*], and the Labour Party had committed itself to Indian independence by 1948. During the interwar period, even Conservative governments had been prepared to make modest but significant concessions in terms of local self-government in India. After the war, everyone disagreed about where the new national borders should be drawn, but events began moving too quickly for anyone to control. Amid escalating sectarian warfare in which tens of thousands of people died, hasty negotiations rammed through a compromise partition between India and Pakistan in 1947. Open warfare between Muslims and Hindus was already under way near the borders, taking over 1 million lives and producing 12 million refugees before the new nations had celebrated their first anniversaries. Alien imperial rule, combined with an imperial anthropology which hardened the divisions between them, left the peoples of south Asia with enormous post-independence challenges.

In other parts of the British empire, the concept of 'indirect rule' had developed to describe the collaboration between indigenous elites and colonial administrations. This enabled colonies to be run at a lower cost (always desirable) and appeared to be a more virtuous system than others. One of indirect rule's most famous advocates, Lord Frederick Lugard, became governor of Nigeria in 1914 [*Doc. 21*]. Writing later about his policies, he expressed particular interest in the Muslim rulers of northern Nigeria (the southern peoples were mostly Christian). Concerned that Muslims were prone 'to waves of fanaticism', he explained that the best strategy was to ensure that 'the personal interests of the rulers must rapidly become identified with those of the controlling Power' (Samson, 2001a: 193). By catering to some extent to what he called the 'traditions and prejudices' of native rulers, Lugard could offer powerful incentives: entrenched power protected by British authority and military might, new titles and ceremonies, and lucrative commercial arrangements. The advantages for Lugard and the British lay in the exploitation of these relationships in order to bring about European education, medical practices such as vaccination, and the encouragement of wage labour. Europeanisation under collaborative indigenous leadership seemed to be extraordinarily successful in some colonies. Later, when colonial nationalism arose, it became clear that there were deep divisions between those whom the British had favoured, and those they had not.

Besides, 'indirect' rule was never completely indirect. We have already seen the way in which certain Indian cultural practices were forbidden even when British rule claimed to be neutral in religious matters. In western Africa a similar process surrounded the indigenous religious practices known to Europeans as 'fetishism'. Research has since demonstrated that 'fetish' oaths, ceremonies, and gift exchanges were originally related to maintaining social order, to delivering justice, and to other aspects of indigenous social organisation. Under indirect rule, such practices should have been left alone to operate in the interests of keeping law and order for the benefit of the colonial government. However, thanks to anthropology and sociology, 'fetishism' was already loaded with significance. For missionaries, it was evidence of how far Africans had degraded from the original, biblical state of grace, and they complained to the authorities when Christianised Africans felt obliged to take part in 'fetish' ceremonies in their home villages. More secular theorists saw it as evidence of a primitive stage of human spirituality. Colonial officials worried that the sometimes brutal punishments doled out by village leaders were incompatible with the development and progress that they hoped to achieve for Africans. Such concerns led the governor of the Gold Coast to outlaw traditional village courts and punishments in 1887 because, he said, they were based 'as much on fetish as on facts' (Pietz, 1999: 77).

Concerns about 'backwardness' were common in Africa and the Pacific islands, highlighting the degree to which these groups were deemed inferior to the south Asians who, despite the frustrations of their nationalist movements, were at least permitted some degree of self-government within Europeanised political structures. Colonies under indirect rule, on the other hand, were not yet 'ready' for the introduction of these structures, and were therefore much further away from eventual independence. Only after postwar conditions accelerated the process of decolonisation would this picture change, and even then paternalistic attitudes lingered. 'The main asset is the good humoured and easy going outlook of the African', wrote a British official in the Gold Coast a year before independence in 1957; 'with time, careful handling and extreme patience, it should be possible to lead him to recognize where the country's interests lie' (Samson, 2001a: 252, 253).

A similar set of dynamics affected developments in the American-ruled Philippines. Filipinos had welcomed the Americans as liberators from Spanish rule in 1898, only to find themselves under an open-ended American occupation. The American overseas empire at this time was a typical exercise in self-affirming imperial benevolence [*Doc. 16*]. Because imperial power often collided with republican and democratic values [*Doc. 15*], as during the Mexican Wars, American politicians had emphasised a mission of trusteeship which was humanitarian and (supposedly) temporary. American administrators were therefore baffled by the growing hatred of those that they so earnestly wanted to help. One statesman invoked the Marshall judgment in the *Cherokee Nation* case when he said of Filipinos that 'They are merely in a state of Christian pupilage. They are imitative. They are glad to be educated, glad to study some languages other than their own, glad to follow European and American ideals' (Rafael, 1993: 198). Contrary to these predictions, Filipinos began to battle their new rulers with costly enthusiasm, and the Americans stayed because of their belief that no suitable Filipino leadership was ready to take over. In addition, Congress was keen to impose tariffs on the new colonies to enhance the United States' economic advantage over them, and would lose this advantage if independence was granted too quickly. Minority anti-imperialist voices were drowned out by views such as President Roosevelt's which pointed to the benefits of imperial rule: Algeria 'was far better off in every way under French rule', he said, and British India was 'one of the mighty feats to the credit of the white race' (Tilchin, 1997: 217, 219).

Nevertheless, the United States was determined to rule its colonial subjects better than either the British or French, with a clearer sense of the inevitability of independence. Like other imperial powers, however, the United States found it difficult to deliver substantially higher literacy rates or to alleviate poverty despite considerable expenditures on colonial welfare. Like others, it told nationalists that their country must be stabilised before political freedom could be granted. 'Give us the freedom and we will develop ourselves', the nationalists replied (Friend, 1966: 40). One Filipino businessman remarked that the Americans shared with the British, Dutch, and French 'this Kipling mentality' of the white man's burden, whereby 'If the little native has learned to walk erect and make the little noises of democracy, it is all due to the painstaking upbringing he has received', but 'if it crouches in a corner . . . half-dead from too big a dose of innocent tyranny and astute benevolence, then, of course, it is its own miserable fault' (Friend, 1966: 41).

Fortunately for Filipino nationalists, anti-immigrant and labour groups in the United States were supportive of Philippine independence as a means of restricting unwelcome Filipino immigration. Compromise was reached in the shape of a Philippine Commonwealth created in 1935 to give self-government to the Philippines under continued American supervision. The parallel with the British Dominions was clear: some commentators referred to the Philippines as a Dominion, and there was a 'High Commissioner' for the Philippines just as there was for Canada, Australia, New Zealand, and South Africa in Britain. The main benefit of this compromise was strategic: the maintenance of American military and naval bases in the Philippines. During the Second World War Filipinos and Americans fought together until the Japanese surrender in September 1945. Independence came to the Philippines in 1946 amid the development of anti-Communist 'containment' policies and an escalating political distaste for formal imperial rule. There is no doubt that American rule was relatively short-lived compared with the centuries of Dutch, Portuguese, or British dominance in other areas of Asia. There is also no doubt that the difference was one of degree rather than substance. In all cases, a combination of changing domestic attitudes, economic pressures, and shifting international dynamics won out over longstanding notions of racial superiority and imperial duty.

TRUSTEESHIP?

Advocates of imperial rule talked frequently about improving the colonies, but how was this to be measured? As late as the 1960s a sympathetic historian of Africa wrote that 'A century ago, the peoples of Dahomey for the most part still went about naked or dressed only in a vulgar loincloth . . . Now they are dressed, they travel by automobile . . . They have gone from the iron age to the twentieth century' (Aldrich, 1996: 199). Who benefited most from such changes, however, Africans or the European manufacturing industries? Did driving automobiles give Africans legal or political equality with Europeans? Attempts to emulate European attitudes, no matter how sincere, were often regarded as inauthentic by European observers. In other words, racial differ- ence might indefinitely postpone 'development'. During the South African War, a British trader in Malaya overheard some Chinese 'pig-tailed, slit-eyed fellows talking of "we Britishers – our defeats – our successes" '. Furious, he dismissed such talk as 'Damned cheek' (Kiernan, 1969: 69). If loyalty to a shared imperial Britishness was 'damned cheek', we must wonder how disloyalty would have been construed. For all their talk of developing and improving non-European peoples, it seemed that for many Europeans, race predetermined behaviour and therefore made real change impossible. Only a conjunction of overwhelming circumstances, including domestic economic and political concerns, would force the imperial powers to concede independ- ence to groups they had so recently been denigrating.

In some cases, however, imperial Powers found themselves responsible for League of Nations 'Mandates' on condition that these territories be brought to independence. Parts of the world formerly under Ottoman (Turkish) rule, along with Germany's former colonies, were without recognised government after the First World War. Traditionally, conquering empires simply absorbed their defeated enemy's territory, but the United States was uncomfortable with this process in a new era of emphasis on self-determination. It was unclear, however, how these things could be achieved without some sort of European supervision, so the League of Nations created the Mandates as a way of bridging the gap. Mandates were granted to various European governments for administrative purposes, but on the condition that they were brought as quickly as possible to independence: trusteeship on a timetable.

The terms of Mandates differed along racial lines. 'Class A' mandates, with the most rapid projected self-government, were all primarily Arab areas from the former Ottoman empire and they were turned over to Britain and France exclusively. Arabs were perceived to be naturally 'readier' for self-government than Africans or Pacific islanders, whose Mandates featured much longer time-lines. The French in Syria (which then included Lebanon), and the British in Mesopotamia (Iraq) and Palestine (Israel and Jordan), introduced forms of government that were an uncomfortable mixture of indigenous and European priorities. During the First World War, Britain had promised through T.E. Lawrence ('Lawrence of Arabia') and others that Arabs would be permitted to form an independent state after the war in return for their assistance against the Turks. This approach reflected a longstanding admiration of Arabic culture in British intellectual circles, and an equally longstanding hostility to what the British regarded as Turkish effeminacy and barbarism. These attitudes had been convenient during the 'Great Game' of the late Victorian period, during which Britain and Russia vied with one another to erode the failing Ottoman empire. Turks had 'weak and pathetic' characters, according to one old campaigner, together with a 'passive hatred of the Christian world, combined with an intense dislike of all change' (Auchterlonie, 2001: 11). Arabs were portrayed, in contrast, as undemocratic but proud and admirable. Amid the British invasion of Egypt in 1882, the Victorian diplomat Arthur Nicolson reminded his countrymen of the proud intellectual heritage of the Arab world: 'Bagdad [was] a bright shining light in the East, foretelling the dawn in the grim darkness of medieval Europe' (Auchterlonie, 2001: 22). There was general agreement, however, that in more recent times Islam had become a restrictive force. An old Indian Army campaigner believed that 'A Moslem, so long as he remains a Moslem, must acquiesce in a moral and intellectual life which is incompatible with progress and humanity' (Auchterlonie, 2001: 20).

Only French or British institutions could save Arabs from themselves, it seemed. The British invasion of Egypt in 1882 had financial motives, especially where control of the Suez Canal was concerned, but it also reflected classic trusteeship ideology. Turkish rule had failed to improve Arabs; British rule would do better. During the First World War Britain and France secretly agreed to divide up former Turkish territory in the Middle East, yet British negotiators also promised Arab leaders an independent state in order to encourage them to rise in revolt against the Turks. Rise they did – as Lawrence of Arabia's career made plain – but the promised reward remained elusive. In 1917 the British foreign secretary Arthur Balfour promised Jews a 'national homeland' in Palestine, generating more questions about British intentions.

After the war, the parcelling out of French and British Mandates in the region seemed to confirm to Arabs that they were still under someone else's control: first the Ottoman Turks'; now the Europeans'. In Syria, the French refused to recognise the self-proclaimed King Faisal Hussein (son of the revered Sherif Hussein of Mecca), insisting that the modernisation of Syria must take a republican form. The British had no aversion to monarchy, and imported Faisal as King of Iraq in hopes of uniting Iraq's disparate population under the rule of a prestigious Muslim dynasty. The role of anthropology in Iraq was crucial: the explorer, archaeologist, and ethnographer Gertrude Bell catalogued its various sects and ethnicities for the Mandate government, and became one of Faisal's leading advisers after he was proclaimed king in 1921. There was trouble with the Kurds, and rebellion by some of the desert sheikhs, but Bell believed that the only hope for Arab advancement was under British guidance: a contradictory position which she herself recognised. 'I'm convinced that no country in the world can work a mandate,' she wrote. 'The Arabs won't submit to any diminution of their sovereign rights such as being placed in tutelage under the L[eague] of N[ations]' (Bell, [1928]: 644). The trouble was that, as we have seen, 'tutelage' seemed to be the only mode in which most Europeans and Americans knew how to operate. When the political implications of this were joined by the growing activities of European and American oil companies, suspicion grew that the 'development' policies of the Mandate were not primarily in Arab interests. After independence in 1932 the Iraqi monarchy lasted only until 1958 when a military revolt overthrew the government. A combination of European social science and European 'tutelage' had failed to create a sustainable democracy in Iraq, generating anti-European resentment in the process.

In the meantime, even more conspicuous failures attended British efforts in the Mandate of Palestine. Having encouraged both Arab and Zionist nationalists during the war, the British now faced an enormous problem of their own creation: how to fulfil the terms of the Mandate when massive Jewish immigration was provoking an increasingly hostile reaction among the indigenous Arabs. The Mandates demonstrated the entrenched power of the victorious empires after the war, but they also enhanced the resentment of European paternalism in international affairs, and delayed decolonisation when European meddling produced increasingly insoluble problems. Claude Condor of the Palestine Exploration Fund had written in 1882 that 'The British nation seems to abound in men specially fitted to govern Orientals by their tolerance, patience, good-humour, honesty, justice and firmness of character' (Auchterlonie, 2001: 15). It would be Israeli nationalism, however, that seized the initiative in Palestine. Having presided over escalating terrorism and civil conflict, Britain hastily withdrew in 1948 and the self-proclamation of the state of Israel precipitated a regional war. The presumption that Britons knew best how 'to govern Orientals' was in tatters.

PART THREE   ASSESSMENT

CHAPTER SIX

CONCLUSIONS

The pace of decolonisation accelerated in the 1960s and 1970s, but empires differed widely in their handling of this process. For those whose metropolitan homelands were inextricably linked with overseas territory, colonial independence movements struck at the heart of national identity. French, Dutch, and Portuguese governments fought prolonged, costly civil wars rather than make concessions to local nationalists in areas of their empires that were particularly prestigious. The American and British governments were more willing to see independence as an eventual outcome for their overseas territories, but often delayed it for reasons which included the notion that subject peoples were not yet 'ready' for modern nationhood.

The question is: how much did racial issues influence decolonisation after the Second World War? The most superficial answer seems to be: not very much. Cold War politics cut across traditional distinctions between the European and non-European world. Both superpowers featured multi-racial populations in which white elites predominated, but in their overseas operations racial categories mattered less than ideological ones. What often counted most was not a country's racial demography, but whether it fell into the American or Soviet sphere of influence. In their global power struggle, both superpowers proved willing to cater to local political initiatives, even dictatorships, to promote their ideological and economic goals. Were the new superpowers simply reinvented imperial Powers with the addition of nuclear arsenals and decreased peer competition? Now that the Cold War has ended scholars are more prepared to see substantial continuity between earlier and later American or Russian expansionism. Claims by both sides that they bore no resemblance to the 'old' imperial Powers are being treated with scepticism. For the 'second-rank' European Powers, however, postwar economic and political challenges proved decisive whether they liked it or not. Some recognised this: a British colonial official writing from the Gold Coast (Ghana) in 1956, a year before independence, declared that 'The comforting myth that the Gold Coast was likely to be a well-behaved child that would be a credit to its parent has always, as you know, seemed to me to bear little relation to the facts. The [African-led] Government is in the hands of knaves.' He added, however, that 'The practical question now is ... whether we can maintain reasonable working relations with them' (Rathbone, 1992: 293). This new pragmatism arose from a combination of changing economic and political circumstances, as well as from a rising criticism of racism and imperialism [*Doc. 23*].

RELUCTANT DECOLONISATIONS

There is no question that, in some cases, persistent racial prejudices could prolong or exacerbate the struggle for independence. Nationalists in the Belgian Congo, for example, would have welcomed even a reluctant movement toward self-government, reminding us that in some empires the notion of trusteeship delivered little more than despotism. Despite talk of civilisation and development for the Congo [*Doc. 14*], the colony's first priority was rubber extraction. The Belgians had restructured indigenous politics to suit their purposes; a 1906 decree said that native custom and indigenous authority would be recognised in the Congo, but the definition of 'custom' lay with the colonial authorities and their anthropologists. This situation aggravated the atrocities of the rubber trade. Although some chiefs were vocal in demanding reform, others were profiting personally and politically from the forced labour and compulsory production systems of the trade. They also supplied troops to the enforcement agencies who murdered and mutilated those who failed to meet the rubber quotas [*Doc. 17*].

Some Belgian liberals tried to build political organisations together with middle-class African *évolués* (literally 'evolved' or Europeanised people). Most, however, would have agreed with the settler who said:

> Nothing in the history of the Congolese justifies any sort of rights for them over the country as a whole. They have never created anything, not a motor, not a wheel-barrow, nothing. We have lifted them from cannibalism and slavery. It is we who have unified, pacified and organized the country. (Anstey, 1966: 172)

Racist attitudes, combined with ethnic divisions and the absence of a substantial, European-educated elite, allowed Belgian administrators to procrastinate about granting greater self-rule. They made only minor changes to the system, including the introduction of local elections in 1957, but in the following year the Brussels International Exhibition brought a number of Congolese to Belgium where they shared grievances and hopes with other Africans, especially the newly-independent Ghanaians. They saw Europeans performing manual labour, and were waited on by Europeans in restaurants. These interactions gave a powerful boost to nationalism in the Congo and within two years the Belgians were gone, leaving chaos in their wake.

One of the most reluctant decolonisations involved French-ruled Algeria. Just before the beginning of the Algerian war of independence in 1954, the future French president François Mitterrand declared that 'From Flanders to the Congo there is one law, one single nation, one Parliament. This is the Constitution and it is our will' (Clayton, 1994: 13). At a French colonial conference in 1944 at Brazzaville, in French Equatorial Africa, some of the French officials were black – certain parts of the empire had retained voting rights for the National Assembly in Paris – but there were no representatives of indigenous authority as such. In retrospect, the conference has been seen as an important milestone in French decolonisation, but many at the time welcomed it as an endorsement of French imperial unity [*Doc. 22*].

Much was made of the French *mission civilisatrice*, yet over 90 per cent of the indigenous population of Algeria remained illiterate after over a century of French rule. 'In day-to-day life the colons consistently spoke of and to the Moslem population in disparaging terms, the *sale race* – dirty people' (Clayton, 1994: 26). Even for *évolués*, the only road to genuine respect seemed to be the road to war. Encouraged by the recent success of nationalist forces in French-ruled Indo-China (the roots of what would become the Vietnam War), Algerians battled the *colons* and the French military until 1962 when the ongoing war brought down the French government itself. The Algerian scholar Frantz Fanon has called his nation's history part of the 'Manichean world' of imperialism, in which 'the settler paints the native as a sort of quintessence of evil' (Betts, 1991: 76) and there is no doubt that the Algerian War both reflected and strengthened prejudices against North Africans.

Portugal proved even more reluctant to relinquish the profitable parts of its empire. In Angola, colonial rule had spread into the interior after a series of brutal military campaigns against the Ovimbundu people in the 1890s. Resource extraction required labour and, as we have seen, forced labour in Angola could be little different from slavery. 'Neither Portuguese officials nor Ovimbundu representatives were required to know each other's language, laws, or customs' (Heywood, 2000: 36) and the Portuguese encouraged tribal rivalry in order to guarantee a steady flow of captive labour and to harden their position as the main power-brokers in the region.

After the Second World War, Portugal used some of its Marshall Plan funding to invest in Angolan infrastructure, but the new roads and mines were built by hundreds of thousands of Africans working under compulsion. British missionaries reported 'pregnant women, many with babies strapped to their backs, and children as young as six, who performed roadwork in many parts of the highlands' (Heywood, 2000: 79). Nationalist resentment exploded in 1961, taking the Portuguese by surprise. The war lasted until 1974 amid horrific atrocities, and there can be no doubt that the profitability of forced African labour was Portugal's main motive for resisting decolonisation. Links between Angolan nationalists and Communist funding was merely new gloss on a very old story of racist exploitation.

The Americans, like the British, were fond of comparing their status as progressive trustees with the halting steps of other imperial powers. A closer look at decolonisation reveals a far from straightforward picture, however. It is provocative to suggest that the integration of Hawai'i and Alaska was a 'decolonisation', but this is the best word to describe a process with so many similarities to other empires of integration. In this case, the main difference is the fact that integration was successful in the long term. The reason for this difference, and for the delay in granting full political rights to these territories, was race relations.

After annexing the territories of Hawai'i and Alaska, the United States delayed the granting of full statehood to an extent out of all proportion to the experience of other states in the union. Hawai'i and Alaska did not become full-fledged states until 1959, by which time their racial demographics and politics had changed significantly since annexation. Voting rights in Hawai'i had been linked, among other things, to language proficiency in English or Hawai'ian, in a move designed to prevent Hawai'i's growing Asian population from gaining substantial political power. We have seen how powerful 'yellow peril' fears were in the United States and other countries. Only after the Second World War, when Hawai'ian Asians had proved themselves to be loyal Americans, did these attitudes begin to abate. In Alaska, a minority white population grew dramatically during and after the Second World War through the presence of American military forces and an expanding petroleum industry. In both cases, racial anxieties had delayed the granting of full political rights.

Racial tensions grew violent in the case of the British colonies whose white populations remained minorities. By 1960 Britain had granted independence to India, Ghana (formerly the Gold Coast in western Africa), and Malaya (today's Malaysia). The British Commonwealth had expanded to include the new African and Asian governments as well as the Dominions, although not without strong objections from apartheid South Africa (which eventually withdrew from the Commonwealth in disgust). Britain had accepted the principle of black majority rule in its African colonies, and the pace of decolonisation accelerated during the 1960s. This hardly squares with ongoing racism, it would seem. Nevertheless, those African colonies with powerful white minorities featured a prolonged and painful struggle for independence. Here the British were caught in a trap of their own making. Having been willing enough in the early twentieth century to allow whites to rule over a majority black population in South Africa, Kenya, and Rhodesia, they were now faced with a considerable dilemma. The British government might have changed its outlook to favour African majority rule, but white elites in African colonies most certainly had not. With the exception of a relatively small number of liberals, whites would rather fight than lose power. It took the Mau-Mau insurrection of the 1950s in Kenya to convince the British that independence would have to be granted sooner rather than later, whether white colonial politicians agreed or not.

The Rhodesian government fought this process to the bitter end, issuing a unilateral declaration of independence in 1965 – the first in the British empire since the American declaration of 1776 – in order to maintain white political privileges. 'I don't believe in black majority rule ever in Rhodesia,' vowed Prime Minister Ian Smith, 'not in a thousand years' (Samson, 2001a: 267). The British government dragged its feet, unwilling to go to war with white British subjects, but also unwilling to endorse their plans for Rhodesia's future. African members of the Commonwealth precipitated a boycott which was taken up by the United Nations. 'I will not be bullied', declared Margaret Thatcher when she became British prime minister in 1979, but the threat of sanctions against the British government itself by lucrative trading partners like Nigeria was decisive in resolving the problem of Rhodesia. Like many British officials before her, she discovered that she had to do business with African nationalists sooner or later, and this shift in British attitudes helped to bring about Zimbabwean independence in 1980.

It had taken over fifteen years of bloody civil war to reach this point, and there can be absolutely no doubt that the Rhodesian conflict was primarily about race. In South Africa, too, a white minority government had become entrenched under the different social and historical circumstances of the early twentieth century. What worked in 1910 would not work in 1980, however, and even in South Africa a similar combination of international pressures and civil insurrection was challenging apartheid. Free elections in 1994 produced South Africa's first black president, Nelson Mandela, and saw the return of South Africa to the Commonwealth. The examples of Rhodesia and South Africa are salutary reminders that imperial ideologies of trusteeship or pupilage meant little if white minorities on the ground were prepared to do battle to maintain racial privilege.

THE END OF EMPIRE?

At the beginning of the twentieth century, the British diplomat and writer Wilfrid Blunt wrote a scathing criticism of European imperialism:

> The Emperor of Germany gives the word for slaughter and the Pope looks on and approves. In South Africa our troops are burning farms under Kitchener's command, and the Queen and the two Houses of Parliament and the bench of bishops thank God publicly and vote money for the work. The Americans are spending fifty millions a year on slaughtering the Filipinos; the King of the Belgians has invested his whole fortune on the Congo, where he is brutalising negroes to fill his pockets. . . . The whole white race is reveling openly in

violence, as though it had never pretended to be Christian. God's equal curse on them all! So ends the famous nineteenth century into which we were so proud to have been born. (Samson, 2001a: 200–1)

Even allowing for journalistic licence, this summary of comparative imperialism is painfully accurate in its identification of links between racism and imperialism. The nineteenth century, so proud of its place in the story of human progress, seemed to Blunt to have ended in criminal exploitation and bloodshed. Much worse was to come during the newly-born twentieth century. While it is true that by 1980 most of the largest European and American colonies had become independent, eighty years is a very brief term in the history of modern imperialism, and we must therefore ask: did the legacy of imperial race relations vanish as quickly as the colonies themselves [*Doc. 26*]?

We have already seen how decolonisation in the colonies of settlement did not necessarily mean decolonisation for the indigenous populations of those colonies. For these people and their ancestors, the alleged achievement of self-government in the nineteenth century was mainly a myth. Only in the 1960s did national referenda give voting rights to aboriginal citizens in Australia and Canadia citizens, for example. From the point of view of many aboriginal activists in these countries, decolonisation has barely begun. Controversy also surrounds the legacy of imperialism and racism in Latin America, especially in the former Portuguese colony of Brazil. As we have seen, the Portuguese empire-builders prided themselves on their successful avoidance of racism. Has their legacy been different as a result?

Many nineteenth-century Brazilians claimed that differences in social or economic status was more significant than differences in skin colour. Before slavery was abolished in 1888, to refer to a Brazilian as 'black' was to call him or her a slave; whether the person was of entirely African ancestry or not was irrelevant. As in the West Indies, various words were developed to describe free people of African or Indian ancestry. One Brazilian wrote that 'We have been able to fuse all races into a single native population because Portuguese colonization assimilated the savage races instead of trying to destroy them' (Reichmann, 1999: 7). The circumstances of Brazilian independence helped to foster this sense of national unity. Brazil's white and mixed-race elite was much less resentful about imperial policy than their Spanish counterparts were. The Portuguese royal family fled to Brazil after Napoleon's invasion in 1808, and it was Brazilian-born Prince Pedro who declared Brazilian independence in 1822. By the twentieth century, the notion of a racially egalitarian Portuguese legacy was well entrenched [*Doc. 25*].

Recent scholarship has challenged the image of a peaceful, egalitarian transition to independence, however. Miscegenation did not necessarily mean equality: Portuguese colonists often married Indian women, but rarely married Africans. This meant that it was much easier for *mestizo* children to join the elite; *mulattos*, on the other hand, often retained the 'black' slave identity of their mothers. The ongoing marginalisation of darker-skinned Brazilians testifies to the lingering presence of colonial racial structures. During the 1970s there was extensive debate among Brazilian scientists about the growing number of Brazilians of African ancestry; projections suggested that this group would reach 60 per cent of the total population by 2000. The result of this debate was a vigorous population control campaign aimed exclusively at noticeably black communities (Fiola, 1990: 5). Why would such issues even be investigated, let alone feared, in an alleged racial democracy? It has become increasingly difficult to regard Brazilian society as profoundly different from other post-independence states in this respect. The concept of *branqueamento* ('whitening') meant that miscegenation could be combined with upward mobility in some mixed-race portions of the population. Nevertheless, such mobility was defined by whiteness, demonstrating that a failure to breed 'up' out of African or Indian ancestry would relegate people to a lower place in the social scale. The Brazilian concept of *amor sem cor* ('love without colour boundaries') does not seem quite so liberating when seen from this angle.

In other cases, post-independence race relations were immediately troubled by the continued privileged position of groups favoured by colonial administrations. The Dutch East Indies had always been an artificial construction, composed of assorted kingdoms and principalities drawn together by outside rule. After 1949, the new Indonesian government reflected the ongoing power of Javanese interests in the archipelago; Java had always been the heart of the old colony. Non-Javanese found that independence did not necessarily bring liberation from these internal power structures. Neighbouring Malaysia featured similar problems when it achieved independence from the British in 1957. Having encouraged massive immigration by ethnic Chinese in order to meet labour demands, the British found themselves fighting a Communist-backed insurrection during the 1950s which had significant Chinese support. Racial tensions remained after the uprising was over: 'The different races in Malaya think of themselves primarily as Malays, Chinese or Indians and only secondarily, if at all, as Malayans,' wrote one colonial official. 'The process of nation-building, although recognised as essential . . . has so far made slow progress' (Samson, 2001a: 279–80). The British would have preferred a slower pace, due to the lack of readiness for unified independence, but it was impossible to stem the tide of nationalism in the indigenous Malay population. Attempts to create an inclusive political identity failed, both before and after independence, not least because of strong Malay pressure to restrict land ownership to Malays. The Chinese-majority population of Singapore broke away from Malaysia in 1965 to become an independent republic.

It was often Asians who found themselves abandoned, rather than liberated, by decolonisation. In eastern Africa, where the British had imported large numbers of Indian indentured labourers in the nineteenth and early twentieth centuries, the concept of African majority rule was daunting. Would racial minority rights be respected? After independence, racially exclusive nationalisms arose in some former colonies, as when 'Africanisation' campaigns produced the expulsion of Asians from Kenya and Uganda in the 1960s and 1970s. In the south Pacific colony of Fiji, the colonial use of indentured labour had produced a similar dilemma. The British had ensured that indigenous Fijians held exclusive rights to land ownership, but Fijians of Indian ancestry increased in number during the twentieth centuries. The British policy of 'indirect rule' through indigenous elites bore bitter fruit. Coups in 1987 ushered in an ethnic Fijian military dictatorship and prompted substantial Indo-Fijian emigration. The large-scale diasporas of Indians and Chinese through imperial labour systems generated profound demographic change, creating enormous problems for new governments trying to create national identity and unity. If ethnic or race-based nationalism was preferred, as it usually was, this by no means meant that a colony's troubles were over once the European rulers had left.

In east-central Africa the Germans had taken an anthropological, 'indirect rule' approach to colonial government which made unification extremely difficult after independence. Ruanda and Urundi (now Rwanda and Burundi) occupied a strategic location in eastern Africa, and were eventually divided between Britain and Germany. The first German colonial Resident, Dr Richard Kandt, took an anthropological interest in its inhabitants after his arrival in 1907. Like many theorists of the day, he used the model of European feudalism in order to analyse the relative status of the different peoples of the region: the Tutsi, whom he considered the aristocrats, the Hutu, the commoners, and the pygmy Twa people, who were dismissed as 'the lowest caste, an ancient people despised, feared, hated by the other natives' (Louis, 1963: 148). The Germans approved of what they considered to be an admirable system of tribute and military service under a Tutsi king, and the Tutsi welcomed the enforcement of their status by the German authorities. Although the Hutu were extremely dissatisfied with being relegated to a permanent semi-serfdom, they supported German persecution of the Twa. German rule was casting into stone ethnic categories and social relationships which had once been more fluid. When control of the colony passed to Belgium after Germany's defeat in the First World War, the Belgians continued to rule through the Tutsi elite, ensuring that ethnic hatred would intensify through decolonisation and beyond. Europeans did not invent ethnic boundaries in Africa or elsewhere, but European rule enhanced and codified these boundaries to an unprecedented extent. Colonial anthropology has left a poisonous legacy.

In all of these cases the language of 'independence' and 'decolonisation' conceals as much as it reveals. Racial policies introduced under imperial rule generated social and political structures which might or might not have been transformed by independence movements. For racial minorities, too often they were not. The modern empires moved people around the world in unprecedented numbers, creating multi-racial populations that faced unprecedented challenges in nation-building. Arbitrarily-drawn colonial borders often ignored the geographies of ethnicity or trade. In addition, European notions of nationalism were profoundly contradictory. Notions of civic nationalism based on collective democratic participation were contradicted by Romantic conceptions of 'blood and soil' nationalism in which belonging was defined in biological or cultural terms. Colonial nationalisms also differed in this respect. This is why (confusingly) we can speak of 'Indian nationalists', 'Hindu nationalists', and 'Muslim nationalists' in colonial India, for example. The first of these phrases describes a political-national identity while the other two are culturally exclusive.

Such tensions are not unique to the colonial world. Some European attempts at inclusive nationalism were successful, as in the nineteenth-century creation of Germany and Italy. Other attempts proved to be relatively short lived, such as the nation of Yugoslavia which broke apart amid civil war and genocide in the 1990s. In this case, too, the issue of imperialism is deeply implicated. The Muslim empire of the Ottomans, the expansionist Orthodox empire of the Russians, and the Roman Catholic empire of the Austro-Hungarians all met in the Balkans, generating waves of inclusive and exclusive strategies of power which saw particular ethnic groups dominate others over time. No wonder many liberal Yugoslav nationalists hoped for a better future under a united flag; no wonder such powerful forces were arrayed against their hopes. Under imperial rule, religious change, labour systems, gender relations, and local political power are all subject to manipulation. The legacy of this manipulation can be protracted and bitterly costly.

'THE WEST' AND 'THE REST'

I have said in the introduction to this book that 'people make race'. If race or ethnicity is considered to be of primary importance, then shared ancestry will be the 'common sense' definition of belonging to a particular community. In other situations, where a different shared identity has become more powerful, ethnic or racial differences are less important. People decide whether or not racial differences are significant and in what ways. We have seen to what extent the issue of race was related to the expansion of European imperialism: empires did not invent discrimination, but they did much to increase and institutionalise it. Origin debates, in which either racism or imperialism is claimed to be of paramount significance, should not distract us from the insight that 'it is in the unique relationships and in the transmission of ideas between a relatively small intellectual elite in America and Europe, and in the colonial administrations in Africa, the Middle East and Asia at this time that we may find the origins of the modern conception of race' (Brown, 2003: 204).

Racism arose in relationship with imperialism, and it continues to operate in the context of power relations whether these are specifically 'imperial' or not.

In some obvious cases, the old imperial Powers continue to rule remnants of their former empires. Many people do not realise how extensive these remnants are. France retains substantial territory in the south Pacific, including the large island of New Caledonia off the north-eastern coast of Australia, and the islands of French Polynesia (including Tahiti) where it has conducted nuclear testing. French Polynesia might be declared to be part of metropolitan France, but its inhabitants are keenly aware that no French government would explode a nuclear device near Paris. French Polynesia's remoteness from Europe, its relative insignificance for French voters, and generous subsidies for local residents have combine to perpetuate the imperial relationship. Some parts of the Pacific and Caribbean still retain various degrees of direct American influence. In Cuba this includes a leased naval base at Guantanamo Bay. American Samoa, acquired in 1900 through a partition of the Samoan islands with Britain and Germany, remains under the authority of the Department of the Interior and is exempted from key provisions of the US constitution. The US Virgin Islands, purchased from Denmark in 1917, are also 'unincorporated' in terms of constitutional rights. As one historian observes: 'the nonwhite race of the population made the territories unsuitable for assimilation into the Union, but incapable of self-government at the same time. In that status limbo most territories were placed . . . and there many territories remain today' (McFerson, 1997: 91).

The United Nations, having proclaimed its hopes for the eradication of colonialism by the year 2000, has called on the United States and other imperial powers to accelerate the move to independence in their overseas territories. Rising popular criticism after the Second World War prompted American governments to talk more about 'development' than 'civilisation', and to spend more money on infrastructure in the colonies (now renamed 'territories'). Progress toward actual independence has been slow or nonexistent in some cases, however; the United States is not alone in facing significant dilemmas when considering how (or if) to grant independence to tiny populations whose standard of living might fall significantly once metropolitan subsidies are withdrawn. Sometimes there are significant advantages to remaining a colony, as the people of Gibraltar and Bermuda have made clear in recent referenda endorsing British rule. However, in colonies with significant independence movements, such as French-ruled New Caledonia, the case for ongoing foreign rule is more difficult to make, and cannot help but draw attention to the fact that in such cases Europeans are continuing to rule non-Europeans whether they like it or not.

One of the primary characteristics of imperial racism was the assumption of a baseline against which strangers could be defined. 'We' had civilisation; 'they' had culture. Distinctions were made between 'European' and 'non-

European', 'white' and 'non-white', or, more recently, 'the West' and 'the rest'. In each case, Europeans and North Americans believed that they knew best how to describe and enable global systems of ordering, including the ordering of peoples into various kinds of hierarchies. We have seen how this process could emphasise either human universals or human differences; in fact, these two approaches are mutually dependent and cannot exist without reference to the other. Notions of universalism are meaningful because they can be distinguished from essentialised notions of difference: 'brothering' depends on its distinction from 'othering'.

European and North American views on international affairs these days often feature universalist language, emphasising global processes of economic and social change which, although defined by European history and culture, are presumed to be the best forms of development for all of the world's peoples. Sometimes the assumption that 'the West knows best' produces painfully ironic results. The paradox of protection by invasion remains as pointed today in Iraq as it did after the British invasion of Egypt at the height of Victorian imperialism. 'When we offer them advice, it will always be for their own good,' wrote one British official after the invasion of 1882, 'and the more speedily they improve under it, the more speedily we shall leave the country. The more they resent our counsel and follow their own devices, the longer we shall have to remain' (Auchterlonie, 2001: 18). Trapped by a paradox of their own creation, British forces remained in the Suez Canal zone until forced out by the humiliating Suez Crisis of 1956. As I have noted elsewhere, 'one person's humanitarian intervention is another's neocolonialism' and 'relationships between benevolent intentions, armed force, and national prestige remain as precarious today as they were over a century ago' (Samson, 1998: 175). Despite widespread decolonisation, European and North American influence has maintained its global reach and significant divisions between 'haves' and 'have nots' remain along familiar lines. Should these divisions be breached in favour of more unified political, economic, and social standards? Many people might simply assume that this is common sense, without realising that globalised plans for humanity are inevitably rooted in imperial history. Non-Europeans might or might not appreciate these plans, especially when they bear significant similarities to plans expressed by the old imperial Powers. As a Pacific islander once put it with respect to American rule in his part of the world: 'It is said that an American likes to walk tall even though we may be short, and that he occasionally takes a giant step or two for mankind even though mankind may not have asked him to' (Weeks, 2002: 125).

It would be telling only half a story, however, if we did not also consider the ways in which empire changed the metropolitan powers themselves. Growing numbers of immigrants from former imperial territories migrated to the imperial homelands after the Second World War. The presence of growing populations of West Indians and south Asians in Britain, or Algerians in

France, were not necessarily welcomed. Kenyan Asians, for example, often preferred to migrate to Britain rather than face increasing discrimination in Kenya. As British subjects, with British passports, they were legally entitled to do this. British attitudes toward immigration from the former colonies had changed substantially since the Second World War, however. Increasingly restrictive legislation was passed during the 1960s which protected the right of white expatriates to return to Britain while curtailing the number of non-white migrants. Britishness was no longer a global, multi-racial identity held by 'British subjects', nor was it guaranteed by the holding of a British pass-port. It was now debated in terms of race. Even non-white people born in Britain might not be considered truly British; the notorious comments of the Conservative politician Enoch Powell are a case in point: 'The West Indian or Indian does not, by being born in England, become an Englishman. In law he becomes a United Kingdom citizen by birth; in fact he is a West Indian or an Asian still' (Paul, 1997: 178). Other voices protested against such views; another Conservative politician declared that they were not only 'dis-crimination based on racial origin' but also 'a denial . . . of one of the basic rights of a citizen, namely to enter the country of which he is a citizen' (Paul, 1997: 180). Here are the two familiar and fundamentally contradictory views of nationality: communities based on shared faith, citizenship, or other non-biological ties, and communities related by blood. The British government eventually revised its stance on Asian immigration from Africa, and when Uganda began expelling Asians in the 1970s, attitudes in Britain had become somewhat more welcoming. Whether immigrants have felt able to participate in British national life to the extent that they would wish is, of course, another question.

Many countries today are proudly 'multicultural', and it is worth consid-ering this term in light of our study of race and empire. Multiculturalism is meant to demonstrate diversity and tolerance, yet it depends on the identifica-tion of ethnic and cultural difference. Careful attention is paid to descriptive terminology. 'Indians' in Canada have become 'First Nations'; 'Negroes' in the United States are now 'African-Americans'. Making new labels usually represents an attempt to disassociate the present from the past, but the prob-lem is that these labels have been replaced rather than rejected. Sincere efforts are being made to eliminate discrimination against particular racial groups, and this is only to be encouraged, but such efforts mitigate racism rather than eliminating it. As long as we group people into racial or ethnic categories, insisting on particular labels and qualifications for membership, we perpetu-ate the importance of race in ordering our collective life.

We also perpetuate the idea of a racial baseline from which all others are described as different. The well-known hyphenated identities of the United States reveal the dilemma in a particularly visible way. Americans pride themselves on being inclusive, egalitarian people, and in many ways they are.

Nevertheless, anyone with non-Anglo-Saxon background has a hyphenated ethnic identification, revealing that Anglo-Saxons continue to be the presumed baseline. There are 'Chinese-Americans' and 'Irish-Americans' but there are no 'English-Americans'. Significantly, people of aboriginal descent are also hyphenated as Native-Americans even though they were the original inhabitants of the soil. New Zealand, whose indigenous population enjoyed more rights than most, is the only former settler colony whose labelling system uses the indigenous identity as the baseline, and this development is relatively recent. The Maori are the indigenous inhabitants and have always been called Maori. All the rest are *pakeha* (non-Maori), although both Maori and *pakeha* are New Zealanders. The commonplace use of an indigenous word to describe the non-indigenous population is significant, revealing the extensive participation of Maori in New Zealand's national life. Even in this case, however, racial labelling retains primary importance.

Correct labelling is the subject of intense debate and emotion in most countries today, just as it was during the colonial period. Fears of individuals 'passing' into the wrong group have been replaced by admonitions against denying 'roots'. In Canada, the threat of cultural marginalisation, combined with historical grievances stemming from British conquest in the eighteenth century, has produced a modern separatist movement in Québec. In this context, Canadian nationalism is seen as a hegemonic process which has stifled the national identity of Québec, disguising the extent to which the unique society of French Canadians has been besieged by English Canada. These different constructions of national identity have been called the 'two solitudes' of Canadian history.

It is easy to see why activists use strategies of labelling and belonging in order to gather political momentum, but it is important to point out that such strategies can reinforce racial or ethnic boundaries even as they seek to expose and denounce them. As Kenan Malik puts it, 'We live in a world which at one and the same time abhors the creation of apartheid racial barriers but applauds the maintenance of cultural diversity, a world in which the aim of much social and educational policy is to ensure cultural separation' (Malik, 1996: 149). None of these ironies can be fully appreciated unless we realise how much the 'postcolonial' present is entangled with the imperial past. The legacy of empire is an immensely complex subject, yet it is crucial to understanding today's world. Despite the achievement of political independence, former colonies still experience the effects of attitudes and structures introduced by colonial rule. Today's world must still contend with links between skin colour and prosperity, not only in terms of 'the West' and 'the rest', but within national borders as well. Race is not the only insightful guide to inequality, to be sure: differences of class, gender, and age also divide 'haves' from 'have-nots'. This book has concentrated on race because it is a useful way of understanding modern imperial history; not because it is the only way.

A focus on race can help to illustrate why today's nations should be regarded as ongoing conversations in which we reassess and renegotiate our relationships with one another until we are satisfied that all are included in the nation's benefits. It may be that more options exist than we yet realise, but few of them will be explored if we continue to accept the 'common sense' view that race is natural and racial disparity is inevitable. For centuries, thinkers have struggled to conceptualise forms of identity which transcend race or ethnicity as a focus for nationalism. The difficulties faced by the European Union, however, demonstrate how difficult the construction of new configurations can be. To confront the modern world's entanglement with history is to make a good beginning. It is easy to scorn the flagrant racisms and imperialisms of the past, as though such things magically disappeared after the Second World War, or after the collapse of the Soviet Union. The truth is that many people still seem to prefer a world in which physical appearance reveals a 'fact' called race. We expect race to mean something, and therefore it does. The tragedy is that our actions so often live down to this expectation. The hope is that that they don't have to.

PART FOUR   DOCUMENTS

The Portuguese began slave trading in the fifteenth century, and this account from 1444 is one of the earliest observations we have of the arrival of African slaves for sale in Europe. The Portuguese chronicler Gomes Eannes mixes sympathy with more discriminatory judgements.

O, Thou heavenly Father . . . I pray Thee that my tears may not wrong my conscience; for it is not their religion but their humanity that maketh mine to weep in pity for their sufferings. And if the brute animals, with their bestial feelings, by a natural instinct understand the sufferings of their own kind, what wouldst Thou have my human nature to do on seeing before my eyes that miserable company, and remembering that they too are of the generation of the sons of Adam?

On the next day, which was the 8th of the month of August, very early in the morning, by reason of the heat, the seamen began to make ready their boats, and to take out those captives, and carry them on shore, as they were commanded. And these, placed all together in that field, were a marvelous sight; for amongst them were some white enough, fair to look upon, and well proportioned; others were less white like mulattoes; others again were as black as Ethiops, and so ugly, both in features and in body, as almost to appear (to those who saw them) the images of a lower hemisphere. But what heart could be so hard as not to be pierced with piteous feeling to see that company? For some kept their heads low and their faces bathed in tears, looking one upon another, others stood groaning very dolorously, looking up to the height of heaven, fixing their eyes upon it, crying out loudly, as if asking help of the father of Nature . . .

The Infant [Prince Henry] was there, mounted upon a powerful steed, and accompanied by his retinue, making distribution of his favours, as a man who sought to gain but small treasure from his share; for of the forty-six souls that fell to him as his fifth, he made a very speedy partition of these.

And certainly his expectation was not in vain; for, as we said before, as soon as they understood our language they turned Christians with very little ado; and I who put together this history into this volume, saw in the town of Lagos boys and girls (the children and grandchildren of those first captives, born in this land) as good and true Christians as if they had directly descended, from the beginning of the dispensation of Christ, from those who were first baptised.

Gomes Eannes de Zurara, *The Chronicle of the Discovery and Conquest of Guinea*, trans. Charles Raymond Beazley and Adgar Prestage (New York: Burt Franklin for the Hakluyt Society, [1896]), vol. I, pp. 80–3.

The Spanish court convened a debate in 1550 between the philosopher Juan Ginés de Sepúlveda, author of a treatise arguing that colonial conflict constituted a 'just war' against barbarism, and Bartolomé de las Casas, a Dominican friar and missionary already known for his championship of Indian rights.

De Sepúlveda: Now compare these [Spanish] traits of prudence, intelligence, magnanimity, moderation, humanity, and religion with the qualities of these little men in whom you will scarcely find even vestiges of humanity; who not only are devoid of learning but do not even have a written language; who preserve no monuments of their history . . . and who have no written laws but only barbaric customs and institutions. And if we are to speak of virtues, what moderation or mildness can you expect of men who are given to all kinds of intemperance and wicked lusts, and who eat human flesh? . . .

Could one give more convincing proof of the superiority of some men to others in intelligence, spirit, and valor, and of the fact that such people are slaves by nature? . . .

Such, in sum, are the disposition and customs of these little men – barbarous, uncivilized, and inhumane; and we know that they were like this before the coming of the Spaniards. We have not yet spoken of their impious religion and of the wicked sacrifices in which they worshiped the devil as their God, believing that they could offer no better tribute than human hearts . . . How can we doubt that these peoples, so uncivilized, so barbarous, contaminated with so many infidelities and vices, have been justly conquered by such an excellent, pious, and just king as the late Ferdinand the Catholic, and the present Emperor Charles, and by a nation that is most humane and excels in every kind of virtue?

Las Casas: [But] it is clear that no nation exists, no matter how rude and uncivilized, barbarous, gross, savage or almost brutal it may be, that cannot be persuaded into a good way of life and made domestic, mild, and tractable – provided that diligence and skill are employed, and provided that the method that is proper and natural to men is used: namely, love and gentleness and kindness . . .

For all the peoples of the world are men, and the definition of all men, collectively and severally, is one: that they are rational beings. All possess understanding and volition, being formed in the image and likeness of God . . . and this is true not only of those that are inclined toward good but of those that by reason of their depraved customs are bad . . .

Thus all mankind is one, and all men are alike in what concerns their creation and all natural things, and no one is born enlightened. From this it follows that all of us must be guided and aided at first by those who were born before us. And the savage peoples of the earth may be compared to uncultivated soil that readily brings forth weeds and useless thorns, but has within itself such natural virtue that by labor and cultivation it may be made to yield sound and beneficial fruits.

Benjamin Keen, ed., *The Colonial Origins*, vol. I of *Latin American Civilization*
(Boston: Houghton Mifflin, 1974), pp. 176–8.

DOCUMENT 3   *CALVIN'S CASE*

This judgment of 1608, given by the court of King's Bench in England, attempted to clarify the question of English jurisdiction over persons born outside England. In the process, it claimed that Christian laws should prevail in a conquered non-Christian territory. This view would be decisively overturned in the eighteenth century.

Every man was either a subject born, or (temporarily or perpetually) an alien friend or similarly an alien enemy. All pagans were perpetual enemies to Christendom in law and the law presumed they will not be converted.

And upon this ground there is a diversity between a conquest of a kingdom of a Christian king, and the conquest of a kingdom of an infidel; for if a king come to a Christian kingdom by conquest . . . he may at his pleasure alter and change the laws of that kingdom, but until he doth make an alteration of those laws, the ancient laws of that kingdom remain. But if a Christian king should conquer a kingdom of an infidel, and bring them under his subjection, there . . . the laws of the infidel are abrogated; for that they be not only against Christianity, but against the law of God and of nature . . . and in that case, until certain laws be established amongst them, the king by himself, and such judges as he shall appoint, shall judge them and their causes according to natural equity, in such sort as kings in ancient time did . . .

A.F. Madden and D.K. Fieldhouse, eds, *Empire of the Bretaignes, 1175–1688*,
vol. I of *Select Documents on the Constitutional History of the British
Empire and Commonwealth: The Foundations of a Colonial System of
Government* (Westport, CN: Greenwood Press, 1985), p. 36.

DOCUMENT 4   **FRENCH AND INDIANS MEET IN BILOXI**

Pierre le Moyne, Sieur d'Iberville, claimed the area of Biloxi Bay for France in 1699, securing the Mississippi delta for what would eventually become the colony of Louisiana. This account of the ceremonies in 1699 demonstrates both interaction and incomprehension.

A week later – as soon as news of the arrival of the French spread among the savages neighbouring to these – they came with the chiefs of several villages and sang their calumet [pipe] of peace, as all the nations do with people whom they have not seen before, but with whom they wish friendship and peace. . . .

The chiefs of these savages . . . came ceremoniously into our fort, singing the while, to present the calumet to M. d'Hyberville, our commander, who did indeed draw some puffs on that calumet after the manner of the savages. Then, as a mark of honor, they rubbed white dirt over the faces of M. d'Hyberville, his brothers, and several other officers. The feast of the calumet lasted three days, during which the savages sang and danced three times a day. On the third day they sank a stake in the clearing in front of our fort and danced around it . . . When they had thus arrived before the stake, they laid M. d'Hyberville on the ground upon a deer skin, and made him sit on it; and one of their chiefs, placed behind him, put his hands on M. d'Hyberville's shoulders and rocked him as if he had been an infant needing sleep. . . .

The French then went to the King's warehouse by order of M. d'Hyberville and brought knives, glass beads, vermilion, guns, lead, powder, mirrors, combs, kettles, cloaks, hats, shirts, *braguets*, leggings, rings, and other such trinkets . . . The savages were also given axes and picks. After this M. d'Hyberville went off to his quarters, leaving the savages before the fort dividing the presents and examining them with astonishment, not knowing the uses of the greater part of them. We took keen pleasure in watching their bewilderment.

Fleur de Lys and Calumet: Being the Penicaut Narrative of French
Adventure in Louisiana, ed. and trans. Richebourg Gaillard McWilliams
(Baton Rouge: Louisiana State University Press, 1953), pp. 5–7.

DOCUMENT 5   **MONTESQUIEU ON THE INFERIORITY OF AFRICANS**

Charles de Secondat, baron de Montesquieu, was one of France's leading philosophers of the early Enlightenment. His quest for a rational understanding of legal systems was liberal for its time, although he was clearly vulnerable to prejudice in racial matters. The final sentence exposes an irony that Christian antislavery campaigners would exploit later in the eighteenth century.

Were I to vindicate our right to make slaves of the negroes, these should be my arguments:–

The Europeans, having extirpated the [indigenous] Americans, were obliged to make slaves of the Africans, for clearing such vast tracts of land.

Sugar would be too dear if the plants which produce it were cultivated by any other than slaves.

These creatures are all over black, and with such a flat nose that they can scarcely be pitied.

It is hardly to be believed that God, who is a wise Being, should place a soul, especially a good soul, in such a black ugly body.

It is so natural to look upon color as the criterion of human nature, that the Asiatics, among whom eunuchs are employed, always deprive the blacks of their resemblance to us by a more opprobrious distinction [castration]. . . .

The negroes prefer a glass necklace to that gold which polite nations so highly value. Can there be any greater proof of their wanting common sense?

It is impossible for us to suppose these creatures to be men, because, allowing them to be men, a suspicion would follow that we ourselves are not Christians.

Charles de Secondat, baron de Montesquieu, *The Spirit of the Laws*, trans. Thomas Nugent
(New York, NY: The Colonial Press, 1899), vol. I, pp. 238–9.

DOCUMENT 6   WARREN HASTINGS PROMOTES RESPECT FOR INDIAN CULTURE

As governor-general of Bengal, Warren Hastings followed EIC precedent by running his government along mainly Indian lines. In this letter from 1774, written to his friend, the British Chief Justice, Lord Mansfield, Hastings reveals his respect for Indian culture; a respect no longer tolerated by many at home.

Among the various plans which have been lately formed for the improvement of the British interests in the provinces of Bengal, the necessity of establishing a new form of judicature, and giving laws to a people who were supposed to be governed by no other principle of justice than the arbitrary wills, or uninstructed judgments, of their temporary rulers, has been frequently suggested; and this opinion I fear has obtained the greater strength from some publications of considerable merit in which it is too positively asserted that written laws are totally unknown to the Hindus . . .

From whatever cause this notion has proceeded, nothing can be more foreign from truth . . . It would be a grievance to deprive the people of the protection of their own laws, but it would be a wanton tyranny to require their obedience to others of which they are wholly ignorant, and of which they have no possible means of acquiring a knowledge . . .

It was judged advisable for the sake of giving confidence to the people, and of enabling the courts to decide with certainty and despatch, to form a compilation of the Hindu laws with the best authority which could be obtained; and for that purpose ten of the most learned *pundits* [scholars] were invited to Calcutta . . .

This code they have written in their own language, the Sanscrit . . . The two first chapters I have now the honour to present to your Lordship with this, as a proof that the inhabitants of this land are not in the savage state in which they have been unfairly represented, and as a specimen of the principles which constitute the rights of property among them . . . With respect to the Mahomedan law, which is the guide at least of one fourth of the natives of this province, your Lordship need not be told that this is as comprehensive, and as well defined, as that of most states in Europe, having been formed at a time in which the Arabians were in possession of all the real learning which existed in the western parts of this continent.

Ramsay Muir, *The Making of British India 1756–1858*
(Manchester: Manchester University Press, 1915), pp. 144–5.

DOCUMENT 7   AN OPPONENT OF ABOLITION

This text by Edward Long was published amid the gathering abolition move-ment in Britain. Long refutes the environmental theories of Buffon, among others, preferring more essentialist explanations of African inferiority. The result was a brutally racist argument in favour of the continuation of slavery.

The particulars where [Africans] differ most essentially from Whites are, first, in respect to their bodies, viz. The dark membrane which communicates that black colour to their skins, which does not alter by transportation into other climates, and which they never lose . . . Secondly, A covering of wool, like the bestial fleece, instead of hair. Thirdly, The roundness of their eyes, the figure of their ears, tumid nostrils, flat noses, invariable thick lips, and general large size of the female nipples, as if adapted by nature to the peculiar con-formation of their childrens mouths. Fourthly, The black colour of the lice which infest their bodies . . . It is known, that there is a very great variety of these insects; and some say, that almost all animals have their particular sort. Fifthly, Their bestial or fetid smell, which they all have in a greater or less degree . . .

I shall next consider their disparity, in regard to the faculties of the mind. Under this head we are to observe, that they remain at this time in the same rude situation in which they were found two thousand years ago. In general, they are void of genius, and seem almost incapable of making any progress in civility or science. They have no plan or system of morality among them. Their barbarity to their children debases their nature even below that of brutes. They have no moral sensations; no taste but for women; gormondizing, and drinking to excess; no wish but to be idle . . . They are represented by all authors as the vilest of the human kind, to which they have little more pretension of resemblance than what arises from their exterior form. . . .

When we reflect on the nature of these men, and their dissimilarity to the rest of mankind, must we not conclude, that they are a different species of the same *genus*? . . .

Among them of so savage a disposition, as that they scarcely differ from the wild beasts of the wood in the ferocity of their manners, we must not think of introducing those polished rules and refinements, which have drawn their origin and force from the gradual civilization of other nations that once were barbarous. Such men must be managed at first as if they were beasts; they must be tamed, before they can be treated like men.

Edward Long, *The History of Jamaica, or, General Survey of the Antient and Modern State of That Island with Reflections on its Situation, Settlements, Inhabitants, Climates, Products, Commerce, Laws and Government* (London: T. Lowndes, 1774), vol. II, pp. 351–6, 401.

DOCUMENT 8   AN ENVIRONMENTAL THEORY OF RACE

Like many eighteenth-century theorists, Georges-Louis Leclerc, comte de Buffon, saw humanity as essentially unified, and therefore sought explanations of human difference which did not focus on biological, racial difference.

From the above historical account of all the inhabitants of Europe and Asia, it is apparent, that the differences in colour depend much, though not entirely, upon the climates. There are many other causes which have an influence upon the colour, and even upon the features and corporeal form of different people. The nature of the food is one of the principal causes; and we shall afterwards consider the changes it may produce. Manners, or the mode of living, may also have considerable effects. A polished people, who are accustomed to an easy, regular, and tranquil mode of life, and who, by the vigilance of a wise government, are removed from the dread of oppression and misery, will, for these reasons alone, be more strong, vigorous, and handsome, than savage and lawless nations, where every individual, deriving no succours from society, is obliged to provide for his own subsistence, to suffer alternately the pangs arising from hunger and from surfeits of unwholesome food, to sink under the fatigues of hard labour, to feel the rigours of a severe climate, without possessing the means of alleviating them, to act, in a word, more frequently like a brute than a man. Supposing two nations, thus differently circumstanced, to live under the same climate, it is reasonable to think, that the savage people would be more ugly, more tawny, more diminutive, and more wrinkled, than the nation that enjoyed the advantages of society and civilization.

Georges-Louis Leclerc, comte de Buffon, *A Natural History, General and Particular* (first published 1748–1804), p. 269.

*Joseph-Arthur, comte de Gobineau was a critic of the legacy of the French
Revolution, as well as a race theorist and observer of international relations.
He published a compendium of his views in the multi-volume 'Essai sur
l'inégalité des races humaines' in the 1850s.*

In order to appreciate the intellectual differences between races, we ought first
to ascertain the degree of stupidity to which mankind can descend. We know
already the highest point that it can reach, namely civilization.

Most scientific observers up to now have been very prone to make out the
lowest types as worse than they really are.

Nearly all the early accounts of a savage tribe paint it in hideous colours,
far more hideous than the reality. They give it so little power of reason and
understanding, that it seems to be on a level with the monkey and below the
elephant. It is true that we find the contrary opinion. If a captain is well
received in an island, if he meets, as he believes, with a kind and hospitable
welcome, and succeeds in making a few natives do a small amount of work
with his sailors, then praises are showered on the happy people. They are
declared to be fit for anything and capable of everything; and sometimes the
enthusiasm bursts all bounds, and swears it has found among them some
higher intelligences. . . .

Are however these moral possibilities, which lie at the back of every man's
consciousness, capable of infinite extension? Do all men possess in an equal
degree an unlimited power of intellectual development? In other words,
has every human race the capacity for becoming equal to every other? The
question is ultimately concerned with the infinite capacity for improvement
possessed by the species as a whole, and with the equality of races. I deny both
points. . . .

Civilization is incommunicable, not only to savages, but also to more
enlightened nations. This is shown by the efforts of French goodwill and
conciliation in the ancient kingdom of Algiers at the present-day, as well as by
the experience of the English in India, and the Dutch in Java. There are no
more striking and conclusive proofs of the unlikeness and inequality of races.

Joseph-Arthur comte de Gobineau, *The Inequality of Human Races*, trans. Adrian Collins
(London: William Heinemann, 1915), pp. 154–5, 171.

DOCUMENT 10   THE VIRTUES OF ANGLO-SAXONDOM

*After a world tour in 1866–7, Charles Wentworth Dilke wrote this paean of
praise to what he regarded as the world's dominant race: the Anglo-Saxons.*

In America we have seen the struggle of the dear races against the cheap – the endeavours of the English to hold their own against the Irish and Chinese. In New Zealand, we found the stronger and more energetic race pushing from the earth the shrewd and laborious descendants of the Asian Malays; in Australia, the English triumphant, and the cheaper races excluded from the soil not by distance merely, but by arbitrary legislation; in India, we saw the solution of the problem of officering of the cheaper by the dearer race. Everywhere we have found that the difficulties which impede the progress to universal dominion of the English people lie in the conflict with the cheaper races. The result of our survey is such as to give us reason for the belief that race distinctions will long continue, that miscegenation will go but little way towards blending races; that the dearer are, on the whole, likely to destroy the cheaper peoples, and that Saxendom [*sic*] will rise triumphant from the doubtful struggle.

Charles Wentworth Dilke, *Greater Britain: A Record of Travel in English-Speaking Countries*
(London, Macmillan: 1868), vol. II, pp. 405–7.

DOCUMENT 11   GENDERING SOCIAL EVOLUTIONISM

The British anthropologist Edward Burnett Tylor was one of the first theorists to work with an evolutionary model of human history. This approach enabled him to regard aspects of non-European culture as 'survivals' of an earlier, primitive stage that Europeans had passed through long ago. Note that matrilineal societies are presumed to be inferior to patrilineal ones.

The comparison of peoples according to their social framework of family and tribe has been assuming more and more importance . . .

    If, led by such new evidence, we look at the map of the world from this point of view, there discloses itself a remarkable fact of social geography. It is seen that matriarchal exogamous society, that is, society with female descent and prohibition of marriage within the clan, does not crop up here and there, as if it were an isolated invention, but characterizes a whole vast region of the world. If the Malay district be taken as a center, the system of intermarrying mother-clans may be followed west-ward into Asia, among the Garos and other hill tribes of India. Eastward from the Indian Archipelago it pervades the Melanesian Islands, with remains in Polynesia; it prevails widely in Australia, and stretches north and south in the Americas. This immense district represents an area of lower culture, where matriarchalism has only in places yielded to the patriarchal system, which develops with the idea of property, and which, in the other civilized half of the globe, has carried all before it, only showing in isolated spots and by relics of custom the former existence of matriarchal society. . . .

May it not be inferred from such a state of things, that social institutions form a deeper-lying element in man than language or even physical racetype? This is a problem which presents itself for serious discussion, when the evidence can be brought more completely together.

Regna Darnell, ed., *Readings in the History of Anthropology*
(New York: Harper and Row, 1974), pp. 161, 162–3.

DOCUMENT 12   LAW, PROPERTY, AND CIVILISATION

The American social anthropologist Lewis Henry Morgan turned earlier theories about agriculture and land title into a theory about progress of civilisation. For Morgan, the idea of private property was the cornerstone of civilisation; societies which favoured more collective property rights were therefore backward.

The latest investigations respecting the early condition of the human race are tending to the conclusion that mankind commenced their career at the bottom of the scale and worked their way up from savagery to civilization through the slow accumulations of experimental knowledge. . . .

[For example] the idea of property was slowly formed in the human mind, remaining nascent and feeble through immense periods of time. Springing into life in savagery, it required all the experience of this period and of the subsequent period of barbarism to develop the germ, and to prepare the human brain for the acceptance of its controlling influence. Its dominance as a passion over all other passions marks the commencement of civilization. It not only led mankind to overcome the obstacles which delayed civilization, but to establish political society on the basis of territory and of property. A critical knowledge of the evolution of the idea of property would embody, in some respects, the most remarkable portion of the mental history of mankind. . . .

Lewis H. Morgan, *Ancient Society, or, Researches in the Lines of
Human Progress from Savagery through Barbarism to Civilization*
(Chicago: Charles H. Kerr and Company, 1877), pp. 3–4.

DOCUMENT 13   THE BIRTH OF CULTURAL RELATIVISM

The German anthropologist Franz Boas would transform American anthropology with his theory of cultural relativism. The following extracts are taken from his address to the Anthropology section of the American Association for the Advancement of Science meeting in 1894.

Proud of his wonderful achievements, civilized man looks down upon the humbler members of mankind. He has conquered the forces of nature and compelled them to serve him. He has transformed inhospitable forests into fertile fields. The mountain fastnesses are yielding their treasures to his demands. The fierce animals which are obstructing his progress are being exterminated, while others which are useful to him are made to increase a thousand fold. The waves of the ocean carry him from land to land and towering mountain ranges set him no bounds. His genius has moulded inert matter into powerful machines which wait a touch of his hand to serve his manifold demands. . . .

Other conditions being equal, a race is always described as the lower the more fundamentally it differs from the white race. This becomes clearest by the tendency on the part of many anthropologists to look for anatomical peculiarities of primitive man which would characterize him as a being of lower order, and also by the endeavours of recent writers to prove that there exist hardly any anatomical features of the so-called lowest races which would stamp them as lower types of organisms. Both these facts show that the idea dwells in the minds of investigators that we should expect to find in the white race the highest type of man.

In judging social distinctions the same error is frequently committed. As the mental development of the white race is the highest, it is also supposed to have the highest aptitude in this direction, and therefore its mind is supposed to have the most subtle organization. As the ultimate psychical causes are not so apparent as anatomical characters, the judgment of the mental status of a people is generally guided by the difference between its social status and our own; the greater the difference between their intellectual, emotion and moral processes and those which are found in our civilization the harsher the judgment on the people . . .

Franz Boas, 'Human faculty as determined by race', *Proceedings of the American Association for the Advancement of Science* 43 (1894), pp. 301–2.

DOCUMENT 14   BRINGING 'CIVILISATION' TO THE BELGIAN CONGO

King Leopold of Belgium was offended by criticisms of his Congo Free State. He wrote this letter in 1897 to his colonial agents in the Congo, declaring that Belgium had the highest motives in ruling central Africa.

The task which the State agents have had to accomplish in the Congo is noble and elevated. They have had to carry on the work of civilisation in Equatorial Africa, guided by the principles set forth in the Berlin and Brussels resolutions.

Face to face with primitive barbarity, struggling against dreadful customs, thousands of years old, their duty has been to modify gradually those customs. . . .

I am glad to think that our agents, nearly all of whom are volunteers from the ranks of the Belgian army, always bear in mind the rules of the honorable career in which they are engaged. Animated with a pure sentiment of patriotism, reckoning little of their own blood, they will care all the more for the natives who will find in them the powerful protectors of life and property, the kindly guardians they need so much.

The aim of all of us – I desire to repeat it here with you – is to regenerate, materially and morally, races whose degradation and misfortune it is hard to realise. The fearful scourges of which, in the eyes of our humanity, these races seemed the victims, are already lessening, little by little, through our intervention. Each step forward made by our people should mark an improvement in the condition of the natives.

Louis Snyder, ed., *The Imperialism Reader: Documents and Readings on Modern Expansionism* (Princeton: Van Nostrand [1962]), pp. 236–7.

DOCUMENT 15   THE AMERICAN ANTI-IMPERIALIST LEAGUE

In the immediate aftermath of the Spanish–American War, the American Anti-Imperialist League issued a manifesto written in the style of the American Declaration of Independence.

We earnestly condemn the policy of the present National Administration of the Philippines. It seeks to extinguish the spirit of 1776 in those islands. We deplore the sacrifice of our soldiers and sailors, whose bravery deserves admiration even in an unjust war. We denounce the slaughter of the Filipinos as a needless horror. We protest against the extension of American sovereignty by Spanish methods.

We demand the immediate cessation of the war against liberty, begun by Spain and continued by us. We urge that Congress be promptly convened to announce to the Filipinos our purpose to concede to them the independence for which they have so long fought and which of right is theirs.

The United States have always protested against the doctrine of international law which permits the subjugation of the weak by the strong. A self-governing state cannot accept sovereignty over an unwilling people. The United States cannot act upon the ancient heresy that might makes right. . . .

We hold, with Abraham Lincoln, that 'no man is good enough to govern another without that man's consent. When the white man governs himself, that is self-government, but when he governs himself and also governs another man, that is more than self-government – this is despotism.' 'Our reliance is in the love of liberty which God has planted in us. Our defense is in the spirit which prizes liberty as the heritage of all men in all lands. Those who deny freedom to others deserve it not for themselves, and under a just God cannot long retain it.'

Snyder, *The Imperialism Reader*, pp. 391–2, 393.

DOCUMENT 16 'THE MASTER ORGANIZERS OF THE WORLD'

During a debate in 1900 about the annexation of the Philippines, Senator Albert Jeremiah Beveridge invoked traditional notions of Anglo-Saxon supremacy to justify imperialism as a racial destiny.

Mr. President, the times call for candor. The Philippines are ours forever, 'territory belonging to the United States,' as the Constitution calls them. And just beyond the Philippines are China's illimitable markets. We will not repudiate our duty in the archipelago. We will not abandon our opportunity in the Orient. We will not renounce our part in the mission of our race, trustee, under God, of the civilization of the world. . . .

Mr. President, this question is deeper than any question of party politics; deeper than any question of the isolated policy of our country even; deeper even than any question of constitutional power. It is elemental. It is racial. God has not been preparing the English-speaking and Teutonic peoples for a thousand years for nothing but vain and idle self-contemplation and self-admiration. No! He has made us the master organizers of the world to establish system where chaos reigns. He has given us the spirit of progress to overwhelm the forces of reaction throughout the earth. He has made us adept in government that we may administer government among savage and senile peoples. Were it not for such a force as this the world would relapse into barbarism and night. And of all our race He has marked the American people as His chosen nation to finally lead in the regeneration of the world. This is the divine mission of America, and it holds for us all the profit, all the glory, all the happiness possible to man. We are trustees of the world's progress, guardians of its righteous peace. . . .

Snyder, *The Imperialism Reader*, pp. 393–4.

DOCUMENT 17 HUMANITARIAN OUTRAGE IN THE CONGO

After travelling through the Congo Free State in 1903, the British civil servant Roger Casement published a harsh denunciation of labour conditions in the Congo rubber trade. The Belgian government was forced to convene a commission of inquiry.

And then, N.N., whom I asked again, said: 'Our village got cloth and a little salt, but not the people who did the work. Our Chief ate up the cloth; the workers get nothing. The pay was a fathom of cloth and a little salt for every basket full, but it was given to the Chief, never to the men. It used to take ten days to get the twenty baskets of rubber – we were always in the forest to find the rubber vines, to go without food, and our women had to give up cultivating the fields and gardens. Then we starved. Wild beasts – the leopards killed some of us while we were working away in the forest and others got lost or died from exposure and starvation and we begged the white men to leave us alone, saying we could get no more rubber, but the white men and their soldiers said: "Go. You are only beasts yourselves, you are only nyama (meat)." We tried, always further into the forest, and when we failed and our rubber was short, the soldiers came to our towns and killed us. Many were shot, some had their ears cut off; others were tied up with rope around their necks and bodies and taken away. The white men sometimes at the post did not know of the bad things the soldiers did to us, but it was the white men who sent the soldiers to punish us for not bringing in enough rubber'. . . .

And looking around on the scene of desolation, on the untended farms and neglected palms, one could not but believe that in the main the story was true. From State sentries came confirmation and particulars even more horrifying, and the evidence of a white man as to the state of the country – the unspeakable condition of the prisons at the State posts – all combined to convince me over and over again that, during the last seven years, this 'Domaine Privé' of King Leopold has been a veritable hell on earth.

Roger Casement, The Black Diaries: An Account of Roger Casement's Life and
Times with a Collection of his Diaries and Public Writings, ed. Peter Singleton-Gates
(London, Sidgwick & Jackson [1959]), pp. 112, 118.

DOCUMENT 18   DOING BUSINESS WITH APARTHEID IN SOUTH AFRICA

Lord Milner, as High Commissioner to South Africa, delivered the following speech in Johannesburg in 1903. Although critical of the more extreme forms of racism in white South African society, he supported white minority rule for the foreseeable future.

What is the good . . . of perpetually going on shouting that this is a white man's country? Does it mean that it is a country only inhabited by white men? That, of course, is an obvious absurdity, as the blacks outnumber us as five to one. Does it mean a country which ought only to be inhabited by white men? Well, as an ideal that would possibly be all very well, but as a practical statement it surely is perfectly useless. If it means anything, it means that we ought to try and expel the black population, thereby instantly ruining all the industries of the country. What it does mean, I suppose, if any sane meaning can be applied to it, is that the white man should rule. Well, if that is its meaning, there is nobody more absolutely agreed with it than I; but then let us say that plainly, and do not let us only say it, but let us justify it. There is only one ground on which we can justify it, and that is the ground of superior civilization.

The white man must rule, because he is elevated by many, many steps above the black man; steps which it will take the latter centuries to climb, and which it is quite possible that the vast bulk of the black population may never be able to climb at all. But then, if we justify, what I believe we all hold to, the necessity of the rule of the white man by his superior civilization, what does that involve? Does it involve an attempt to keep a black man always at the very low level of civilization at which he is to-day? I believe you will all reject such an idea. One of the strongest arguments why the white man must rule is because that is the only possible means of gradually raising the black man, not to our level of civilization – which it is doubtful whether he would ever attain – but up to a much higher level than that which he at present occupies.

George Bennett, ed., *The Concept of Empire: Burke to Attlee 1774–1947*
(London: Adam and Charles Black, 1953), pp. 343–4.

DOCUMENT 19   **AN EARLY CALL FOR SELF-GOVERNMENT IN INDIA**

The radical Labour politician Keir Hardie visited India in 1907–8. The discrimination and oppression that he witnessed appalled him. Note, however, that Hardie suggests that Indians deserve greater political rights because they are 'Aryan' relatives of the British.

Let it not be forgotten that the Indian people are of the same Aryan stock as ourselves. Take a gathering of Indians. Remove their graceful, picturesque costumes, and clothe them in coat and trousers, wash the sun out of their skins, and then a stranger suddenly let down into the midst of them would have difficulty in saying whether he was in Manchester or Madras. This fact has a very important bearing upon the question of how far the Indian people can be trusted with the right of self-government.

J. Keir Hardie, *India, Impressions and Suggestions*
(London: Independent Labour Party, 1909), p. 102.

DOCUMENT 20   **CONDEMNING THE CONQUEST OF MOROCCO**

Jean Jaurès was a socialist politician who made the following speech to the Chamber of Deputies in 1912 during a debate about the annexation of Morocco. Jaurès's stance against militarism and imperialism made him an intensely controversial figure and he was assassinated in 1914.

Don't tell me, Gentlemen, that we are subjugating Morocco by these brutal means for the sake of civilization.

I have never painted an idyllic picture of Moslem civilization, and I am fully aware of its chaotic side – the exploitation by an oligarchy of chieftains that exists in some areas. Nonetheless, Gentlemen, you must admit that there has existed a Moroccan civilization capable of evolution and progress, a civilization at once ancient and modern. The Berber tribes, as you know, have been established there for centuries past. They have a fine history, and despise them though we may, they are proud of their tradition. The leading historians of the Moslem world have recounted their exploits and praised their high intelligence. These were the tribes that once conquered Spain; in the city of Fez they raised human thought to a high level of philosophical genius. Again, it was the Moroccans who penetrated to the heart of Africa, establishing in what are now Senegal, Dutch Sudan, and the Niger Colony the foundations of civilization, on which Europe has been able to build. . . .

What has always struck me is the complexity and adaptability of Moroccan society: its readiness to change; the ease with which it has integrated all types of property organization, from collective ownership by tribes to individual ownership by the peasants who plow the land and sow the crops; the vitality of its craftsmen, makers of leather and metal goods working in little shops or in bazaars; the flexibility of a country so receptive to European influence, its farmers sending their goods to the port cities, its children beginning to frequent European schools along the Mediterranean and Atlantic coasts. All of this I welcomed, and it gave hope for a fine future. And let me tell you that I shall never forgive those who have crushed the seeds of peaceful progress by brutal conquest. . . .

Snyder, *The Imperialism Reader*, pp. 156–7.

DOCUMENT 21   INDIGENOUS CULTURE AND 'INDIRECT RULE'

Lord Frederick Lugard formally developed the notion of 'indirect rule' during his governorship of Nigeria in the early twentieth century. Empires had gathered ethnographical information for their own purposes for some time, but in Lugard's doctrine the importance of understanding and reinforcing indigenous culture was given special emphasis. One of Lugard's motives was to work constructively with the Islamic leaders of northern Nigeria.

This identification of the ruling class with the Government accentuates the corresponding obligation to check malpractices on their part. The task of educating them in the duties of a ruler becomes more than ever insistent; of inculcating a sense of responsibility; of convincing their intelligence of the advantages which accrue from the material prosperity of the peasantry, from free labour and initiative; of the necessity of delegating powers to trusted subordinates; of the evils of favouritism and bribery; of the importance of education, especially for the ruling class, and for the filling of lucrative posts under Government; of the benefits of sanitation, vaccination, and isolation of infection in checking mortality; and finally, of impressing upon them how greatly they may benefit their country by personal interest in such matters, and by the application of labour-saving devices and of scientific methods in agriculture . . .

I have throughout these pages continually emphasised the necessity of recognising, as a cardinal principle of British policy in dealing with native races, that institutions and methods, in order to command success and promote the happiness and welfare of the people, must be deep-rooted in their traditions and prejudices. Obviously in no sphere of administration is this more essential than in that under discussion, and a slavish adherence to any particular type, however successful it may have proved elsewhere, may, if unadapted to the local environment, be as ill-suited and as foreign to its conceptions as direct British rule would be.

Lord Lugard, *The Dual Mandate in British Tropical Africa*
(London: Frank Cass and Company, 1965), pp. 210–11.

DOCUMENT 22   THE BRAZZAVILLE CONFERENCE

During the Second World War the Vichy government was defeated in Africa and a colonial conference was convened in 1944. The presence of African officials was significant, and so were hopes that more elected colonial assemblies could be created, and a new colonial parliament established in Paris. There was no discussion of decolonisation, however. Development was to take place only within the integrated context of the French empire.

The Constitutive Elements of the Colonial Society: the Respective Place of the Europeans and of the Natives in Colonization. – Our entire colonial policy will be based upon the respect and the progress of the native society, and we shall have to accept fully and absolutely the demands and consequences implied by this principle. The natives may not be treated as devoid of human dignity, they can be subjected neither to eviction nor to exploitation. However, the colonies are destined, by their very nature, to be inhabited jointly by both Europeans and natives. Although our policy must be subordinated to the full development of the local races, we must also give European activity the place to which it is entitled.

1. The prerequisite for the progress of the African continent is the development of the native populations. The activity of the Europeans and other non-Africans in the colonial territories of Africa must conform to this condition.

2. On the other hand, this progress of the African continent, as it is being contemplated, cannot be achieved without the collaboration of

non-African persons and enterprises to a much greater extent and in greater proportion than at the present time. Consequently, all necessary talent, ability and services will be duly enlisted and utilized. . . .

4.   All the various trades must gradually be taken over by the natives. The Governors-General and the Governors of the territories shall establish, within a brief period, an inventory of the enterprises which will be progressively opened to the natives. . . .

5.   The education of the natives will be directed towards this progressive accession to public office. Proper selection and adequate training will be the dominant tendency in this field.

6.   The necessity for training replacement personnel, as well as the realization of the reforms recommended in all domains by the French African Conference at Brazzaville, make it imperative to launch . . . large-scale recruitment in order to meet the needs of the administrative personnel as well as of the new colonial economy.

Snyder, *The Imperialism Reader*, p. 483.

DOCUMENT 23   **CHALLENGING 'SCIENTIFIC RACISM'**

W.E.B. Du Bois was Director of Special Research, National Association for the Advancement of Colored People, and a pioneering African-American civil rights activist. His book 'Color and Democracy' was published in 1945 and reflects the link between undermining 'scientific racism' and promoting decolonisation.

For the most part, today the colonial peoples are colored of skin; this was not true of colonies in other days, but it is mainly true today. And to most minds, this is of fatal significance; coupled with Negro slavery, Chinese coolies, and doctrines of race inferiority, it proves to most white folk the logic of the modern colonial system: Colonies are filled with peoples who never were abreast with civilization and never can be.

This rationalization is very satisfactory to empire-builders and investors, but it does not satisfy science today, no matter how much it did yesterday. Skin color is a matter of climate, and colonies today are mainly in the hot, moist tropics and semitropics. Naturally, here skins are colored. But historically these lands also were seats of ancient cultures among normal men. Here human civilization began, in Africa, Asia, and Central America. What has happened to these folk across the ages? They have been conquered, enslaved, oppressed, and exploited by stronger invaders. But was this invading force invariably stronger in body, keener in mind, and higher in culture? Not necessarily, but always stronger in offensive technique, even though often lower in culture and only average in mind. . . .

The recent advance of anthropology, psychology, and other social sciences is beginning to show this, and beginning to prove on how false a premise these assertions are based and how fatal a body of folklore has been built upon it. These beliefs have been influenced by propaganda, by caricature, and by ignorance of the human soul. Today these attitudes must be challenged, and without trying to approach anything like completeness of scientific statement we may allude here to certain general matters concerning colonial peoples the truth of which cannot be disputed.

W.E.B. Du Bois, *Color and Democracy* (New York: Harcourt,
Brace and Company, 1945), pp. 18, 25–6.

DOCUMENT 24   GERMAN IMPERIALISM AS A CIVILISING MISSION

This academic study of German imperialism was published when stories of German brutality in the Cameroons and elsewhere were widespread. The study suggests that Africans were better off under European rule than as subjects of a Muslim empire, but is sceptical about the idea of imperialism as 'improvement'.

There are some critics who thoughtlessly say that the natives would have fared much better if the Germans had not come into the Cameroons. Such critics make the statement on the easy assumption that the tropics are a Garden of Eden where the white man plays the serpent's role. In the first place, it should be clear that if the Germans had not occupied the Cameroons, the English or the French would have done so. In the second place, if European powers had not occupied the territory, the presumption is that the Mohammedan Fulbe would have extended the conquest of the Cameroons which they began in the early part of the nineteenth century. Whether Moslem imperialism is better or worse than the Christian imperialism of European powers becomes then a pertinent question, which cannot here be definitely answered. I would point out, however, that Islam made slaves of the conquered people, confiscated their cattle, built no roads, schools, or hospitals for the benefit of the defeated. Over against that type of rule one may place the taxation, labour, and land policies of the European imperialist – policies which, after all, let the natives retain some land and some freedom. One would also have to consider the great sums of money spent on schools and hospitals, on roads and other aids to transportation. All these things taken together might appear to make the native more content with European imperialism.

What the impact of European civilization was on native culture will never be fully known. Exceedingly little is known about the world of the native before the white man's arrival. The very presence of the white man introduces factors that make a study of the native's intimate life a great difficulty, if not an impossibility . . .

It needs only to be pointed out that history means change in all places and at all times, even in Africa. Who shall say what is lost and what is gained as pattern follows pattern in time's kaleidoscope of change?

Harry R. Rudin, *German Administration in the Cameroon, 1884–1914: A Case Study in Modern Imperialism* (New Haven: Yale University Press, 1938), pp. 420–1.

DOCUMENT 25   **PORTUGAL'S NON-RACIST EMPIRE?**

The notion that Portugal's empire was uniquely racially tolerant was well established by the twentieth century. In this defence of ongoing Portuguese imperialism, the economist A.J. Alfaro Cardoso (who had worked in Angola) invoked the familiar notion of a 'civilising mission' in Africa.

It is a fact commented upon by everybody that in the Portuguese colonies, whether localized in Africa, Asia or Australasia, a peaceful atmosphere has prevailed now for centuries, in startling contrast to the state of affairs at present observed in the same continents, in territories governed by other nations.

This fact is the outcome of our policy of assimilation of native peoples, markedly realistic and based upon an experience of long centuries of civilizing action, by means of which we are gradually raising them to our level so that in time we will make them all as Portuguese as the Portuguese of the Mother-Country, distinct from these only in their colour . . .

This raw native has to be looked at as an adult with a child's mentality – and as such he must be considered. He needs to be tutored as if he were a minor, taught to feed and clothe himself properly and to withstand the dangers that face him on all sides, shown how to get the most out of his own land by the best methods, guided in the choice of work suited to his abilities – in short, educated, physically, morally and professionally.

What he consequently requires is protection and teaching, until he grows up and, as a civilized man, can take his place beside us.

Bearing this in mind, the enlightened action of the Portuguese in Africa has been characteristically 'paternal,' slowly but surely improving the native's standards of living and bringing him towards our sphere of life and into closer touch with ourselves, so that gradually he will come to adopt our culture, language and faith.

For this purpose our Government and the Missions it subsidizes maintain, throughout the Colony, a large number of schools where Africans learn to speak, read and write our language; [also provided are] experimental farms where they are taught to cultivate their lands and raise their cattle, and work-shop schools where such trades as carpentry, masonry, painting, printing and so on, are instilled into them.

That is the reason why we find to-day, in Angola, a high percentage of natives exercising the most varied professions, such as those given above. They are not only semi-skilled, but skilled artisans of all types. Everywhere in the territory we see them at work, and the fact that they feel equally at home with their white masters is the foundation on which we build our peaceful colonizing policy.

The result of the foregoing is that we do not practise racial discrimination. What we want to see is that the individual, be he white, yellow or black, should possess moral and civic education and culture – should be, in a word, a civilized man.

All those who reach our standards enjoy among us the same rights, and stand in a position of perfect equality with us, irrespective of the colour of their skins.

Snyder, *The Imperialism Reader*, pp. 497–8.

DOCUMENT 26   *READER'S DIGEST* PROMOTES THE BENEFITS OF COLONIALISM

As late as 1960, when this article titled 'Don't Decry Colonialism' appeared in 'Reader's Digest', there was still substantial support for ongoing imperial rule. For many Europeans and North Americans, postwar decolonisation was neither inevitable nor desirable, and Cold War geopolitics made it easier than ever to view independence movements as dangerous.

One of the most thrilling dramas of human history is unfolding under our eyes in Africa today. We are witnessing a continent more than three times the size of the United States, a vast storehouse of resources and manpower, plunging into self-rule, unready and explosive, while native politicians inflame men of unbelievable ignorance and Communist agents wait hopefully to take over from the politicians. The truth about this great drama, in which millions of black men are trying to claw their way up into civilization, has been obscured by a barrage of propaganda alleging that Western 'colonialism' is resisting freedom and supporting enslavement. When compared with the facts these allegations turn out to be nonsense.

Colonialism is today a dead duck throughout the world, except in Moscow and Peiping. In Africa, 130,000,000 black men are now free citizens of the Belgian Congo, Cameroons Republic, Dahomey, French Equatorial Africa, Ghana, Guinea, Kenya, Madagascar, Mali, Niger, Nigeria, Somalia and British Somaliland, Sudan, Tanganyika, Togoland and Volta, all of which have gained self-rule in the past four years or are in the final stages of achieving it.

In countries like Rhodesia and Nyasaland the issue is still unsolved. But only in the Union of South Africa is a vicious type of colonialism still in existence, inflicted by a Nazi-type government which is trying to keep 9,600,000 black men in bondage. For the rest of Black Africa, the only enslavement left is to age-old tribal fetishes, witch doctors and primitive ignorance.

Still, Communist mouthings about colonialism not only have poisoned public opinion in neutral nations but have affected some Americans, who think of the word in connection with the American Revolution against British rule. They seem to forget that the men who wrote our Declaration were among the most idealistic, educated and politically enlightened men of their day, and that our new citizens had brought with them the best of the civilization of the Old World. In contrast, the vast majority of Africans today are uneducated and uncivilized. The struggle is to find enough of them, in any country, capable of self-government, and to educate enough of the voters to resist witch doctors and extremists.

Snyder, *The Imperialism Reader*, p. 137.

GLOSSARY

Ab une sanguine   'of one blood'; Latin slogan of the British antislavery movement.

Amor sem cor   'love without colour boundaries'; Brazilian concept expressing racial tolerance.

Apartheid   'apartness'; twentieth-century racial segregation policies in South Africa.

Assimilado   'assimilated' or 'civilised'; term used in Portuguese Angola and elsewhere to denote non-Europeans who were Europeanised.

Blijvers   'belongers'; Dutch plantation managers or owners and colonial officials who lived in colonies permanently.

Bon sauvage   'noble savage'; an interpretation of non-European peoples used as a foil for European corruption and decadence.

Branqueamento   'whitening'; Brazilian term for upwardly mobile miscegenation.

Capitaines des sauvages   'native leaders'; term used to describe the Métis in New France who acted as translators and facilitators for French colonists.

Casta   a social/ethnic category used to describe and distinguish different population groups in the Spanish empire.

Chefferie   'district'; Belgian colonial administrative term.

Citoyen   'citizen'; used to denote citizens of the French empire, who were mostly Europeans, in opposition to the non-European *sujet* ('subject').

Code de l'indigénat   separate legal system governing indigenous peoples in the French north African empire; abolished in 1928 in Algeria and in 1946 in the rest of the French empire.

Colon   'colonist'; used to denote French colonists in Algeria.

Conquistadores   'conquerors'; Spanish explorers who set out to conquer the Americas.

Creole   term used in the West Indies and parts of America to denote people of European or African descent born in the New World colonies (people of non-indigenous ancestry).

Crillos   'native'; Spanish term used to denote a colonial-born person of European descent.

Cunhadismo   'in-lawism'; Portuguese designation by which marriages into Indian families gave traders a wide range of social and economic connections.

Diwani   'civil rulership'; term used to describe the taxation rights and other powers granted by the Mughal emperor to the EIC in Bengal.

Encomienda   labour system in the early Spanish New World empire that relied heavily on slavery and Indian and African labour.

Engagés forcés   forced labour.

Évolués 'evolved ones'; Europeanized non-Europeans in the French empire.

Fatwa a decree carrying Muslim clerical endorsement

Hottentots Dutch term used to describe the Khoi peoples of southern Africa.

Indio 'Indian'; administrative designation denoting indigenous peoples in the Spanish and Portuguese New World empires.

Kulturvölker 'cultural peoples'; used by German anthropologists to denote Europeans (used in opposition to *Naturvölker* ('natural peoples'), denoting non-Europeans).

Lebensraum 'living space'; used by German theorists who presented German territorial expansion as natural and inevitable.

Libertos term used in Portuguese Angola to distinguish free labourers from slaves.

Limpieza de sangre 'purity of blood'; term used among the Spanish royalty and aristocracy following the reconquest of Spain from the Moors.

Lingua franca 'Frankish tongue'; refers to any language in widespread use.

Mahdi 'the expected one'; popular name given to Mohammed Ahmed Ibn-el-Sayed, Muslim nationalist leader of Sudan.

Mamelucos mixed-race Portuguese-Indians in Brazil.

Mameluke of mixed Indian and European ancestry.

Mau Mau an oath-taking society which spread rapidly in Kenya in the 1950s, resulting in the killing of Europeans and Africans loyal to them, and prompting a state of emergency.

Mazombo Brazilian Portuguese term used to denote a locally-born person of European descent.

Mestizos 'of mixed ancestry'; term used in Latin America to denote people of mixed Indian and European parentage.

Métis people of mixed native and European descent in New France and British North America (now Canada).

Métissage 'mixing', 'crossing'; used to denote racial or ethnic mixing.

Mission civilisatrice 'civilising mission'; French expression for imperial trusteeship.

Mouvement National Congolais Congolese National Movement, established by Patrice Lumumba in 1958.

Mulattos people of mixed European and African parentage.

Não-assimilado 'non-assimilated' or 'non-civilised'; term used in Portuguese Angola to denote Africans required to perform compulsory labour.

Naturvölker 'natural peoples'; used by German anthropologists to denote non-Europeans (used in opposition to *Kulturvölker* ('cultural peoples'), denoting Europeans).

Nawab provincial ruler within the Mughal empire.

Négritude 'celebrating blackness'; cultural movement in France after the First World War.

Obedezco pero no cumplo 'I obey but do not execute'; Spanish phrase used by colonial officials to delay the implementation of metropolitan instructions.

Pakeha 'non-Maori'; term used to describe non-Maori settlers in New Zealand.

Puissance musulmane 'Muslim power'; French expression used to describe the aspiration of identifying the French empire with respect for Islam.

Res nullius 'empty things'; legal phrase used to describe lands technically considered empty because the inhabitants did not cultivate them in a manner understood by Europeans.

Sale race 'dirty people'; term used by French Algerian colonists to describe Muslim Algerians.

Sati 'widow suicide'; a traditional cultural practice in India, eventually banned by the British.

Schutzgebietsgesetz German colonial law.

Serviçaes term used in Portuguese Angola to distinguish free labourers from slaves.

Sociedad de castas social organisation of breeds established in the Spanish New World empire, which placed Spaniards at the top and black slaves at the bottom.

Sous-chefferie 'sub-district'; Belgian colonial administrative term.

Sujet 'subject'; used to denote subjects of the French empire, mostly non-Europeans, in opposition to the European *citoyen* ('citizen').

Trekkers Dutch colonial plantation owners who retired to the Netherlands after farming.

Übermenschen 'supermen'; term used by Friedrich Nietzsche to describe his conception of a new nobility.

Ubuhake Rwandan clientele system, which contained a cattle agreement, whereby Hutus could obtain cattle (means of wealth) by working for Tutsis.

Voudoun 'voodoo', a set of hybrid religious practices of west African origin which were modified by slave societies in the Americas.

Wahriki traditional Maori woven floor mat.

Weltoffen 'open to the world'; term used by German advocates of colonisation.

Yellow peril term used in Australia and New Zealand to describe the demographic, economic, and military threat of Asia.

WHO'S WHO

Aristotle (384–322 BCE). Greek philosopher. He identified civility with urban life, labelling other types of communities 'barbarian'. He proposed the inevitability of slavery due to the natural superiority of rational, civilised society over others.

Bastian, Adolf (1826–1905). German anthropologist and a founder of ethnology. He was a mentor of Franz Boas and he believed in universal psychic processes and ideas linking all humans. He sought to reveal rules of cultural development common to all human societies.

Bismarck, Otto von (1815–98). Founder of the unified Germany (1871), and first Chancellor of Germany (1871–90). He oversaw the establishment of a German colonial presence in Africa and helped initiate the 'Scramble for Africa'. He hosted the Berlin Conference (1884).

Blumenbach, Johann (1752–1840). German anatomist and founder of modern physical anthropology. He wrote *The Natural Variety of Mankind* (1775), in which he built upon the traditional taxonomy of man developed by Linnaeus to provide a standard classification for the so-called races of man based on the anthropological study of cranial morphology.

Boas, Franz (1858–1942). German-American anthropologist. Famous for his fieldwork on the north-west coast of North America, he advocated cultural relativism and argued that any search for general laws of human development must take into account the specific historical circumstances influencing each culture's development.

Bonaparte, Napoleon (1769–1821). Emperor of France (1804–14). He assumed power in the aftermath of the French Revolution, and after leading an unsuccessful campaign to conquer Egypt in 1798–9, he occupied much of Europe during the Napoleonic wars of 1804–15.

Bougainville, Louis Antoine de (1729–1811). First French explorer to circumnavigate the globe. He helped popularise the myth of the 'noble savage' using descriptions of Pacific Islanders.

Bowen, Sir George Fergasun (1821–99). Governor of New Zealand (1868–73). He played a key role in ending struggles between Maoris and colonists.

Broca, Paul (1824–80). French surgeon and renowned physical anthropologist. He studied and helped advance cranial anthropometry and comparative primate anatomy, attempting to prove that mulattos were sterile.

Buckle, Henry Thomas (1821–62). British historian. He wrote *History of Civilization in England* (1857–61), in which he argued that environment was the most important factor in determining human development.

Buffon, Georges Louis Leclerc, comte de (1707–88). French anatomist and ethnologist. Author of *Natural History* (1749–67), he emphasised the unity of human species. He also noted the fertility of mixed-race people and advocated degeneration theory to explain physical and cultural differences.

Carey, William (1761–1834). British missionary to India with the Baptist Missionary Society. He arrived in Bengal in 1793 and eventually helped established 20 churches and missionary stations across India. He worked to improve social conditions in India and was a key figure in the fight to outlaw infanticide and *sati* (widow suicide).

Chamberlain, Houston Stewart (1855–1927). English cultural critic and racial theorist. Living and working in Germany, he wrote *The Foundations of the Nineteenth Century* (1899), which linked racial survival with the establishment of viable nation-states. He believed that a lack of unified nationalism would lead to racial decline.

Charles X (r. 1824–30). King of France. To distract his increasingly disenchanted subjects, Charles attempted to shore up his regime through an invasion of Algiers in 1830, inaugurating the French empire in North Africa.

Clive, Robert (1725–74). Commander of the East India Company's forces. Clive's victory in Bengal in 1757 laid the foundations of British territorial rule in India.

Cook, James (1728–79). British explorer. Cook made three voyages to the Pacific during which he claimed Australia and New Zealand for Britain and made observations of Pacific peoples which would prompt British missionary activity in the region.

Cornwallis, Charles (Lord) (1738–1805). British general and statesman and governor-general of Bengal (1786–93). He introduced reforms in the civil and military administrative structures of India which had the effect of marginalising Eurasians.

Crowther, Samuel Adjai (1809–91). West African missionary and member of the Church Missionary Society of Sierra Leone. He was the first Anglican bishop of African ancestry (consecrated 1864).

Cuvier, Georges (1769–1832). French anatomist and conservative creationist theorist. He resisted the idea of ranking various animal species, including humans, yet believed that it was possible to rank human races.

Darwin, Charles (1809–82). English naturalist and founder of evolutionary theory. He published his theory of evolution in *The Origin of Species* (1859), and expanded his theories to include human evolution in *The Descent of Man* (1871). He emphasised the unity of humanity as a single species. His theory of the 'struggle for survival' inspired Social Darwinism.

Davenport, Charles Benedict (1866–1944). American zoologist and eugenicist. He established the Eugenics Record Office in Cold Spring Harbor, New York.

Dilke, Sir Charles Wentworth (1843–1911). British author. He wrote *Greater Britain* (1869), which stressed the natural superiority of Europeans and their right to expand into other territories.

Dom Affonso (r. 1506–43). Ruler of the ancient kingdom of Congo. He converted to Roman Catholicism and modelled his court and society on Portuguese lines. His pro-Portuguese stance was not reflected by his successors because of increased racial hostility amid the growing slave trade in the region.

Durkheim, Émile (1858–1915). Pioneering French sociologist. Seeking to discover general laws of social development, he theorised about religion being the basis of social identity and communication and emphasised a shared human history in which societies progressed at different paces.

Equiano, Olaudah (?–1797). Former African slave who purchased his freedom and rose to prominence in the British antislavery movement. His published memoirs drew attention to the voices of Africans themselves in recounting their experience of slavery and their aspirations for freedom.

Fanon, Frantz (1925–61). Psychiatrist and political author. Born in Martinique, he became a key figure in the Algerian independence movement of the 1950s. He wrote *The Wretched of the Earth* (1961), one of the most famous books written on decolonisation.

Forster, Johann Reinhold (1729–98). German naturalist. He took part in Captain James Cook's second voyage of discovery. He argued that Pacific islanders provided evidence of the infant human condition.

Freud, Sigmund (1856–1939). German pioneer of psychoanalysis. He proposed that human sexuality was the key to psychology. He believed that failure to understand the biology of human conception was a sign of social backwardness.

Galton, Sir Francis (1822–1911). Founder of British eugenics movement. He was a cousin of Charles Darwin and authored *Hereditary Genius* (1869).

Gandhi, Mohandas Karamchand (1869–1948). Indian nationalist leader. A British-trained lawyer, he practised law in South Africa 1893–1915. He became the moral leader of the Indian National Congress 1920–48, and advocated civil disobedience to force concessions from the British.

Gobineau, Joseph-Arthur (comte de) (1816–82). French diplomat and author. He wrote *Essai sur l'inégalité des races humaines* (1853). He was a proponent of racial essentialism and North European supremacy.

Gordon, Charles (1833–85). British general and leader of British–Egyptian forces in the Sudan. Gordon was killed under siege at Khartoum by anti-European Sudanese nationalists. His imperial 'martyrdom' was one motive for Britain's determination to conquer the Sudan.

Haddon, Alfred Cort (1855–1940). British anthropologist. As leader of the Cambridge University Expedition to the Torres Strait Islands (1898), he developed and modified functionalist anthropology.

Hastings, Warren (1732–1818). Governor-general of Bengal. At a time when Bengal was still under EIC rule, Hastings was recalled in 1785 and later tried for corruption. Although he was acquitted, the trial drew attention to debates about the EIC's approach to governance.

Hegel, Georg Wilhelm Friedrich (1770–1831). German idealist philosopher. A disciple of Immanuel Kant, he was a proponent of an inborn, essential human spirit and national character. He believed that nineteenth-century European Romantic nationalism was the highest form of cultural development.

Herder, Johann Gottfried von (1744–1803). German historian. Author of *Outlines of a Philosophy of the History of Man* (1784–91), he introduced the concept of *Kultur* ('culture') and argued that history primarily concerned the formation and development of particular national cultures.

Hidalgo y Costilla, Miguel (1753–1811). Mexican Roman Catholic priest. He led the unsuccessful Mexican Revolution of 1810.

Hobbes, Thomas (1588–1679). English political theorist. He wrote *The Leviathan* (1651), in which he argued that humanity was naturally disposed to warfare and conquest, and that peoples with unrecognisable forms of government were fit for conquest.

Home, Henry (Lord Kames) (1696–1782). British naturalist and race theorist. He believed that Africans were a separate species of humanity.

Ibn-el-Sayed, Mohammed Ahmed (1844–85). Muslim religious and nationalist leader in the Sudan. He was nicknamed 'The Mad Mullah' by the British. His followers enjoyed significant military victories before being defeated by General Kitchener's forces at Omdurman (1898).

Jinnah, Mohammad Ali (1876–1948). Member of the Indian National Congress, 1908–20 and President of the Muslim League, 1934–48. He led the campaign for a separate Muslim state in south Asia. He became the first governor-general of Pakistan.

Kandt, Richard, Dr (1867–1913). First German colonial Resident of Rwanda 1907. He was an ethnographer, responsible for formalising distinctions between Hutu and Tutsi for colonial administrative purposes.

Kant, Immanuel (1724–1804). German philosopher and one of the earliest theorists of Romantic nationalism. Author of *On the Different Races of Men* (1775), he stressed the essential, biological nature of national character and argued against miscegenation.

Khan, Sir Saiyyid Ahmad (1817–98). Muslim statesman and educator in British India. He remained loyal to Britain during the Rebellion of 1857. He attempted to Europeanise Indian Muslims through the establishment of colleges and the translation of English works.

Kitchener, Horatio (1850–1916). British general. As commander-in-chief of British forces in the Sudan, Kitchener presided over the defeat of Sudanese nationalist forces at Omdurman in 1898. He would become a Field Marshal and leader of Britain's armed forces in the First World War.

Las Casas, Bartolomé de (1474–1566). Spanish Roman Catholic missionary to the Americas. In 1550 he participated in a debate about Spain's treatment of indigenous peoples in the Americas. He was a staunch defender of the natural rights of Indians.

LeBon, Gustave (1841–1931). French psychologist. He travelled through Europe, Asia, and North Africa and wrote about archaeology and anthropology as well as psychology. Author of *Les Lois psychologiques de l'évolution des peuples* (1894), he argued that character was inherited and thus objected to out-breeding and the subsequent weakening of races.

Leroy-Beaulieu, Paul (1843–1916). Ardent advocate of French colonial expansion. He wrote *De la colonisation chez les peuples modernes* (1874).

Linnaeus, Carl (1707–78). Swedish naturalist. He created the first (and still dominant) systematic classification of all plants, animals, and minerals, which he laid out in his *Systema Naturae* (1758). He amassed a huge collection of botanical specimens collected by explorers around the world, and was best known for creating the genus *Homo* and order Primates, which included the non-human and human primates together.

London, Jack (1876–1916). American socialist and novelist. He used the term 'yellow peril' in his popular novels.

Long, Edward (1734–1813). Colonial official in Jamaica. He wrote *The History of Jamaica* (1774). He was an opponent of antislavery and argued that Africans were naturally inferior to Europeans. He suggested that Africans were related to the great apes.

Lugard, Lord Frederick (1858–1945). British colonial administrator. He joined the British East Africa Company in 1889 and became governor of Nigeria (1912–19). He was an outspoken advocate of indirect rule in Britain's African colonies.

L'Ouverture, Toussaint (*c.* 1743–1803). Black leader in Saint-Domingue (later Haiti). He led a slave rebellion in Saint-Domingue (1791) and briefly established Haiti as a black-ruled republic.

Lumumba, Patrice (1925–61). Congolese political figure. He organised the *Mouvement National Congolais*, and became the first prime minister of the Democratic Republic of the Congo (1960). He was forcibly removed from office through a military coup and assassinated in January 1961 under circumstances that remain mysterious.

Macaulay, Thomas Babington (Lord) (1800–59). British politician, essayist, and historian. Author of *The History of England from the Accession of James II* (1848–9), he took a cyclical view of the rise and fall of civilisations, but nevertheless promoted Europeanisation in India. He acted as the first law member of the viceroy's council 1834–9.

Maine, Sir Henry (1822–88). British jurist and ethnologist. He believed that India contained vestiges of a more primitive stage of human development. He developed comparative law in the field of anthropology, and created the first centralised Indian law code.

Malinowski, Bronislaw (1884–1942). Polish anthropologist who lived and worked in Britain. Emphasising respect for the rationality of cultures in their own terms, he developed the anthropological theory of 'functionalism' to explain the pragmatic development of cultural features.

Marshall, (Chief Justice) John (1755–1835). Chief Justice of the US Supreme Court (early 1830s). He created the idea of 'domestic-dependent nations' in his final *Cherokee Nation* decision in 1831. He recognised Indian sovereignty but set important limits on it.

Marx, Karl (1818–83). German political and economic theorist. He developed a view of history based on material conditions and class struggle, and believed that race was of little importance compared with class.

Millar, John (1735–1801). Scottish Enlightenment theorist. He advocated an optimistic yet discriminatory belief in the linear progression of human society through various stages, from lower to higher.

Montesquieu, Charles-Louis de Secondat, baron de (1689–1755). French philosopher. Author of *Spirit of the Laws* (1748), he introduced the word 'savage' as a specific category in a social evolutionary scheme. He believed that African slavery was natural.

Morel, Edmond (1873–1924). British socialist, Labour MP, and human rights activist. He helped draw attention to atrocities committed in the Belgian Congo, and founded the Congo Reform Association in 1904. He objected to the use of colonial troops in the First World War.

Morgan, Lewis Henry (1818–81). Pioneering American anthropologist and social evolutionist. He developed a hierarchy of marriage practices through which to analyse social progress.

Mugabe, Robert (1924–). Black nationalist leader and president of Zimbabwe (1980–). He was an advocate of African forms of socialism. He has presided over the forced reallocation of white-owned land.

Müller, Friedrich Max (1823–1900). German-born British philologist and ethnologist. He wrote *Biographies of Words: The Home of the Aryans* (1888), in which he identified what he called an 'Aryan' linguistic family based on Sanscrit. He rejected any automatic connection between language and race.

Niebuhr, Barthold (1776–1831). German diplomat and historian. He wrote *Lectures on Ancient Ethnography and Geography* (1812–13), and advocated German folk *Kultur* as a source of German nationalism and strength.

Nietzsche, Friedrich Wilhelm (1844–1900). German radical philology professor. He worried about the loss of German *Volk* genius as Germany modernised after the Franco-Prussian War. He sought to create a new nobility of *Übermenschen* ('supermen').

Omai (c. 1753–76). Raiatean islander brought back to Europe by Captain Cook's second voyage to the Pacific. He became a symbol (to some) of the ideal 'noble savage'. He returned to Raiatea with Cook's third voyage.

Pocahontas (c. 1595–1617). Daughter of Powhatan, chief of the Algonquian Indians in Virginia and key figure in negotiations between them and the Jamestown settlers. She converted to Christianity and married Virginian tobacco planter John Rolfe in 1614, which led to the making of peace between the English and Indians. She travelled to London in 1616.

Potatau (*c.* 1800–60). Leader of a Maori rebellion against the colony of New Zealand. He was proclaimed the first King of the Maori in 1858 and ruled until his death in 1860.

Prichard, James Cowles (1786–1848). British anatomist and ethnologist. He emphasised the unity of the human race, and the context of biblical history.

Quezon, Manuel (1878–1944). Filipino statesman. He fought extensively for independence for the Philippines, playing a key role in the passage of the *Jones Act* (1916) which promised future independence. He became the first president of the Philippines (1935–44).

Radcliffe-Brown, A.R. (1881–1955). British anthropologist. He researched and taught in Australia in the early twentieth century. He extended Malinowski's functionalist theory of kinship.

Raffles, (Sir) Stamford (1781–1826). British entrepreneur and expansionist. He purchased Singapore in 1819 from the Sultan of Johor. He encouraged both Chinese and Indian immigration to Singapore, thus establishing the island's multicultural character.

Ratzel, Friedrich (1844–1904). German anthropologist. He wrote *Anthropogeographie* (1891), *Politische Geographie* (1897), and *Der Lebensraum* (1904). He grew to embrace ideas of racial essentialism and interracial struggle for living space (*Lebensraum*).

Ripley, William Z. (1867–1941). Author of *Races of Europe* (1899). He used skull measurements to identify a number of putative European racial groups.

Roosevelt, Theodore (President) (1858–1919). President of the United States (1901–9). He was the first president to pursue extensive overseas territorial expansion. He believed in the struggle of races in the Pacific region.

Rousseau, Jean-Jacques (1712–78). French philosopher and author. He revived notions of 'noble savages' to argue that the institutions of advanced civilisation corrupted humanity.

Roy, Ram Mohun (1772–1883). Hindu ruler and modernist in British India. He founded a club for debating the reform of Indian society. He was an advocate of Indian Europeanisation.

Salazar, Antonio de Oliveira (1889–1970). Portuguese dictator. He led a military coup in 1926 and ruled Portugal until 1968. His government enacted legislation requiring Africans under Portuguese rule to perform forced labour and enhancing the power of European-born colonial officials.

Scholes, Theophilus (*c.* 1854–1937). Scot who had lived in Jamaica; doctor trained in Scotland and Belgium. He wrote various works on contemporary politics, including *The British Empire and Alliances or Britain's Duty to her Colonies and Subject Races* (1899). He was a vocal opponent of British racism.

Sepúlveda, Juan Ginés de (1489–1573). Official Spanish court historian. He acted as a spokesman for Spanish colonists in America. He debated with the Dominican priest and advocate of indigenous rights Bartolomé de las Casas in 1550.

Sitting Bull (*c.* 1831–90). American Indian (Hunkpapa Lakota) Chief. He denied the US federal government's right to define 'Indian territory', and eventually crossed into Canada to evade capture following the Battle of Little Bighorn (1876).

Smith, William Robertson (1846–94). British orientalist and theologian. He argued that religious beliefs revealed the heart of social organisation. He was charged with heresy after questioning the literal truth of some parts of the Bible.

Spencer, Herbert (1820–1903). British philosopher and sociologist. He was the key proponent of 'Social Darwinism' and developed the notion of the 'survival of the fittest' based on Darwin's evolutionary theory.

Thierry, Augustin (1795–1856). French nationalist and historian. Author of *History of the Conquest of England by the Normans* (1821–5), he espoused the theory of an inherited French culture. He attempted to demonstrate that inborn French superiority had allowed the Normans to conquer the British Isles.

Tocqueville, Alexis de (1805–59). French politician. He advocated the expansion of the French empire outward from Algeria, based upon the model of American continental expansion.

Von Trotha, General Adrian Dietrich Lothar (1868–1940). German naval officer. He ordered the extermination of the Herero people in German South-West Africa.

Weber, Max (1864–1920). German sociologist. He contrasted the individualism and fervour of European capitalism and Protestantism with what he perceived to be the passive nature of Hinduism and Buddhism.

Wellesley, Richard (1798–1805). First Marquess Wellesley. As governor-general of Bengal his military campaigns expanded British rule in India.

GUIDE TO FURTHER READING

Although 'Race and Empire' is organised chronologically, many of the relevant reference works do not break down by chronological period. They are grouped here by categories instead. The recommended readings concentrate on the concept of race; there are many other approaches to the study of imperialism, and the following lists are therefore extremely selective.

Few primary source collections exist which take a broad, comparative approach to modern imperial race relations, but important exceptions are Barbara Harlow and Mia Carter, eds, *Imperialism and Orientalism: A Documentary Sourcebook* (Oxford: Blackwell, 1998); A.L. Macfie, ed., *Orientalism: A Reader* (New York, NY: New York University Press, 2000); and Louis Snyder, *The Imperialism Reader: Documents and Readings on Modern Expansionism* (Princeton, NJ: Van Nostrand [1962]). Primary source material on the British empire can be found in Antoinette Burton, ed., *Politics and Empire in Victorian Britain: A Reader* (New York, NY: St Martin's Press, 2001); Catherine Hall, ed., *Cultures of Empire: Colonizers in Britain and the Empire in the Nineteenth and Twentieth Centuries: A Reader* (London: Routledge, 2000); and Jane Samson, ed., *The British Empire* (Oxford: Oxford University Press, 2001).

EMPIRES

The best recent introductions to the comparative study of modern empires include C.A. Bayly, *The Birth of the Modern World, 1780–1914: Global Connections and Comparisons* (Oxford: Blackwell, 2004); Muriel Chamberlain, *Longman Companion to the Formation of the European Empires 1488–1920* (London and New York: Longman, 2000); Marc Ferro, *Colonization: A Global History* (London: Routledge, 1997); Andrew Porter, *European Imperialism, 1860–1914* (London: Macmillan, 1994); and John C. Weaver, *The Great Land Rush and the Making of the Modern World, 1650–1900* (Montreal: McGill-Queen's University Press, 2003).

RACE

Overviews of the history of the concept of race are found in Michael Banton and Jonathan Harwood, *The Race Concept* (London, 1975); George M. Fredrickson, *Racism: A Short History* (Princeton, NJ: Princeton University Press, 2002); Ivan Hannaford, *Race: The History of an Idea in the West* (Baltimore, MD: Johns Hopkins University Press, 1995); Kenan Malik, *The Meaning of Race: Race, History and Culture in Western Society* (New York, NY: New York University Press, 1996); Philip Mason, *Patterns of Dominance* (London and New York, NY Institute of Race Relations, 1970); and Edward Said, *Orientalism* (New York, NY: Pantheon Books, 1978).

More detailed studies of racial science include Lee D. Baker, *From Savage to Negro: Anthropology and the Construction of Race, 1896–1954* (Berkeley, CA:

University of California Press, 1998); E. Barkan, *The Retreat of Scientific Racism: Changing Concepts of Race in Britain and the United States Between the World Wars* (Cambridge: Cambridge University Press, 1992); Terry Jay Ellingson, *The Myth of the Noble Savage* (Berkeley, CA: University of California Press, 2001); Margaret T. Hodgen, *Early Anthropology in the Sixteenth and Seventeenth Centuries* (Philadelphia, PA: University of Pennsylvania Press, 1964); Adam Kuper, *The Invention of Primitive Society* (London: Routledge, 1988); Harold E. Pagliaro, ed., *Racism in the Eighteenth Century* (Cleveland, OH: Cleveland Press of Case Western Reserve University, 1973); Leon Poliakov, *The Aryan Myth: A History of Racist and Nationalist Ideas in Europe* (New York, NY: Basic Books, 1971); Nancy Stepan, *The Idea of Race in Science: Great Britain 1800–1960* (London: Macmillan, 1982); and George W. Stocking, *Victorian Anthropology* (New York, NY: The Free Press, 1987).

On the concept of whiteness see Theodore W. Allen, *The Invention of the White Race* (London, 1994); Richard Dyer, *White* (London: Routledge, 1997); and George M. Fredrickson, *White Supremacy* (Oxford: Oxford University Press, 1981).

RACE AND EMPIRE

Comparative studies of the relationship between race theory and imperialism include Talal Asad, ed., *Anthropology and the Colonial Encounter* (New York, NY: Ithaca Press, 1973); Nicholas B. Dirks, *Colonialism and Culture* (Ann Arbor, MI: University of Michigan Press, 1992); Frank Füredi, *The Silent War: Imperialism and the Changing Perception of Race* (New Brunswick, NJ: Rutgers University Press, 1998); W.R. Johnston, S. Paul, A. Strong, and M. Thomson, *Imperialism and Racism in the South Pacific* (Sydney: William Brooks, 1983); Victor Kiernan, *The Lords of Human Kind: European Attitudes Toward the Outside World in the Imperial Age* (London: Weidenfeld & Nicolson, 1995); Alan J. Levine, *Race Relations Within Western Expansion* (Westport, CT: Praeger, 1996); Robert Ross, ed., *Racism and Colonialism* (The Hague: Martinus Nijhoff, 1982); Hugh Tinker, *Race, Conflict and the International Order: From Empire to United Nations* (London: Macmillan, 1977); and Robert Young, *Colonial Desire: Hybridity in Theory, Culture and Race* (New York and London: Routledge).

Special attention should be drawn to Anthony Pagden's work on the early modern period in *The Fall of Natural Man: The American Indian and the Origins of Comparative Ethnology* (Cambridge: Cambridge University Press, 1982); *European Encounters with the New World, from Renaissance to Romanticism* (New Haven, CT: Yale University Press, 1993); and *Lords of All the World: Ideologies of Empire in Spain, Britain and France c. 1500–c. 1800* (New Haven, CT: Yale University Press, 1995).

More focused studies are provided in P.E.H. Hair, *Africa Encountered: European Contacts and Evidence, 1450–1700* (Aldershot: Ashgate, 1997); John M. MacKenzie and Hermann J. Hiery, eds, *European Impact and Pacific Influence: British and German Colonial Policy in the Pacific Islands and the Indigenous Response* (London: I.B. Tauris, 1997); H. Glenn Penny and Matti Bunzel, eds, *Worldly Provincialism: German Anthropology in the Age of Empire* (Ann Arbor, MI: University of Michigan Press, 2003) and Nicholas Thomas, *Colonialism's Culture* (Princeton, NJ: Princeton University Press, 1994).

One of the most vibrant approaches to this subject involves a focus on gender: see Jennifer S.H. Brown, *Strangers in Blood: Fur Trade Company Families in Indian*

Country (Vancouver: University of British Columbia Press, 1980); Julia Clancy-Smith and Francis Gouda, eds, *Domesticating the Empire: Race, Gender and Family Life in French and Dutch Colonialism* (Charlottesville, VA: University of Virginia Press, 1998); Graham Dawson, *Soldier Heroes: British Adventure, Empire, and the Imagining of Masculinities* (London: Routledge, 1994); Anne McClintock, *Imperial Leather: Race, Gender, and Sexuality in the Colonial Contest* (London: Routledge, 1995); Adele Perry, *On the Edge of Empire: Gender, Race, and the Making of British Columbia 1849–1871* (Toronto: University of Toronto Press, 2001); Margaret Strobel, *European Women and the Second British Empire* (Bloomington, IN: Indiana University Press, 1991); and Sylvia van Kirk, *Many Tender Ties: Women in Fur-Trade Society in Western Canada, 1670–1870* (Winnipeg: Watson & Dwyer, 1980).

The articles of anthropologist Ann Stoler are particularly important; see her 'Sexual affronts and racial frontiers: European identities and the cultural politics of exclusion in colonial Southeast Asia', *Comparative Studies in Society and History* 34 (1992), pp. 514–51, and '"Mixed-bloods" and the cultural politics of European identity in colonial Southeast Asia', in Jan Nederveen Pieterse and Bhikhu Parekh, eds, *The Decolonization of Imagination* (London: Zed Books, 1995), pp. 128–48.

Studies of imperial labour systems include Winthrop D. Jordan, *White Over Black: American Attitudes Toward the Negro, 1550–1812* (Chapel Hill, NC: University of North Carolina Press, 1968); Martin A. Klein, *Slavery and Colonial Rule in French West Africa* (Cambridge: Cambridge University Press, 1998); Suzanne Miers and Martin Klein, eds, *Slavery and Colonial Rule in Africa* (London: Frank Cass, 1999); Philip D. Morgan, 'The black experience in the British empire, 1680–1810', *Oxford History of the British Empire*, vol. 2, *The Eighteenth Century*, pp. 465–86; Kay Saunders, ed., *Indentured Labour in the British Empire 1834–1920* (London: Croom Helm, 1984); Stuart B. Schwartz, *Slaves, Peasants, and Rebels: Reconsidering Brazilian Slavery* (Urbana, IL: University of Illinois Press, 1992); and James Walvin, *Slaves and Slavery: The British Colonial Experience* (Manchester: Manchester University Press, 1992).

REFERENCES

The following list includes only those works referred to directly in the text. Expanding it to reflect the range of works consulted for research purposes would have made the list unmanageable.

Alberta, Aboriginal Affairs and Northern Development (2001) *Memorandum of Understanding, Alberta Grand Council of Treaty 8 First Nations and Government of Alberta*. Edmonton, AB: Aboriginal Affairs and Northern Development.

Aldrich, Robert (1996) *Greater France: A History of French Overseas Expansion*. Basingstoke: Macmillan.

Anstey, Roger (1966) *King Leopold's Legacy: The Congo Under Belgian Rule 1908–1960*. London: Oxford University Press for the Institute of Race Relations.

Appiah, Anthony (1995) 'Race', in Frank Lentricchia and Thomas McLaughlin eds, *Critical Terms for Literary Study*. Chicago, IL: University of Chicago Press.

Auchterlonie, Paul (2001) 'From the Eastern Question to the death of General Gordon: representations of the Middle East in the Victorian periodical press, 1876–1885', *British Journal of Middle Eastern Studies* 28:1, pp. 5–24.

Augstein, H.F. (1990) 'From the land of the Bible to the Caucasus and beyond', in Waltraud Ernst and Bernard Harris, eds, *Race, Science and Medicine, 1700–1960*. London: Routledge.

Ballantyne, Tony (2002) *Orientalism and Race: Aryanism in the British Empire*. New York, NY: Palgrave.

Barkan, E. (1992) *The Retreat of Scientific Racism: Changing Concepts of Race in Britain and the United States Between the World Wars*. Cambridge: Cambridge University Press.

Bayly, C.A. (1991) 'Maine and change in nineteenth-century India', in Alan Diamond, ed., *The Victorian Achievement of Sir Henry Maine: A Centennial Reappraisal*. Cambridge: Cambridge University Press.

Bayly, C.A. (2003) 'The Orient: British historical writing about Asia since 1890', in Peter Burke, ed., *History and Historians in the Twentieth Century*. Oxford: Oxford University Press, pp. 88–119.

Bayly, Susan (2000) 'French anthropology and the Durkheimians in colonial Indochina', *Modern Asian Studies* 34, pp. 581–622.

Bell, Gertrude [1928] *The Letters of Gertrude Bell*. New York, NY: Boni and Liveright.

Betts, Raymond F. (1982) 'The French colonial empire and the French world-view', in Robert Ross, ed., *Racism and Colonialism*. The Hague: Martinus Nijhoff.

Betts, Raymond F. (1991) *France and Decolonisation*. London: Macmillan.

Blackburn, Robin (1997) 'The Old World background to European colonial slavery', *William and Mary Quarterly* 54:1, pp. 65–102.

Bley, Helmut (1996) *Namibia Under German Rule*. Hamburg: LIT.

Boxer, C.R. (1963) *Race Relations in the Portuguese Colonial Empire 1415–1825*. Oxford: Oxford University Press.

Boxer, C.R. (1965) *The Dutch Seaborne Empire 1600–1800*. London: Hutchinson & Co.

Braude, Benjamin (1997) 'The sons of Noah and the construction of ethnic and geographical identities in the medieval and early modern periods', *William and Mary Quarterly* 54:1, pp. 103–42.

Brown, Jennifer (1988) 'Métis', *The Canadian Encyclopedia*. Edmonton, AB: Hurtig.

Brown, M. (2003) 'Ethnology and colonial administration in nineteenth-century British India: the question of native crime and criminality', *British Journal for the History of Science* 36:2, pp. 201–20.

Bulbeck, Chilla (1992) *Australian Women in Papua New Guinea: Colonial Passages 1920–1960*. Melbourne and Cambridge: Cambridge University Press.

Burns, E. Bradford (1995) 'Brazil: frontier and ideology', *Pacific Historical Review* 64, pp. 1–18.

Cairns, Alan C. (2001) *Citizens Plus: Aboriginal Peoples and the Canadian State*. Vancouver: UBC Press.

Cannadine, David (2001) 'Ornamentalism', *History Today* 51:5, pp. 12–19.

Canny, Nicholas (1998) 'England's New World and the Old, 1480s–1630s', in Nicholas Canny, ed., *The Origins of Empire*, vol. 1 of *The Oxford History of the British Empire*. Oxford: Oxford University Press.

Carmack, Robert M., Gasco, Janine and Gossen, Gary H. (1996) *The Legacy of Mesoamerica: History and Culture of a Native American Civilization*. Upper Saddle River, NJ: Prentice Hall.

Clayton, Anthony (1994) *The Wars of French Decolonization*. London: Longman.

Cohen, William B. (1980) *The French Encounter with Africans: White Response to Blacks, 1530–1880*. Bloomington, IN: Indiana University Press.

Collin, Richard H. (1985) *Theodore Roosevelt, Culture, Diplomacy, and Expansion*. Baton Rouge: Louisiana State University Press.

Copland, Ian (2001) *India 1885–1947: The Unmaking of an Empire*. London: Longman.

Craton, Michael, Walvin, James and Wright, David, eds (1976) *Slavery, Abolition and Emancipation: Black Slaves and the British Empire, A Thematic Documentary*. London: Longman.

Dalrymple, William (1998) *The Age of Kali: Indian Travels and Encounters*. London: HarperCollins.

Dickason, Olive P. (1997) *The Myth of the Savage, and the Beginnings of French Colonialism in the Americas*. Edmonton, AB: University of Alberta Press.

Dyer, Richard (1997) *White*. London: Routledge.

Elliott, John (1992) *The Old World and the New 1492–1650*. Cambridge: Canto.

Feldman, Marcus W., Lewontin, Richard C. and King, Mary-Claire (2003) 'Race: a genetic melting-pot', *Nature* 374; doi: 10.1038/424374a (electronic version).

Fiola, Jan (1990) *Race Relations in Brazil: A Reassessment of the 'Racial Democracy' Thesis*. Amherst, MA: University of Massachusetts at Amherst.

Friend, Theodore (1966) *Between Two Empires: The Ordeal of the Philippines, 1929–1946*. New Haven, CT: Yale University Press.

Gong, G.W. (1984) *The Standard of 'Civilization' in International Society*. Oxford: Clarendon Press.

Great Britain, House of Commons (1837) *Report of the Select Committee on Aborigines (British Settlements)*. London: Government Printer.

Greene, Jack P. (1998) 'Empire and identity from the Glorious Revolution to the American Revolution', in P.J. Marshall, ed., *The Eighteenth Century*, vol. 3 of *The Oxford History of the British Empire*. Oxford: Oxford University Press.

Hall, Kim F. (1995) *Things of Darkness: Economies of Race and Gender in Early Modern England*. Ithaca, NY: Cornell University Press.

Hannaford, Ivan (1995) *Race: The History of an Idea in the West*. Baltimore, MD: Johns Hopkins University Press.

Heywood, Linda (2000) *Contested Power in Angola, 1840s to the Present*. Rochester, NY: University of Rochester Press.

Hobson, J.A. (1988) *Imperialism: A Study*. London: Unwin Hyman.

Horsman, Reginald (1981) *Race and Manifest Destiny: The Origins of American Racial Anglo-Saxonism*. Cambridge, MA: Harvard University Press.

Howe, K.R. (1993) 'The intellectual discovery and exploration of Polynesia', in Robin Fisher and Hugh Johnston, eds, *From Maps to Metaphors: The Pacific World of George Vancouver*. Vancouver, BC: University of British Columbia Press.

Huntington, Samuel P. (1997) *The Clash of Civilizations and the Remaking of World Order*. New York, NY: Touchstone.

Huttenback, Robert A. (1976) *Racism and Empire: White Settlers and Colored Immigrants in the British Self-Governing Colonies 1830–1910*. Ithaca, NY: Cornell University Press.

Isaacman, Allen and Roberts, Richard, eds, (1995) *Cotton, Colonialism, and Social History in Sub-Saharan Africa*. London: James Currey.

Jordan, Winthrop D. (1974) *The White Man's Burden: Historical Origins of Racism in the United States*. New York, NY: Oxford University Press.

Judd, Denis (1972) *The British Raj*. London: Wayland Publishers.

Khodarkovsky, Michael (2002) *Russia's Steppe Frontier: The Making of a Colonial Empire, 1500–1800*. Bloomington, IN: Indiana University Press.

Kiernan, Victor (1969) *The Lords of Human Kind: European Attitudes Towards the Outside World in the Imperial Age*. London: Weidenfeld & Nicolson.

Landes, David S. (1998) *The Wealth and Poverty of Nations: Why Some Are So Rich and Some Are So Poor*. New York, NY: W.W. Norton.

Lindqvist, Sven (1996) *Exterminate All the Brutes*. New York, NY: New Press.

Lindqvist, Sven (1997) *The Skull Measurer's Mistake: And Other Portraits of Men and Women Who Spoke Out Against Racism*. New York, NY: New Press.

Lorcin, Patricia (1999) 'Imperialism, colonial identity, and race in Algeria, 1830–1870', *Isis*, 90:4, online version at http://web11.epnet.com

Louis, William Roger (1963) *Ruanda-Urundi 1884–1919*. Oxford: Clarendon Press.

Lowenthal, David (1973) 'Free colored West Indians: a racial dilemma', in Harold E. Pagliaro, ed., *Racism in the Eighteenth Century*. Cleveland Press of Case Western Reserve University.

McFerson, Hazel M. (1997) *The Racial Dimension of American Overseas Colonial Policy*. Westport, CN: Greenwood.

Malcomson, Scott L. (2000) *One Drop of Blood: The American Misadventure of Race*. New York: Farrar Straus Giroux.

Malik, Kenan (1996) *The Meaning of Race: Race, History and Culture in Western Society*. New York, NY: New York University Press.

Marks, Shula (1981) '"Bold, thievish, and not to be trusted": racial stereotypes in South Africa in historical perspective', *History Today* 31, pp. 15–21.

Marshall, P.J., ed. (1998) *The Eighteenth Century*, vol. 2 of *The Oxford History of the British Empire*. Oxford: Oxford University Press.

Marshall, P.J. and Williams, Glyndwr (1982) *The Great Map of Mankind: British Perceptions of the World in the Age of Enlightenment*. London: J.M. Dent & Sons.

Miller, J.R. (2000) *Skyscrapers Hide the Heavens: A History of Indian–White Relations in Canada*. Toronto, ON: University of Toronto Press.

Murphy, Agnes (1968) *The Ideology of French Imperialism 1871–1881*. New York, NY: Howard Fertig.

Müller, Friedrich Max (1899) *India: What Can it Teach Us?* London: Longmans, Green, and Co.

Muthu, Sankar (2003) *Enlightenment Against Empire*. Princeton, NJ: Princeton University Press.

Nordholt, Henk Schulte (1999) 'The making of traditional Bali: colonial ethnography and bureaucratic reproduction', in Peter Pels and Oscar Salemink, eds, *Colonial Subjects: Essays on the Practical History of Anthropology*. Ann Arbor, MI: University of Michigan Press.

Pagden, Anthony (1995) *Lords of All The World: Ideologies of Empire in Spain, Britain and France c. 1500–c. 1800*. New Haven, CT: Yale University Press.

Paul, Kathleen (1997) *Whitewashing Britain: Race and Citizenship in the Postwar Era*. Ithaca, NY: Cornell University Press.

Phelan, John Leddy (1960) 'Authority and flexibility in the Spanish imperial bureaucracy', *Administrative Science Quarterly* 5:1, pp. 47–65.

Pietz, William (1999) 'The fetish of civilization: sacrificial blood and monetary debt', in Peter Pels and Oscar Salemink, eds, *Colonial Subjects: Essays on the Practical History of Anthropology*. Ann Arbor, MI: University of Michigan Press.

Porter, Andrew (1999) 'Trusteeship, anti-slavery, and humanitarianism', in Andrew Porter, ed., *The Nineteenth Century*, vol. 3 of *The Oxford History of the British Empire*. Oxford: Oxford University Press.

Rafael, Vincente L. (1993) 'White love: surveillance and nationalist resistance in the U.S. colonization of the Philippines', in Amy Kaplan and Donald E. Pease, eds, *Cultures of United States Imperialism*. Durham, NC and London: Duke University Press.

Rathbone, Richard, ed. (1992) *Ghana*. London: HMSO.

Reichmann, Rebecca, ed. (1999) *Race in Contemporary Brazil: From Indifference to Inequality*. University Park, PA: Pennsylvania State University Press.

Reynolds, Henry (1989) *Dispossession: Black Australians and White Invaders*. Sydney: Allen & Unwin.

Reynolds, Henry (2001) *An Indelible Stain? The Question of Genocide in Australia's History*. Ringwood: Penguin.

Ribeiro, Darcy (2000) *The Brazilian People: The Formation and Meaning of Brazil*. Gainesville, FL: University Press of Florida.

Richter, Daniel K. (1998) 'Native peoples of North America and the eighteenth-century British empire', in P.J. Marshall, ed., *The Eighteenth Century*, pp. 347–71.

Robinson, David (2000) *Paths of Accommodation: Muslim Societies and French Colonial Authorities in Senegal and Mauritania, 1880–1920*. Athens, OH: Ohio University Press.

Robinson, Jane (1999) *Parrot Pie for Breakfast: An Anthology of Women Pioneers*. Oxford: Oxford University Press.

Samson, Jane (1998) *Imperial Benevolence: Making British Authority in the Pacific Islands*. Honolulu, HI: University of Hawai'i Press.

Samson, Jane, ed. (2001a) *The British Empire*. Oxford: Oxford University Press.

Samson, Jane (2001b) 'Ethnology and theology: nineteenth-century mission dilemmas in the South Pacific', in Brian Stanley, ed., *Christian Missions and the Enlightenment*. Grand Rapids, MI: William B. Eerdmans.

Sarich, Vincent and Miele, Frank (2004) *Race: The Reality of Human Difference*. Boulder, CO: Westview Press.

Segrè, Claudio G. (1974) *Fourth Shore: The Italian Colonization of Libya*. Chicago, IL: University of Chicago Press.

Sinha, Mrinalini (1995) *Colonial Masculinity: The 'Manly Englishman' and the 'Effeminate Bengali' in the Late Nineteenth Century*. Manchester: Manchester University Press.

Slade, William (1914) 'The Maori of New Zealand' in James Colwell, ed., *A Century in the Pacific*. Sydney: William H. Beale.

Stocking, George W. (1987) *Victorian Anthropology*. New York, NY: The Free Press.

Stocking, George W. (1995) *After Tylor: British Social Anthropology, 1888–1951*. Madison, WI: University of Wisconsin Press.

Stoecker, Helmuth (1987) 'The position of Africans in the German colonies', in Arthur J. Knoll and Lewis H. Gann, eds, *Germans in the Tropics: Essays in German Colonial History*. New York, NY: Greenwood Press.

Stoler, Ann (1992) 'Sexual affronts and racial frontiers: European identities and the cultural politics of exclusion in colonial southeast Asia', *Comparative Studies in Society and History* 34, pp. 514–51.

Strobel, Margaret (1991) *European Women and the Second British Empire*. Bloomington, IN: Indiana University Press.

Sweet, James H. (1997) 'The Iberian roots of American racist thought', *William and Mary Quarterly* 54:1, pp. 143–66.

Taylor, Jean (1983) *The Social World of Batavia: European and Eurasian in Dutch Asia*. Madison, WI: University of Wisconsin Press.

Thapar, Romila (1980) 'Durkheim and Weber on the theories of society and race relating to pre-colonial India', in UNESCO, *Sociological Theories: Race and Colonialism*. Paris: UNESCO.

Tiger, Lionel and Fox, Robin (1998) *The Imperial Animal*. New Brunswick, NJ: Transaction Publishers.

Tilchin, William N. (1997) *Theodore Roosevelt and the British Empire: A study in Presidential Statecraft*. New York, NY: St Martin's Press.

Tinker, Hugh (1977) *Race, Conflict and the International Order: From Empire to United Nations*. London: Macmillan.

Van Den Boogaart, Ernst (1982) 'Colour prejudice and the yardstick of civility: the initial Dutch confrontation with black Africans, 1590–1635', in Robert Ross, ed., *Racism and Colonialism*. The Hague Martinus Nijhoff.

Van Kirk, Sylvia (1999) 'The native wives and daughters of five founding families of Victoria', in Alan Frost and Jane Samson, eds, *Pacific Empires: Essays in Honour of Glyndwr Williams*. Melbourne: Melbourne University Press.

Van Young, Eric (2001) *The Other Rebellion: Popular Violence, Ideology, and the Mexican Struggle for Independence, 1810–1821*. Stanford, CA: Stanford University Press.

Wade, Peter (1997) *Race and Ethnicity in Latin America*. London: Pluto Press.

Weaver, John C. (2003) *The Great Land Rush and the Making of the Modern World, 1650–1900*. Montreal, PQ: McGill-Queen's University Press.

Weeks, Charles J. (2002) 'The New Frontier, the Great Society, and American imperialism in Oceania', *Pacific Historical Review* 71:1, pp. 91–125.

White, Owen (1999) *Children of the French Empire: Miscegenation and Colonial Society in French West Africa 1895–1960*. Oxford: Clarendon Press.

Wilder, Gary (2003) 'Colonial ethnology and political rationality in French West Africa', *History and Anthropology* 14:3, pp. 219–52.

Williams, Robert A. (1990) *The American Indian in Western Legal Thought: The Discourses of Conquest*. New York, NY: Oxford University Press.

Wolfe, Patrick (1999) 'White man's flour: the politics and poetics of an anthropological discovery', in Peter Pels and Oscar Salemink, eds, *Colonial Subjects: Essays on the Practical History of Anthropology*. Ann Arbor, MI: University of Michigan Press, pp. 196–240.

Young, Robert (1995) *Colonial Desire: Hybridity in Theory, Culture and Race*. London: Routledge.

Zimmerman, Andrew (2001) *Anthropology and Antihumanism in Imperial Germany*. Chicago, IL and London: University of Chicago Press.

INDEX

aborigines, Australian, xii, 35–6, 46–7, 78, 100
Abyssinia, 62–3, 80
Admiralty Manual of Scientific Enquiry, 46
Africa, 'scramble' for, 59–63, 136
Africans, stereotypes of, 20, 21–2, 28, 32, 70, 111, 114–15, 116–17, 139, 140
Afrikaners, 48–9, 78
Alaska, 51, 98
Alberta, 49
Algeria, 43, 54–5, 82, 97, 138
Algiers, 51–2, 118, 137
Alsace-Lorraine, 66
American Anti-Imperialist League, 122
American Association for the Advancement of Science, 120
American Revolution, 37, 38, 50, 76, 77–8
American Samoa, 104
American-Mexican Wars, 50–1, 63, 89
Amritsar Massacre (1919), 86
Ancient Law (1861), 44
Anglo-Saxons, 43, 46, 72–3, 118–19, 123
Angola, 21, 55, 97–8, 130–1
Anthropogeographie (1891), 72, 142
Anthropological Society of London, 69
anthropology, 28, 43–6, 69, 70–1, 80–1, 84–5, 88, 92, 102, 120, 136, 138, 140, 142
Antilles, 38
anti-Semitism, 45
apes, 28, 32, 140
Arabs, 91–2
Argentina, 64
Aristotle, 14, 15, 17, 19, 27, 136
art, 14
Aryans, 43–4, 72, 125, 141
Ashanti, 59–60
assimilation, 50, 81–3, 130–1
Assiniboia colony, 37
Australia, xii, 34, 35–6, 46–7, 52, 74, 78, 100, 119
Austro-Hungarian empire, 103
Aztecs, 77

Baden-Powell, Robert, 59–60
Balfour, Arthur, 91
Bali, 84
Balkans, 103
barbarians, 14, 19, 27, 28, 136

Bastian, Adolf, 45, 136
Batavia, 24–5, 41
Battle of Adowa, 62, 63
Battle of Omdurman, 61, 139
Battle of Plassey, 39
Belgian empire, 96, 102, 121–2, 123–4
Bell, Gertrude, 92
Bengal, 39–40, 115–16
Bengalis, 47
Benin, 60
Berlin Anthropological Society, 45
Berlin Conference (1884), 68, 136
Bermuda, 104
Beveridge, Albert Jeremiah, 123
Bible, 13, 20, 29–30, 58, 143
Biloxi Bay, 113–14
Bismark, Otto von, 136
Black Hole of Calcutta (1757), 39
Blumenbach, Johann, 27, 28, 136
Boas, Franz, 75–6, 120–1, 136
Bonaparte, Napoleon, 34, 100, 136
Borneo, 54
Bouganville, Louis Antoine, 136
Bowen, Sir George Fergasun, 136
Boxer Rebellion, 73
Boy Scouts, 60, 74
Brazil, 16, 21, 55, 64, 100–1
Brazzaville, 97, 127–8
British Columbia, 36
British Commonwealth, 98, 99
British empire, 16–18, 22, 24, 31, 35–6, 46–9, 52–4, 56–61, 85–8, 119
  decolonisation in, 54, 98–9, 101–2
  devolution in, 77–9
  in India, 39–41, 44, 47–8, 56–7, 64–5, 85–7, 115–16, 118, 138, 139, 140
  in Middle East, 91–2, 105
  in sub-Saharan Africa, 48–9, 56, 59–61, 87–8, 126–7
British Empire and Alliances (1899), 75, 142
British South Africa Company (BSAC), 49
Broca, Paul, 136
Brussels International Exhibition (1958), 96
Buckle, Henry Thomas, 46, 136
Buddhism, 84, 143
Buffon, Georges-Louis Leclerc, comte de, 27–8, 116, 117, 137
Burundi, 102
Byzantium, 12

MEDIEVAL ENGLAND

The Pre-Reformation Church in England 1400–1530 (Second edition)
Christopher Harper-Bill   0 582 28989 0

Lancastrians and Yorkists: The Wars of the Roses
David R. Cook   0 582 35384 X

Family and Kinship in England 1450–1800
Will Coster   0 582 35717 9

TUDOR ENGLAND

Henry VII (Third edition)
Roger Lockyer & Andrew Thrush   0 582 20912 9

Henry VIII (Second edition)
M.D. Palmer   0 582 35437 4

Tudor Rebellions (Fourth edition)
Anthony Fletcher & Diarmaid MacCulloch   0 582 28990 4

The Reign of Mary I (Second edition)
Robert Tittler   0 582 06107 5

Early Tudor Parliaments 1485–1558
Michael A.R. Graves   0 582 03497 3

The English Reformation 1530–1570
W.J. Sheils   0 582 35398 X

Elizabethan Parliaments 1559–1601 (Second edition)
Michael A.R. Graves   0 582 29196 8

England and Europe 1485–1603 (Second edition)
Susan Doran   0 582 28991 2

The Church of England 1570–1640
Andrew Foster   0 582 35574 5

STUART BRITAIN

Social Change and Continuity: England 1550–1750 (Second edition)
Barry Coward   0 582 29442 8

James I (Second edition)
S.J. Houston   0 582 20911 0

The English Civil War 1640–1649
Martyn Bennett   0 582 35392 0

Charles I, 1625–1640
Brian Quintrell   0 582 00354 7

The English Republic 1649–1660 (Second edition)
Toby Barnard   0 582 08003 7

Radical Puritans in England 1550–1660
R.J. Acheson   0 582 35515 X

The Restoration and the England of Charles II (Second edition)
John Miller   0 582 29223 9

The Glorious Revolution (Second edition)
John Miller   0 582 29222 0

EARLY MODERN EUROPE

The Renaissance (Second edition)
Alison Brown   0 582 30781 3

The Emperor Charles V
Martyn Rady   0 582 35475 7

French Renaissance Monarchy: Francis I and Henry II (Second edition)
Robert Knecht   0 582 28707 3

The Protestant Reformation in Europe
Andrew Johnston   0 582 07020 1

The French Wars of Religion 1559–1598 (Second edition)
Robert Knecht   0 582 28533 X

Philip II
Geoffrey Woodward   0 582 07232 8

The Thirty Years' War
Peter Limm   0 582 35373 4

Louis XIV
Peter Campbell   0 582 01770 X

Spain in the Seventeenth Century
Graham Darby   0 582 07234 4

Peter the Great
William Marshall   0 582 00355 5

EUROPE 1789–1918

Britain and the French Revolution
Clive Emsley   0 582 36961 4

Revolution and Terror in France 1789–1795 (Second edition)
D.G. Wright   0 582 00379 2

Napoleon and Europe
D.G. Wright   0 582 35457 9

The Abolition of Serfdom in Russia 1762–1907
David Moon   0 582 29486 X

Nineteenth-Century Russia: Opposition to Autocracy
Derek Offord   0 582 35767 5

The Constitutional Monarchy in France 1814–48
Pamela Pilbeam   0 582 31210 8

The 1848 Revolutions (Second edition)
Peter Jones   0 582 06106 7

The Italian Risorgimento
M. Clark   0 582 00353 9

Bismarck & Germany 1862–1890 (Second edition)
D.G. Williamson   0 582 29321 9

Imperial Germany 1890–1918
Ian Porter, Ian Armour and Roger Lockyer   0 582 03496 5

The Dissolution of the Austro-Hungarian Empire 1867–1918 (Second edition)
John W. Mason   0 582 29466 5

Second Empire and Commune: France 1848–1871 (Second edition)
William H.C. Smith   0 582 28705 7

France 1870–1914 (Second edition)
Robert Gildea   0 582 29221 2

The Scramble for Africa (Second edition)
M.E. Chamberlain   0 582 36881 2

Late Imperial Russia 1890–1917
John F. Hutchinson   0 582 32721 0

The First World War
Stuart Robson   0 582 31556 5

Austria, Prussia and Germany 1806–1871
John Breuilly   0 582 43739 3

Napoleon: Conquest, Reform and Reorganisation
Clive Emsley   0 582 43795 4

The French Revolution 1787–1804
Peter Jones   0 582 77289 3

The Origins of the First World War (Third edition)
Gordon Martel   0 582 43804 7

The Birth of Industrial Britain *Kenneth Morgan*	0 582 30270 6

EUROPE SINCE 1918

The Russian Revolution (Second edition) *Anthony Wood*	0 582 35559 1
Lenin's Revolution: Russia 1917–1921 *David Marples*	0 582 31917 X
Stalin and Stalinism (Third edition) *Martin McCauley*	0 582 50587 9
The Weimar Republic (Second edition) *John Hiden*	0 582 28706 5
The Inter-War Crisis 1919–1939 *Richard Overy*	0 582 35379 3
Fascism and the Right in Europe 1919–1945 *Martin Blinkhorn*	0 582 07021 X
Spain's Civil War (Second edition) *Harry Browne*	0 582 28988 2
The Third Reich (Third edition) *D.G. Williamson*	0 582 20914 5
The Origins of the Second World War (Second edition) *R.J. Overy*	0 582 29085 6
The Second World War in Europe *Paul MacKenzie*	0 582 32692 3
The French at War 1934–1944 *Nicholas Atkin*	0 582 36899 5
Anti-Semitism before the Holocaust *Albert S. Lindemann*	0 582 36964 9
The Holocaust: The Third Reich and the Jews *David Engel*	0 582 32720 2
Germany from Defeat to Partition 1945–1963 *D.G. Williamson*	0 582 29218 2
Britain and Europe since 1945 *Alex May*	0 582 30778 3
Eastern Europe 1945–1969: From Stalinism to Stagnation *Ben Fowkes*	0 582 32693 1
Eastern Europe since 1970 *Bülent Gökay*	0 582 32858 6

The Khrushchev Era 1953–1964
Martin McCauley   0 582 27776 0

Hitler and the Rise of the Nazi Party
Frank McDonough   0 582 50606 9

The Soviet Union Under Brezhnev
William Tompson   0 582 32719 9

NINETEENTH-CENTURY BRITAIN

Britain before the Reform Acts: Politics and Society 1815–1832
Eric J. Evans   0 582 00265 6

Parliamentary Reform in Britain c. 1770–1918
Eric J. Evans   0 582 29467 3

Democracy and Reform 1815–1885
D.G. Wright   0 582 31400 3

Poverty and Poor Law Reform in Nineteenth-Century Britain
1834–1914: From Chadwick to Booth
David Englander   0 582 31554 9

The Birth of Industrial Britain: Economic Change 1750–1850
Kenneth Morgan   0 582 29833 4

Chartism (Third edition)
Edward Royle   0 582 29080 5

Peel and the Conservative Party 1830–1850
Paul Adelman   0 582 35557 5

Gladstone, Disraeli and later Victorian Politics (Third edition)
Paul Adelman   0 582 29322 7

Britain and Ireland: From Home Rule to Independence
Jeremy Smith   0 582 30193 9

TWENTIETH-CENTURY BRITAIN

The Rise of the Labour Party 1880–1945 (Third edition)
Paul Adelman   0 582 29210 7

The Conservative Party and British Politics 1902–1951
Stuart Ball   0 582 08002 9

The Decline of the Liberal Party 1910–1931 (Second edition)
Paul Adelman   0 582 27733 7

The British Women's Suffrage Campaign 1866–1928
Harold L. Smith   0 582 29811 3

War & Society in Britain 1899–1948
Rex Pope   0 582 03531 7

The British Economy since 1914: A Study in Decline?
Rex Pope   0 582 30194 7

Unemployment in Britain between the Wars
Stephen Constantine   0 582 35232 0

The Attlee Governments 1945–1951
Kevin Jefferys   0 582 06105 9

The Conservative Governments 1951–1964
Andrew Boxer   0 582 20913 7

Britain under Thatcher
Anthony Seldon and Daniel Collings   0 582 31714 2

Britain and Empire 1880–1945
Dane Kennedy   0 582 41493 8

INTERNATIONAL HISTORY

The Eastern Question 1774–1923 (Second edition)
A.L. Macfie   0 582 29195 X

India 1885–1947: The Unmaking of an Empire
Ian Copland   0 582 38173 8

The United States and the First World War
Jennifer D. Keene   0 582 35620 2

Women and the First World War
Susan R. Grayzel   0 582 41876 3

Anti-Semitism before the Holocaust
Albert S. Lindemann   0 582 36964 9

The Origins of the Cold War 1941–1949 (Third edition)
Martin McCauley   0 582 77284 2

Russia, America and the Cold War 1949–1991 (Second edition)
Martin McCauley   0 582 78482 4

The Arab–Israeli Conflict
Kirsten E. Schulze   0 582 31646 4

The United Nations since 1945: Peacekeeping and the Cold War
Norrie MacQueen   0 582 35673 3

Decolonisation: The British Experience since 1945
Nicholas J. White   0 582 29087 2

WORLD HISTORY

China in Transformation 1900–1949
Colin Mackerras   0 582 31209 4

Japan Faces the World 1925–1952
Mary L. Hanneman   0 582 36898 7

Japan in Transformation 1952–2000
Jeff Kingston   0 582 41875 5

China since 1949
Linda Benson   0 582 35722 5

South Africa: The Rise and Fall of Apartheid
Nancy L. Clark and William H. Worger   0 582 41437 7

The Collapse of the Soviet Union
David R. Marples   0 582 50599 2

Race and Empire
Jane Samson   0 582 41837 2

US HISTORY

American Abolitionists
Stanley Harrold   0 582 35738 1

The American Civil War 1861–1865
Reid Mitchell   0 582 31973 0

America in the Progressive Era 1890–1914
Lewis L. Gould   0 582 35671 7

The United States and the First World War
Jennifer D. Keene   0 582 35620 2

The Truman Years 1945–1953
Mark S. Byrnes   0 582 32904 3

The Korean War
Steven Hugh Lee   0 582 31988 9

The Origins of the Vietnam War
Fredrik Logevall   0 582 31918 8

The Vietnam War
Mitchell Hall   0 582 32859 4

American Expansionism 1783–1860
Mark S. Joy   0 582 36965 7

The United States and Europe in the Twentieth Century
David Ryan   0 582 30864 X

The Civil Rights Movement
Bruce J. Dierenfield   0 582 35737 3